Selling
Serenity

Upton®
BOOKS

Selling
Serenity

Life Among the
Recovery Stars

By Andrew Meacham

BOOKS

A division of

SIRS-Mandarin, Inc.
P.O. Box 2348
Boca Raton, FL 33427

© 1999 by SIRS-Mandarin, Inc. All rights reserved
Printed in the United States of America

Library of Congress Cataloging-in-Publication Data

Meacham, Andrew.
   Selling serenity : life among the recovery stars / by Andrew Meacham.
      p.   cm.
   Includes bibliographical references and index.
   ISBN 0-89777-708-5
   1. Alcoholics—Rehabilitation—United States. 2. Recovering alco-
holics—United States—Case studies. 3. Alcoholics Anonymous.
I. Title.
HV5279.M43   1999
362.292'0973—dc21   97-44281
                                                             CIP

Linda Manis, Managing Editor
Anastasia DeBeck, Assistant Editor
Michelle McCulloch, Book Design

For Robert Colegrove and Katherine Miller Meacham

Acknowledgments

The lion's share of credit for encouraging me in the development of this book and providing much useful criticism goes to Lynne Appleton of Florida Atlantic University. It was she who suggested including myself in the narrative, at least as an observer. Next come my editors, Linda Manis and Anastasia DeBeck, without whose help I would not have been able to pick through reams of articles and studies cited herein, many of these works having been dug up years after I first encountered them. For source material as well as personal support I am especially thankful to Alan Jacobs and Marguerite Babcock, two insightful people in their respective fields of psychotherapy and substance abuse treatment. Sidney Willens provided valuable case material for the chapter dealing with reparenting therapy. Feedback from Milan Korcok, Jeren Goldstein, Peter Meinke and Kathy Meacham has also fueled the manuscript in various stages of development. Clayton Hall provided support in gloomy, even seemingly hopeless times despite his own declining health.

Paradoxical as it may seem in a book critical of recovery publishers and their work, I must also thank Health Communications (HCI) presidents Gary Seidler and Peter Vegso for hiring me in 1986. I was sincere in my six years of work at HCI, but am equally sincere now in studying lines of thought which are decidedly less recovery-oriented. Eleanor Goldstein of Social Issues Resources Series (SIRS) approached me with the book idea that has captured my attention since 1993, and my appreciation goes out to her as well.

Finally, I recognize and thank the many people who have talked at length to me about past or present allegations of sexual abuse made against them, which I believe they did not commit. Their warmth, consistency and support for each other inspires me. I am also grateful to those inside and outside of 12-step programs who have talked candidly of personal and philosophical difficulties they encountered with certain fundamentalist strains of addiction theory and practice in Alcoholics Anonymous meetings and chemical dependency treatment centers. Their honesty has helped me realize that I am not alone in my perceptions. Knowing (intellectually, at least) that I am not alone gives me the strength to delve deeper into the mysteries of addiction and profit making; the search for spiritual cures for addiction; and a massive generational willingness to believe the unbelievable, to "cast out demons" and to make demons out of thousands who have committed no crimes yet live as convicted felons. To those in prison or serving lengthy house arrests, know that you, too, are not alone and not forgotten. Society is at last beginning to address injustices done to you and countless others in the name of healing.

TABLE OF CONTENTS

Introduction

S ometime in early 1992 I received a book about how to sue your parents for sexual abuse. Editors receive free unsolicited books almost every day, most of which get shelved with scarcely a backward glance. This one, for whatever reason, caught my eye.

Why would an adult want to sue his or her parents for sexual abuse that happened 20 or 30 years ago? There could be legitimate reasons, starting with the obvious: An injury had occurred. But the linchpin of this particular book, as well as the flood of uncritical books, articles and TV movies about to descend on America, was not the kind of abuse or injury that typically fills up civil court dockets. These authors were talking about sexual abuse that they claim was repressed for decades, then materialized in fragments as the alleged incest survivor worked to recover the memories.

At the time, the information seemed apropos for mention in *Changes*, the magazine for which I wrote and served as associate editor. Sexual abuse was the emerging hot topic of the day and *Changes* targeted adults who had been brought up in dysfunctional families. I called the book's authors, a pair of lawyers in Oswego, Washington, and learned that their state was about to extend its statute of limitations for sexual abuse lawsuits to allow for something called "delayed discovery." The case for making such a change in the law seemed compelling.

If what the authors and a growing host of "trauma experts" were claiming was true—and years of child rape, torture and forced participation in heinous acts, including murder, could be wiped from the victim's conscious memory as a survival mechanism—then existing systems of legal redress were indeed unfair. By the time memories of traumatic childhood experiences were recovered, the statute of limitations had long since expired. Thus it seemed the very severity of the injuries was hindering the victims' access to justice. Under Washington's new statute, sexual abuse survivors would have three years to sue for damages after the abuse was remembered.

The new law had been pioneered almost single-handedly by a Washington couple. After Patricia Barton recovered her memories of being molested by her father and learned of her powerlessness to sue, she and husband Kelvin lobbied state legislators for years until somebody listened. Their success in getting the law changed seemed like a grassroots victory over a system that has often been proved indifferent to domestic abuse, particularly against women and children. I spoke with the Bartons, wrote a short news story about their case and ran it in *Changes*. To my lasting chagrin, I headlined the article "Abuse survivors sue perpetrators"—mainly because I could not fit the word "alleged" into the available headline space. But, hell, it was a survivor's magazine and I figured no one would care.

No one did. I forgot about sexual abuse survivors and their recovered memories and proceeded to work on the other dozens of stories on my plate. Along with *Changes*, my employer, Health Communications, Inc. (HCI), also published a monthly newspaper for addiction professionals along with a magazine for family therapists interested in addiction issues. Similar to the stories of recovered memories of abuse, the topics covered in these publications attracted their share of controversy.

By the early 1990s, the 1980s-inspired "war on drugs" had lost some of its lustre as a social cure-all or even as a workable idea. High-visibility figures, such as William F. Buckley and Baltimore mayor Kurt Schmoke, were openly advocating a once-unthinkable strategy of legalization for at least some drugs. On the so-called "demand" side of the equation, a $2- billion-a-year treatment industry found itself suddenly tottering under increased pressures brought on by market saturation and managed care. Hospital-based treatment chains were going bankrupt, and those who would survive were scrambling for creative ways to fill empty beds. Thus, in the early 1990s, whether as a result of inspiration or financial need, "codependency" emerged as a watchword for mental health consumers as did "sex addiction," "workaholism," eating disorders and "original pain," among other afflictions, diseases and dysfunctions.

No one came right out and said that being a man or a woman qualified one for treatment; although one would have thought so, judging from the proliferation of books, tapes and conferences offering help for "women's issues," and, later, "men's issues." With each successive wave of books came fame and popular credibility for a fairly small pool of authors, mostly therapists with Masters degrees, punctuated by the occasional M.D. or Ph.D. psychologist. Instead of setting trends through experimentation and research, many treatment programs appeared to follow the public's lead, offering programs for whatever issues were selling in the newly created "Addiction and Recovery" bookstore categories. On the afternoon talk shows, a generation of alcoholics apologized to their children, followed by the next generation of adult children confronting their parents with traumatic memories, multiple personalities and tales of satanic slaughter.

The more that popular self-help book authors, or "recovery stars" as I call them, marketed the idea that readers were sick in ways they did not realize, the more each new wave of sickness was said to "underlie" previous diseases: Codependency underlies addiction; "original trauma" underlies codependency.

I watched these developments with fascination and a vague dread for the future. Codependency did not come about as an outgrowth of universally accepted addiction knowledge. On the contrary, most of the addiction field's fundamental claims had been hotly debated in academic and medical journals for decades. Even today, addiction scientists can scarcely determine who is likely to become an alcoholic or drug addict, which addicts can stop on their own and who needs what kind of treatment.

Important gains have been made in understanding the reinforcing properties of alcohol and drugs on the brain; yet no one seems to know why some people tend to abuse substances more heavily than others, despite similar genetic makeups and social backgrounds. Without *a priori* knowledge of who becomes an alcoholic, existing definitions border on the tautological: If you ask the question, "Why does the homeless man drink the way he does?" and I reply, "He drinks that way because he is an alcoholic!", I have not provided an explanation so much as a restatement of what was already known (i.e., that alcoholics drink heavily and chronically, and that this individual apparently drinks in the same manner). It is equal to saying "These furry rodents drown themselves each year because they are lemmings;" or, "He murdered 13 women because he is a serial killer!"

Tautologies are considered meaningless because they offer no information other than what is already known. A genuine explanation might involve the biological processes which cause lemmings to migrate in the first place, or a portrait of a killer's psychological world and his underlying beliefs about women. At least that would carry more weight than a label.

If medicine cannot diagnose an alcoholic on any basis other than that the person drinks entirely too much and that his life revolves around drinking, it is hard to see how the field has, for all of its elegant research and detailed treatment plans, evolved very much beyond tautological explanations for alcoholism and addiction. A disease diagnosis based so much on arbitrary social standards—a diagnosis still riddled with controversy, which can predict only what it already sees—may not represent the bedrock knowledge upon which further speculations should be launched. Yet that is exactly what happened during the late 1980s and early 1990s. Recovery authors diagnosed with a level of certainty that the alcoholism field's most distinguished researchers do not claim for themselves even now.

If you asked a recovery star about critical reactions to the term "codependency," you were likely to get a wise nod in reply followed by, "Yeah, but I'll bet people were saying the same thing about alcoholism in the 1930s." Meanwhile, the list of "-isms" and dependencies continued to grow: "religious addiction," "rage-a-holics" and the "disease of control." From the inside, it became difficult to determine whether the recovery field was making exciting discoveries

(as we at HCI often wrote a bit disingenuously), or clamber-
ing after new diseases as insurers discontinued paying for
old ones such as alcoholism.

But then, recovery had always been a field of dreams. At
the first conference I covered for Adult Children of Alcoholics (ACoAs) in 1987, HCI had gone all out and placed a
merry-go-round inside the Sheraton Twin Towers in Orlando, Florida. More than a thousand conventioneers wan-
dered the hotel ballrooms and exhibit area for three days,
some of them clutching teddy bears so that their "inner
children" would feel safe. I watched as adults in pajamas
gathered around two HCI authors for a scheduled event
called "Bedtime Stories for Adult Children."

For someone who had spent the previous eight years in
heavy construction work (my philosophy degree qualified
me for little else), this was admittedly a strange sight. But it
was my first conference and I was thrilled at the chance to
be turned loose, writing about whatever I saw fit to cover. I
too felt a keen sense of excitement, a sense of being in on
something big.

The term "adult children" was originally short for Adult
Children of Alcoholics. It came about partly because of the
growth of what I call the expanded recovery movement—
the problems and long-term effects of growing up with
alcoholism. As the movement grew through skyrocketing
book sales and a burgeoning treatment industry offering
services for an ever-expanding client base, adult children
became shorthand not only for children of alcoholics but
also for adults who were brought up in other types of
"dysfunctional families." I sometimes fumbled over intro-
ductions when calling strangers on the phone. I would tell
people I was writing a story for *Changes*, a magazine for
adult children of dysfunctional families. We did not mean to

imply, of course, that our readers were in some way children. We were simply affirming their past so that they—and we—might all get on with a happier future.

Despite the awkwardness in attempting to describe what we were doing, these were heady times. At conferences, book authors frequently introduced each other as brave "pioneers" who had crossed many a conceptual mountain, trodden the bleakest of funding deserts and weathered a storm of skepticism along the way. One prominent recovery star presented a slide show, complete with graduation-march music and childhood photographs of founding board members of the National Association for Children of Alcoholics.

Selling Serenity is the story of a movement characterized by zeal and compassion, a wealth of genuine insights but also oversimplification and overdiagnosis. It is the story of financial chaos and temperance, of quasi-religious certainties and bone-chilling doubts about the most fundamental concepts of trauma and repression, addiction and recovery, and even the meaning of family. I will lead the reader on a step-by-step journey from a national concern over drinking and drug abuse, through related problems and eventually to buried trauma and an epidemic of questionable recovered memories of sexual abuse.

Though these topics may seem unrelated, the same people were present throughout. The same hospital chains that treated addiction patients in the late 1980s treated patients for repressed trauma in the 1990s. And the onslaught of new illnesses to be treated, from codependency to satanic ritual abuse, conveniently came at a time when funding for addiction services had begun to dry up.

As the commercial recovery movement passes its peak, a core of goodness remains. People are still able to walk into a support group in almost any town or city and find others who will help them, for free. This is clearly a positive development. Yet it remains important to discern just what went wrong, and where. I was able to put aside my philosophical reservations about recovery for years so long as people were being helped and my own paychecks continued to arrive on Friday. But soon after the story about the Bartons appeared in *Changes*, I began to hear more and more questions regarding the accuracy of recovered memories. I talked to self-described survivors who had only recently remembered their past abuses, as well as those who had retracted their memories and numbers of bewildered family members. It bothered me that HCI's authors—the recovery stars—seemed to be coming down almost unilaterally on the side of "believing the survivors" in an increasingly polarized climate. Eventually, doubts about the enterprise in which we were engaged forced me to leave HCI. What I have produced since is but a tentative whisper in a dialogue that I hope will continue.

Meanwhile, my former employers have left recovery for bigger and better things. At this writing, *Chicken Soup for the Soul* and spinoff titles (for mothers, women, teen-agers and Christians) occupy five slots on *USA Today*'s top 20 book sellers, including three in the top 10. I am told that my former boss, Gary Seidler, has moved to Beverly Hills.

The rest of us must not simply "move on" from recovery without a serious look into its presuppositions and its tone of righteous reformism that belies its medical-sounding language. Academic and popular fads will always come and go. Only to the extent that the reach of new movements tends to exceed their grasp and that self-righteousness is an inescapable part of human nature, are we unable to prevent other people from coming to harm in new ways.

Alleged witches have been burned at the stake and suspected communists have had their careers and reputations ruined over hysteria. Many people have died estranged from their loved ones over false accusations. For accusers who later come to change their minds about the abuse, there can be no sense of closure when the person they accused has since died. For them, and especially for the young who have been led into questionable accusations against day care workers and others, we owe it to ourselves to sort through the madness of what has happened. In an age of emotional narcissism and drive-thru diagnoses what we need is a return to reason.

CHAPTER ONE

A Treatment Industry Mobilizes

In 1990, two California school districts banned the book *Little Red Riding Hood* because of an illustration showing a young girl in red carrying a picnic basket containing, among other items, a bottle of wine.

The "war on drugs" that President Reagan had declared in 1986, which gained momentum as the "number-one issue" for a successful Bush campaign in 1988, was well on its way to becoming a protracted guerilla skirmish.

The California school district decision reflected a ripple of concern spreading across the country. The attention was not on alcohol or drugs but on their influences and long-term effects. During the early 1970s, few people thought about waging a war on drugs. People of that generation saw drugs as something to be enjoyed. Their capacity to "alter consciousness" was beneficial to discovering the different possibilities in viewing life. Certainly ill consequences could result, but few thought of drugs as bad in and of themselves.

Obviously, things changed. Various social factors created a rethinking of the carefree 1960s, which included an expanded appreciation for the potential of addiction. By the time President Reagan declared his war on drugs, the public was ready for an attitudinal change. Though alcohol, a distinctly devastating drug, would survive the assault, it too came under fire. The National Council on Alcoholism (now the National Council on Alcoholism and Drug Dependence), in particular, increased pressure on politicians to spread the message that alcoholism was the nation's number one health problem, that alcoholics needed treatment and that the government and private insurance should help provide funding for that treatment.

Though passions ran deep among alcohol reformers, none advocated a return to Prohibition, at least not from any public platform. Times had changed since that singular evening of June 6, 1900, when Carry Nation randomly opened her Bible to Isaiah and read, "Arise, shine, for thy light is come!"[1] At dawn, Nation drove her horse and buggy to Kiowa, Kansas, walked into a saloon and began heaving bricks. She later returned with a hatchet.

The battle that started in the late 1980s and continues today is far subtler. Prevention campaigns sought to change the way people thought about alcohol, particularly young people. Temperance forces showed their resolve, some through prevention and others through punishment:

• Alcohol manufacturers lost a protracted battle with the National Council on Alcoholism (NCA) and related interests in 1989, when mandatory warning labels on all alcoholic beverages became law.[2]
• Between 1985 and 1990, more than half the states instituted tax hikes of 20% to 25% on alcoholic beverages.[3]
• In 1989, State Senator Thomas Sharp recommended that Delaware resurrect the whipping post, banned since 1961,

for drug pushers. Sharp's defeated proposal called for "no more than thirty lashes, well laid across a bare back."[4]

"Alcohol in the '90s will take the place that tobacco assumed in the '80s—a growing social ostracism and condemnation,"[5] said David Musto, a medical historian at Yale University. Though Prohibition will most likely remain a failed experiment, some historians think America is in the midst of a "new temperance movement." A Gallup poll released in December 1987 revealed that 87% of Americans regarded alcoholism as a disease, up 10% from five years before. Belief that alcoholism is hereditary jumped 13% (from 50% to 63%); and relatively few respondents were willing to blame socioeconomic or educational factors as part of the cause of alcoholism. George Gallup said "the findings are of great importance because they point to the fact that information campaigns have obviously penetrated to all levels of society."[6]

Among physicians, the move toward generalizing "addictive disease" was well under way. An American Psychiatric Association (APA) committee convened for the Betty Ford Center's 1987 Annual Conference and revised the APA's *Diagnostic and Statistical Manual* to include broadened criteria for "dependence on a psychoactive substance,"[7] designed to include alcohol and other drugs. The APA's original three criteria—"a pattern of pathological use of the substance for one month or longer, and an impairment of social relationships" and "the physiological syndrome of tolerance and withdrawal,"[8]—indicating dependence grew to nine; diminishing the importance of withdrawal symptoms and dividing dependence into three categories: mild, moderate and severe.

Shortly thereafter, the American Medical Association

(AMA) followed suit, passing a resolution which "resolved that the American Medical Association endorses the proposition that drug dependencies, including alcoholism, are diseases, and that their treatment is a legitimate part of medical practice."[9] The American Medical Society on Alcohol and Other Drug Dependencies (AMSAODD) (itself an outgrowth of the AMA) treatment supporters called the resolution historical, citing such common phenomena as cross-addiction and poly-drug abuse among addicts.

Official recognition from the AMA was regarded as long overdue by treatment industry insiders. Jess Bromley, an internal medicine specialist and the resolution's author, said that the resolution "legitimizes the original postulates of the 12 Steps through the canons of medicine."[10] During an interview for a *U.S. Journal* article regarding the AMA's decision, Bromley was asked if he would call a broken finger a disease.

"A broken finger is a disease of trauma,"[11] he replied.

The definition for "disease" in *Dorland's* Illustrated *Medical Dictionary* agrees with Bromley's:

> Any deviation from or interruption of the normal structure or function of any part, organ, or system (or combination thereof) of the body that is manifested by a characteristic set of symptoms and signs and whose etiology, pathology and prognosis may be known or unknown.[12]

Bromley was correct; the AMA came closer than ever before to embracing the concept of alcoholism as a disease, as formulated by the laity in Alcoholics Anonymous (AA) some 50 years earlier. The AMA had been inching toward that direction since their 1956 resolution, which called alcoholism an "illness," and in 1966 they upgraded the condition to disease status.

The AMA's unification of alcoholism and all drug addiction under a single disease label placed treatment providers in good stead. Among those pleased with the new resolution was Rick Esterly, a knowledgeable observer of insurance trends and chief executive officer of The Caron Foundation in Wernersville, Pennsylvania.

"Treatment professionals have known for years that alcohol and drug dependencies are closely related," Esterly said. "The AMA adding its official recognition will, I think, add more evidence to those arguments. Eventually, all insurance companies will come around to developing a substance abuse program, rather than the alcohol-and-other-drug programs we see now."[13] Esterly noted that Blue Cross and Blue Shield of Pennsylvania had already unified its alcohol and drug classifications earlier that year. He was optimistic that other third-party payers would now follow suit. The treatment field's members hoped, as a result, that fewer alcoholics and addicts would "fall through the cracks" because they could not afford treatment.

The problem was that scientists were not much closer than they ever had been to explaining why or how it is that some people become addicts and alcoholics whereas others do not. Nor were they refining their knowledge of premorbid alcoholism characteristics to meet challenges as presented by Vincent Dole in the December 1980 issue of *Scientific American*:

No one really understands addictive behavior. . . . The lack of a basic understanding of the addictive process becomes obvious to anyone who examines the confusion of programs seeking to deal with the drug epidemic. As with efforts to control plagues in the Middle

Ages, today's governmental policies toward addiction are politically determined, contradictory and ineffective. The situation is not likely to improve until the biological factors underlying addiction have been discovered.[14]

What Is Addiction?

Most of the broader recovery concepts drew their credibility from alcoholism theory. Yet the concept of alcoholism as a disease has never truly lost its controversial status, an issue many in the treatment field avoid discussing. A large percentage of those in the treatment industry believed their profession was under attack by researchers, greedy insurance companies and a still-flourishing ignorant public who chose the wrong side of the dichotomous "bad-versus-sick" portrayal of alcoholics.

Recent research suggests that the line between an alcoholic and an occasional problematic drinker may be close to invisible. The same is true for other behaviors we call addictions. "Everyone engages in addictive behaviors to some extent because such things as eating, drinking, and sex are essential to survival and highly reinforcing,"[15] said G. Alan Marlatt, Ph.D., director of the Addictive Behaviors Research Center at the University of Washington. "We get immediate gratification from them and find them very hard to give up indeed. That's a pretty good definition of addiction."[16]

"In science nothing is ever nailed down,"[17] said Carlton Erickson, a biochemical researcher at the University of Texas at Austin. Erickson, who has closely followed the literature on alcoholism since the early 1970s, attempted to replicate recent studies claiming to have found a gene for alcoholism, which had mixed results at best.

According to Erickson, as researchers have refined their

definitions and descriptions of alcoholism, several key concepts have been changing:

● The tendency to become alcoholic is probably inherited, but alcoholism cannot be guaranteed simply by having an as-yet-undiscovered gene. Elements of environment, conditioning and choice enter in.

● The field still lacks a diagnostic test separating the alcohol abuser from the alcoholic. "This isn't a too-often, too-much disease, it's an 'I-can't-stop disease,' " Erickson said. "One guy can drink a quart of booze a day and you still don't know he's an alcoholic. Someone else could drink four drinks a day and be one."

● The image of alcoholism as a "progressive" disease, as in an upward-curving line on a graph, has fallen out of favor. Rather, alcoholics may drink in cycles of progression and cutbacks. "The AA model says once you have it, you always have it. But, really, you could achieve remission. There's nothing that says alcoholism can't come and go."

● "Treatments today are called shotgun," Erickson said, in that they apply a single model to a multi-faceted and variable target in clients. As for the "emotional addictions," such as sex, love or codependency, he opined, "that is a misuse of the term 'addiction.' "[18]

During the 1980s, research on heroin and cocaine addicts broadened the concept of addiction. One of the first signs of change was the reshaping and comparative de-emphasizing of the importance of withdrawal symptoms as a necessary feature of addiction. First, it was found that withdrawal symptoms were not experienced across the board by heroin users, some of whom had been able to moderate their use of the drug. Second, withdrawal excluded a wide range of classic addiction indicators such as escalation of use, craving and continued use despite adverse consequences.

But if there was one drug which changed the way professionals looked at addiction and its symptoms, that drug may have been cocaine.

"Cocaine is forcing us to confront the meaning of addiction and the reality of a single disease process that is triggered by many different types of psychoactive chemicals,"[19] physician Arnold Washton wrote in a 1987 *U.S. Journal* column. Washton foresaw an expanded view of addictions not dependent on withdrawal symptoms, which cocaine (technically) does not produce. Rather, "the reinforcing effects of the drug, both positive and negative," coupled with changes in brain activity, "lock a person into compulsive cocaine use."[20]

Washton concluded by stating, "Many clinicians now define addiction as loss of control that leads to compulsive use despite adverse effects to the person's health or ability to function."[21]

What Is Disease?

Scientists have long held a considerable understanding of drug-related phenomena such as tolerance and dependence, explaining the cravings that result with the discontinued use of narcotics. What is missing is a definitive explanation of who becomes an addict and why people relapse long after their bodies have stabilized from withdrawal.

While addressing the disease concept of alcoholism at a 1991 meeting of the American Society on Addiction Medicine, Daniel Flavin, medical-scientific director for the National Council on Alcoholism and Drug Dependence said, "What we are talking about is really more of a philosophical issue than a scientific one."[22] A defender of the disease concept, Flavin added that debate is therefore inevitable and legitimate.

> We know, basically, that alcohol has direct toxic effects on various organ systems; that it's directly or indirectly associated with significant morbidity and mortality; that there is a potential for a physiologic dependence syndrome characterized by increased tolerance and withdrawal; and that these may also be influenced by non-physiologic mechanisms . . . and that there really is no universally accepted theory of alcohol addiction at the present time, given our current data.[23]

Behavioral theories portray addiction as a response to social conditioning or as a desire to escape a negative environment. Genetic theories probably hold the most hope for supplying the field with the answers needed to explain addiction. The search continues for a "genetic marker," which would separate potential addicts from non-addicts.

> We know that there is genetic vulnerability in some but not all individuals addicted to alcohol. As a group, alcoholics are not pre-morbidly different from those who are not alcoholic, and studies that were done by Vaillent and others have conclusively looked at this question. There is a lack of a single distinctive pattern of use which leads to dependence. Problematic alcohol consumption is often progressive but not always progressive.[24]

For Flavin, it was important to choose "a definition of disease consistent with our present level of knowledge."[25]

This is a challenge; too specific a definition risks outdistancing the current data and possibly missing individuals who otherwise would be considered alcoholic, while too broad a definition opens the field to charges of being vague or meaningless.

The Unification of Addictions

In 1987, the AMA decided that all drug dependencies were diseases. Hence its resolution, placed as it was on the delegates' "consent calendar" (traditionally reserved for rubber-stamp issues), was not much of a political risk. Indeed, the AMA's relatively tepid 1956 resolution may have required more courage relative to the times.

The resolution avoided naming any specific drugs, leaving open the possibility that "dependence" on antidepressants or coffee or nicotine gum could qualify one for hospitalization—though it is doubtful that many would have entertained such a notion. According to Max Schneider, a past president of the AMSAODD and a senior statesman in the alcoholism field, the word "drugs" referred to heroin, cocaine, PCP and marijuana.[26]

In a 1987 *U.S. Journal* column, Schneider noted that professional associations, such as the National Association of Alcoholism Treatment Programs (NAATP) and the American Medical Society on Alcoholism (AMSA), were changing their names to reflect the new expanded view of addiction. The NAATP became the National Association of Addictions Treatment Providers; and AMSA revised its name to the American Medical Society on Alcoholism and Other Drug Dependencies, and later to the American Society of Addiction Medicine.

Schneider had mixed feelings regarding these changes: "These objectives are based on noble thoughts and I have no quarrel with them. My concern is the apparent de-emphasizing of the importance of alcohol problems."[27]

Schneider praised the grandparent of them all, the National Council on Alcoholism (NCA), who appeared to be the lone holdout—until they changed their name to the National Council on Alcoholism and Drug Dependence.[28]

These expansions reflected a trend which moved the recovery movement in a new direction. The 1970s were officially over. It was no longer acceptable for an alcoholic in recovery to smoke an occasional joint or for cocaine addicts to drink an occasional glass of wine.

By the late 1980s, recovery had bred through enough generations of multiple meanings and been protected by enough of its authorities to ensure its survival in the eco-system of American English words. There was something magically self-justifying about its resonance, in which the word's very ambiguity added to its appeal.

And just as professional groups changed their names to reflect a broadened understanding of addictions, thousands of men and women around the country began incorporating a broadened understanding of recovery into their everyday lives.

The influence of self-help books and treatment programs for codependency, eating disorders, sexual addiction and sexual abuse caused many groups to rethink their priorities and self-images in an attempt to align with recovery principles. Similar to toddlers learning to stand, 12-Steppers across the country incorporated a more direct form of communication as part of their recoveries. Unspoken traditions, decades-old "rules" in their families-of-origin were assessed, confronted and brought into the light. Excessive involvement in politics, the arts, higher education, athletics, charities or other community projects was now weighed against possible consequences to one's recovery and more than likely pared down.

Toward a Recovering Workplace

By 1987, a quarter of Fortune 500 companies had adopted drug testing, particularly in safety-sensitive jobs involving passengers or heavy machinery. Of the half-dozen testing laboratories contacted, the lowest growth rate for the previous year was 20%. The federal government was one of their largest clients. The Department of Transportation began testing its employees in 1987, and the military stepped up its 1981 testing program. President Reagan ordered widespread random testing for federal employees, despite state and federal judges rulings that such tests violated Fourth Amendment rights on the grounds of unreasonable search and seizure.

Employee Assistance Programs (EAPs), established to help workers with a wide range of everyday needs, were expanded by large companies such as Alcoa, U.S. Steel and Westinghouse. EAPs differed; while some companies chose to run their own programs, others hired independent consultants to administer their EAPs. A 1987 *U.S. Journal* column on EAP issues stated:

> Family counselors will find more family problems, and alcoholism counselors will find more addiction problems than will EAP counselors who have a different orientation. Some EAPs emphasize cost containment. Others emphasize assistance to "troubled employees" through hospital treatment.[29]

Nevertheless, it is fair to say that the scrutiny of every inch of intersection between the employee and any illegal drug—or possibly harmful use of a legal drug such as alcohol—was a key part of most EAPs. If need be, these programs would include such legal or illegal drug use as part of a company's cost containment.

In the above-mentioned article, author Keith McClellan, after allowing for differences in orientations, developed "seven generic functions" that all EAPs should perform, including: "Assessment (ungoverned by law or regulation), Drug screening—medical referral, Health risk appraisal—medical referral and doing 12th Step calls—self-help involvement."[30]

Controversy surrounded the advent of EAPs. Besides the impact of drug testing—which employers could now use to exclude applicants based on recreational, off-duty use of illegal drugs such as marijuana or cocaine—EAPs created a caring-parent image among corporations which was often unwelcome by workers. Even for the one-third of EAPs run by independent contractors, it was difficult for some employees to trust outsiders with personal secrets.

Fiscal Shell Games

The $1.7 billion Anti-Drug Abuse Act of 1986 illustrated the Reagan administration's resolve to attack drug abuse through tougher law enforcement, prevention education and treatment.[31] However, proposed budget cuts announced in 1987 caused supporters of the Act to wonder cynically if the effort hadn't been much more than election-year politics.[32] Most distressing to treatment leaders was the delayed announcement that the more than $262 million reserved for prevention and treatment for Fiscal Year 1987 was actually intended to be dispersed over two years. Block grant money for states and prevention programs for high-risk youth were to be included in the funding.[33]

While officials from the Alcohol, Drug Abuse and Mental Health Administration, a branch of the Health and Human Services Department, and their attorneys claimed the field's leaders had misunderstood the bill's original language, observers from the treatment industry remained unconvinced. Karst Besteman, president of the Alcohol and Drug Problems Association, argued that the administration officials had wanted to cut the treatment budget in half all along.

"The federal budget is a document that has become almost undecipherable,"[34] Besteman complained to the *U.S. Journal* shortly after the White House budget disclosure. "It took us four or five days just to decipher what they had done."[35]

Nonetheless, according to one report, government funds for alcohol treatment, alcohol prevention, drug prevention and drug treatment during 1986 still exceeded $1.6 billion. The lion's share of the tab was paid by the states, not the federal government. The contributions that were offered by the feds were threatened by politicians who previously appeared sympathetic to the treatment cause. Senator Edward Kennedy and Representative Henry Waxman, seeking health coverage for all employees, asked that mandatory alcohol and drug treatment coverage, already in place in 37 states, be dropped for the greater good of more health insurance.[36]

Professional associations fired off letters to Kennedy and Waxman, begging them to reconsider. "With this one unthinking clause," Besteman wrote, "the bill's sponsors are proposing to turn back the clock of concern and consign all alcoholics and drug addicts to the purgatory of overburdened, publicly funded programs or the hell of no treatment."[37]

Unselling Spuds

Although politicians were reluctant to back their anti-drug speeches with financial support, advocacy groups were not. In the Summer of 1987, a coalition of print and broadcast associations met to plan a three-year media assault on drugs. An "unselling" campaign by the National Media Advertising Partnership for a Drug-Free America targeted potential users in the 18- to 34-year-old age group, as well as "influencer groups," such as parents and minority leaders. Their first commercial spot became the most famous: a 30-second film of an egg frying in a skillet, along with the message, "This is your brain on drugs . . . Any questions?"[38]

The partnership was the brainchild of the American Association of Advertising Agencies' executives, who set a $500 million goal of free advertising and air time to be donated by newspapers, magazines and television stations. Operating costs were secured from donations of $25,000 apiece from about 100 corporations; including Chrysler, Ford, Dow Chemical and Standard Oil.[39] Though originally scheduled for three years, the effort was renewed in 1990.

There was one significant omission in the partnership's unselling effort: alcohol. This omission of the single most popular drug of abuse among young people spoke volumes about the alcohol beverage industry's influence and the passions of the millions who keep them in business. And, as those connected with alcohol public policy soon discovered, many industries depend on alcohol manufacturers' good fortunes. Bars and restaurants, the hotel and motel industry, the transportation industry and the grain industry all have a stake in alcohol consumption.

Meanwhile, lobbying groups such as the NCA pressured Congress to mandate warning labels on all alcohol products. The effort eventually succeeded after a few years of wrangling with reluctant politicians. In 1987, Dram Shop Laws governing barroom sales became tougher, expanding to include private party givers or "social hosts" who allowed their guests to drive home intoxicated.[40] Even Spuds MacKenzie, the popular "party animal" mascot of Budweiser beer commercials, got nicked in the fray.

"What's a party animal? A drunk!" declared William McCord, the drug and alcohol commissioner for the state of South Carolina. "To be marketing this to children ought to be criminal."[41]

Similar accusations from other field leaders may have touched a sensitive spot at Anheuser-Busch. After all, most states had recently been exhorted into raising their drinking age to 21, under the possibility of losing federal funds for highways. Budweiser eventually muzzled the Spuds commercials, though spokesmen denied that they had done so in response to pressure.

Alcohol as a Women's Issue

While others were trying out new diagnoses in alcoholism, the market for alcoholism treatment services was being refined. Women in particular were named as an underserved population. Experts noted that AA attendance among women had jumped from near-zero to an estimated 30%. Moreover, women metabolize alcohol more slowly, become intoxicated faster and suffer long-term health complications earlier in their drinking careers than men. A cry of alarm on behalf of women drinkers went out from the NCA, the National Organization for Women (NOW) and the Junior League.

According to some critics; because it was two men who formed AA, it was and still is disproportionately composed of men, targeted toward men and clothed in masculine authoritarian concepts, while the broader recovery movement is largely targeted toward women.

I assisted in designing and evaluating several surveys conducted by Health Communications, Inc. (HCI) over the years, which indicated that women made up about 80% of their readership. An informal scan of audiences at dozens of Adult Children of Alcoholics (ACoA) and codependency conferences across the country reflected a similar proportion of women to men. One could speculate endlessly as to why this was the case. The entire children-of-alcoholics movement was brought about, in part, by a perceived disparity in alcoholism treatment favoring the (male) head of household. There was little or no counseling available for families who were bearing the brunt of the alcoholic's behavior. The treatment that did exist was centered on helping the individual stay sober.

Emphasizing that women, too, could be alcoholic, and that they often hid their disease better than men (if only because society didn't recognize their symptoms), helped shift the balance of treatment in a more equitable direction. The identification of women's alcoholism as a neglected area of study served two purposes: (a) It put treatment marketers in touch with a broader target for their services; and (b) It drew alcoholism treatment closer in line to the expansion of the recovery movement; away from the individual alcoholic and toward groups of people who were adversely affected by the alcoholic's behavior.

The more recovery could be construed as vaguely feminist, the more the market of vaguely dissatisfied women could be tapped and exploited. Emerging research made targeting women easier. New inquiries revealed that standard charts used to project blood-alcohol levels did not apply to women since their reactions to alcohol can fluctuate with menstrual cycles. These findings, available since the early 1980s,[42] were still not widely known.

Sheila Blume, medical director of alcoholism and compulsive gambling programs at an Amityville, New York hospital, claimed that women alcoholics face a "pernicious triple stigma" in their alcoholism: (a) being drunks; (b) women are expected to behave on a generally higher moral plane; and (c) the idea that women become promiscuous after a few drinks.[43]

Blume, Edith Gomberg and other researchers supplied a much needed contribution to the study of genuine differences in women's development of chemical dependency; their likelihood to seek help; variations in both substance abuse and available services according to race, economic class and sexual orientation; and the additional complications brought on by pregnancy with drug-affected infants and fetal alcohol syndrome.[44]

The NCA succeeded in gaining legislation for states to set aside a certain percentage of their federal grant funds to improve services available for women. Representatives of the NCA, NOW and the Junior League met with actress Sharon Gless and her *Cagney & Lacey* producer Barney Rosenzweig, for the screening of a two-part segment about Cagney's drinking and the importance of AA's role in helping her stop.

The broader recovery movement built on the idea of women as a particularly needy group of people. Over the next few years sellers of books, conferences and therapy services refined their advertising and recruiting techniques to identify successful women as also being the neediest and most underserved of anyone.

The Moderation Issue

There seemed to be a pattern among people in the alcoholism and addictions field: The higher you go, the less they know. The more erudite or scientifically trained the interlocutor, the more modest his claims to scientific knowledge would be regarding the precise nature of alcoholism: what it is, how to tell when someone has it and how to distinguish between heavy drinkers and alcoholics.

On the high end were people like Enoch Gordis, former director of what is now the National Institute on Alcoholism and Drug Dependence, who wrote the following in the *Journal of Studies on Alcohol*: "In the case of alcoholism . . . our whole treatment system is founded on hunch, not evidence, and not on science."[45]

At the other end of the continuum are the counselors who work hands-on, witness tragedy and are often in recovery themselves. Based on their case files they wonder how much more evidence is needed to prove that alcoholism is real and that it kills people. Alcohol counselors and the men and women of AA tend to use the most authoritative language when discussing alcoholism.

The studies that have been done estimate that fewer than half of addicts and alcoholics sent for treatment remain clean and sober. According to William Miller, a psychologist and the director of the Center on Alcoholism, Substance Abuse and Addictions at the University of New Mexico, at least four studies found no differences between alcoholics who attended AA meetings and those who received no treatment whatsoever.[46]

"A rather remarkable amount of research has been conducted on the effectiveness of several dozen approaches to the treatment of substance abuse,"[47] Miller told reporter Joann Rodgers in a 1994 issue of *Psychology Today*. Miller and "his colleague, Reed Hester, after a review of treatment outcomes from 1980 to 1990," a period of unprecedented growth in the recovery industry, "concluded that 'despite much more knowledge of what works, treatment for substance abuse hasn't changed much in 40 years.' "[48]

Some of the alternative treatments included brief therapy, aversion therapy, tapering off ("warm turkey"),[49] and an emerging school of drug therapy similar in principle to methadone maintenance for heroin addicts. All of these methods have higher success rates than AA-based treatment, said Miller and Hester, yet they are seldom used.[50]

Miller and Hester also claimed success in teaching some alcoholics to drink moderately. While many of those eventually decided to quit altogether, many others did not, although they did not return to problematic drinking. Even Miller was surprised by these results.[51]

"The prevalent theories were that they would either eventually relapse and lose control of their drinking or that they would quit because moderation did not work,"[52] Miller said. "The old domino theory that one drink equals a drunk proved, for some, to be baloney."[53]

Two of the most infamous studies in this regard were conducted in the early 1970s. In the first, Mark Sobell and Linda Sobell, then of the University of California, followed a group of alcoholics for a number of years and reported that some of them had become controlled drinkers.[54] In 1982, researcher Mary Pendery published a review of the Sobells' work in *Science*, which reported that four of the subjects said to have been drinking successfully had died within 10 years of the study. Though heavy alcohol consumption was thought to have contributed to their deaths this was never firmly established.[55]

Pendery did not mention that six of the subjects in the control group, who received traditional abstinence-oriented treatment, also died. After a congressional investigation and a scientific commission reviewed the original study, the Sobells were exonerated. Other researchers and the American Psychological Association eventually criticized Pendery for citing research out of context.[56] However, her bold stance against the Sobells, and symbolically against controlled drinking research, made her a heroine in the mainstream alcoholism field.

In the mid-1970s, a large national study by the Rand Commission concluded that 22% of the alcoholics in an 18-month survey sample returned to moderate drinking. This report also drew fire from the mainstream treatment field.[57]

The following conclusion reached by philosopher Herbert Fingarette, who reviewed the research in his book *Heavy Drinking: The Myth of Alcoholism as a Disease*, was lost in the outcry over professional ethics in using human subjects.

Placed in context, then, the mortality rate for the controlled drinkers showed that controlled drinking has its risks and failures, but that it may prove to be a significantly more successful method than abstinence for at least some drinkers.[58]

Fingarette also noted that:

Controlled drinking programs for problem drinkers are routinely available in other countries, especially the United Kingdom, Canada, and Norway. In the United Kingdom, for example, three-fourths of the clinics offer controlled drinking as an alternative. But in our country, the ideological preoccupation with the disease concept of alcoholism has forestalled the establishment of programs with goals other than total abstinence.[59]

Opponents as Killers

In a bizarre postscript to the Sobell controversy, Mary

Pendery's body was discovered on April 12, 1994, in her mountain home outside of Sheridan, Wyoming. Pendery had been shot with her own .357 Magnum, apparently by a "friend" who then took his own life. Police found an empty bottle of scotch and an open bottle of wine in the house. The two had met years earlier when Pendery was the director of the alcohol treatment center at the Veterans Administration (VA) Medical Center in San Diego.

In a special issue of *Professional Counselor* eulogizing Pendery's life and accomplishments, editor Cliff Creager reviewed her 10-year effort to prove that the Sobells had falsified survey data on controlled drinking. He employed a phrase by Irving Maltzman, Pendery's graduate school mentor at the University of California-Los Angeles (UCLA) and colleague against the Sobell study, in saying that an "intellectual mafia" opposed to the disease concept of alcoholism had forced Pendery out of the San Diego VA. She eventually relocated to another VA facility in Sheridan. "She and Maltzman fought a mostly lonesome battle for more than a decade," Creager added, "earning the undying gratitude of the addictions treatment field but suffering personal and professional pain at every turn."[60]

A brief accompanying article by Maltzman also lauds Pendery's courage in opposing the psychological establishment, and concludes by asking the following troublesome questions: "Why did she leave her loving family and friends and go alone to an isolated facility? Why did she leave people depending upon her treatment skills? Why did she leave the San Diego VA? Was she harassed into leaving? Why? Why?"[61]

These questions coupled with the article's headline, "Who killed Mary Pendery?"[62] suggest the possibility that Pendery's death was more than a tragic murder-suicide committed by a disturbed individual. It is unclear why Maltzman referred to Pendery's home as an isolated facility.[63] Creager's article reported that Pendery lived alone at the time of her death except for hosting the murder suspect, realtor George Sie Rega of Florida. As for the reasons for Pendery's departure from the VA clinic she founded in San Diego, Creager contends she was indeed forced out by the intellectual mafia opposed to the disease concept. Maltzman isn't quite so sure, but nonetheless paints an apparent murder-suicide with conspiratorial overtones.[64]

These details are included to illustrate the deep-rooted sentiments in the controlled drinking controversy.

Is There a Middle Ground?

It is apparent that a great need exists for broader, more diverse treatment and self-help systems than are available. Rational Recovery (RR), Women for Sobriety and Secular Organizations for Sobriety (SOS) represent significant beginnings in this direction. Perhaps these groups will pave the way for a more expansive treatment methodology, just as AA and treatments built around AA improved on the indifferent or harsh treatments available to alcoholics before the 1950s.

It is possible, however, that the breadth of alcohol problems in this country extends beyond the existing methods of amelioration in treatment or self-help. Until recently, for example, services were not available for people who occasionally overdo happy hour and want to cut back, or for alcoholics who should probably stop drinking but either don't want to or aren't ready to. While "harm avoidance" treatments lack the air of conversion mysticism that seems to appeal to the media and the public at large, there is no reason not to incorporate their use more often.

According to Hester, encouraging data on the possibility for some alcoholics to drink moderately has been available for a long time. "Non-problematic outcomes have been happening for years and been reported," Hester said in a telephone interview, "people don't read the outcome literature." But he added that the likelihood of successful moderation decreases as a person becomes more dependent on alcohol, an observation that he said is approaching "worldwide consensus."[65]

For Barbara McCrady, clinical director of the Center for Alcohol Studies at Rutgers University, abstinence is the only treatment strategy for classical, late-stage alcoholics and a good bet for other problem drinkers. "My preference as a clinician is to work with abstinence because it's safer," McCrady said in an interview. "It's a value decision because by the time people come into treatment, alcohol has been doing stressful things in their lives. Because alcohol is not a terribly important substance, I ask people why they need to continue using it. But clearly some people make a choice to moderate their drinking and it's worked for them."[66]

McCrady also said that attending AA and similar groups can be an important adjunct to treatment.

> People use AA in different ways. There are some people who become longtime AA members who follow very little of the program but are committed because alcohol really harmed their lives. They don't necessarily pay attention to everything other people say, but they see going to meetings as a personal statement, a reaffirmation of a decision they have made to change their lives. It's similar to people who have gotten thin through Weight Watchers and now go to meetings to weigh in once a month. For others it's appropriate to take it all.[67]

The average person struggling with chemical dependency doesn't usually have the opportunity to talk with people like McCrady, Miller, Hester or any of a number of prominent clinicians and researchers who don't subscribe uncritically to a 12-step treatment philosophy for patients with a wide range of drinking problems. Without reading the handful of books that have been published in recent years challenging the scientific accuracy of the disease model and the motives of those who benefit from its near universal application, it is easy for most patients and even many substance abuse counselors to remain in the dark about chemical dependency's most fundamental controversies, and to believe that a naive disease theory and a 12-step (or "Minnesota") model of treatment have somehow been established as the best description of the problem and also the best course of treatment for anyone with an alcohol or drug problem. This is almost certainly not the case.

"Research evidence clearly indicates that there is no shining point of light for a single treatment modality,"[68] said Hester. He continued:

Clearly, the 12-Step model works for some people but not everybody. If you've only got one way to treat a person, you're going to think that that's the appropriate way to treat everybody. If all you've got is a hammer, everything looks like a nail. If you look outside of the United States to Canada, or as far away as East Australia or Europe, nowhere do you see such a single-minded ideological model as in the United States.[69]

During my years as a correspondent in the alcoholism treatment field, I often heard American experts arrogantly describe European treatment as "20 years behind the U.S."[70]

I heard executives representing large hospital chains boasting of their diverse, "multifaceted" programs tailored to the needs of individual clients. More often than not, what they were describing was a single abstinence-oriented 12-step approach applied separately to inpatients, residents of halfway houses and outpatients. But Hester claimed that treatment providers will not improve their success rates until they show more versatility in what they offer patients. "If you don't change content, if you only change the treatment setting, then there is no change in outcomes."[71] This is perhaps a more clinical version of the popular 12-step warning: "If nothing changes, then nothing changes."

A group called Moderation Management (MM) founded by Audrey Kishline is attempting to address these needs. Kishline says people who are unable to follow their conservative drinking guidelines are encouraged to go to AA or another abstinence-oriented group.[72]

It is possible that for a very large number of individuals, moderation may be the treatment outcome of choice. With a few exceptions (only a handful of hospitals in the United States now offer moderation as a treatment goal), the system basically says "use AA or face your problems alone." This seems neither compassionate nor fair. Nor does a one-way treatment philosophy reflect well for a nation with such diverse views.

There are mental health professionals and others who are presently working in this direction by providing less spiritual and other alternative options for drinkers. Alcohol problems cover an enormous range and treatments should reflect that range.

The Best and Worst of Times
Although the late 1980s were boom years for treatment of

addictions, forces were already at work that would dramatically slash and change the face of this treatment. Perhaps the most serious implication for the treatment field was a decision by the Health Care Financing Administration (HCFA) that forced providers to comply with pre-determined Diagnosis Related Groupings (DRGs) in order to qualify for Medicare reimbursement. The DRG system had been in place since 1983, but the 1987 action removed the exemption that had been granted to 325 hospital programs. Under the alcohol and drug DRGs, treatment for specific problems should cost a specific amount, and anything exceeding those estimates would be denied reimbursement. This was quite a blow.[73]

According to a Washington, D.C.-based research firm that studied 11,000 addiction patients, the average length of stay for inpatients in 1987 was 28 days and the average cost for detoxification and rehabilitation was $7,805 per patient.[74] Field mediators tried unsuccessfully to revise the new DRGs, which commanded only 17.6 days worth of reimbursement, and a cap on payments at $4,191.[75]

Perhaps more distressing to the morale of the treatment providers was how the HCFA analysts computed the formulas. The 325 hospitals were originally exempted after persuading HCFA that alcohol and drug services were highly specialized, and thus should not be required to conform to the layman's understanding of rehabilitation.[76] Milan Korcok, a former contributing editor for the *U.S. Journal*, discussed the following in a 1987 *U.S. Journal* article: Michael Ford, then-president of the National Association of Addiction Treatment Providers, saw the actions of the HCFA as a sign of disrespect. "They're (the proposed DRGs) saying that we're not different, that anyone can rehabilitate an alcoholic,"[77] Ford said.

Worse, the DRG system foreshadowed a trend. At the time, most patients were covered by commercial third-party payers such as Blue Cross and Blue Shield while only 5% were covered by Health Maintenance Organizations (HMOs). HMOs and Preferred Provider Organizations (PPOs) work on a capitation system; this means they bid to cover services up to a fixed cost and make or lose money according to how much, or how little, they spend to provide the care. Just as an auto mechanic's *Kelley Blue Book* tells him how much to charge for a used car, HMOs depend on accurate budget forecasts. After all, this was their strongest selling point—the ability to predict and enforce lower costs for health care, meaning lower revenues for providers.

There were reasons for hope. In 1990, Marketdata Enterprises, a research firm based in Valley Stream, New York, estimated gross profits for the entire treatment industry at $3.9 million for 1989. Marketdata estimated that those profits would grow by 9.5% each year for the next five years to $6.2 million by 1995.[78] Marketdata's numbers, however, were mostly the result of interviews with officials from the nation's top 25 treatment center chains and other consultants. This may have influenced their data.

Alcohol and drug associations were already involved in heated rhetoric with HMOs and other insurers who were stepping up their demands for solid data on the necessity and effectiveness of treatment. The field could not produce this data because it did not exist.

The loss of Medicare funds only addressed 5% of the treatment population. The Civilian Health and Medical Program for the Uniformed Services (CHAMPUS) that reimburses health care for all enlisted men and their families also decided to adopt the DRG system, which would cut into treatment still further.[79]

Looking to the federal government for assistance was proving to be a waste of time. "Bush was one of the most transparent leaders," said Milan Korcok, a veteran treatment field writer. "He was always saying we've got to do this and we've got to do that, but in the end, nothing would happen."[80]

"Something has happened to this kinder, gentler nation on the way to the 1990s,"[81] psychiatrist William Hawthorne told a group of physicians at the 11th Betty Ford Center Conference on Chemical Dependency (1991) in Eisenhower, California. Hawthorne, then a vice president for the treatment chain Mediplex Group in Wellesley, Massachusetts, said that there was an active effort to weaken the disease concept of alcoholism and to denigrate treatment.

"The shock troops of that fight are the managed-care organizations," he said. "Today there are probably less than half as many people in treatment as there were a year ago. This means that people who need help are not getting it."[82]

Birth-Order Roles: Wegscheider-Cruse and Adler

Sharon Wegscheider-Cruse, regarded as one of the leading recovery stars, together with her husband, physician Joseph Cruse, started Onsite Training and Consulting in Rapid City, South Dakota. She has written several books and made scores of conference speeches over the years. Though few outside of recovery circles know her name, on the inside she is like a beacon, a statue of liberty.

In her book *Another Chance: Hope and Health for the Alcoholic Family*, Wegscheider-Cruse describes four "family roles" of the children in alcoholic families, beginning with the perfectionistic "Hero" child who dreams unrealistically of rescuing his or her family. That the family cannot be rescued does not deter the Hero from trying, not only during childhood and adolescence but throughout his or her adult life. "The oldest son or daughter usually plays the Hero," [83] Wegscheider-Cruse writes.

Next is the "Scapegoat," the rebellious, often underachieving child. Scapegoats crave attention and fame as much as Heroes. They obtain this by defying the wishes of their parents, teachers, employers and God himself. The Scapegoat learns a twofold message from the Hero, who is the first child: the good things, the honors and awards, have been taken, and "they aren't worth the effort anyway. His anger and low self-esteem have left him with little motivation to try to achieve academically or in any other way."[84]

"The second child in the family ends up playing the Scapegoat,"[85] Wegscheider-Cruse writes. She describes two more roles—the all-but-invisible "Lost Child" and the "Mascot," whose antics provide comic relief for people desperately in need of something to laugh about.[86]

In 1982, the NCA honored Wegscheider-Cruse with the Marty Mann Award, a year after Science and Behavior Books published *Another Chance*. Other recovery authors have credited her over the years for the development of these four family roles and for her contribution to the realization that it is not just a liver or a reputation an alcoholic destroys but the chance for family members to explore life's ups and downs without nervous preoccupation, anxiety and dread. Unlike the alcoholic, who even if suffering from a disease still chooses to remain decimated by it, these families have done nothing to deserve the treatment they endure at the hands of the drinker. On the other hand, in little "enabling" ways, family members may be doing a great deal to reinforce the behavior.

To make note of these disparities between perception and reality and set down the results in an orderly list was a genuine accomplishment. Wegscheider-Cruse's *Another*

Chance resounds with the urgency of a morning reveille, inviting professionals to look deeper into their caseloads and help family members affected by alcoholism to practice healthier behaviors.

The psychiatrist Alfred Adler, who studied under Freud and was a seminal influence on modern psychology, may have contributed to this broadened understanding of family roles, particularly those determined by birth order. In his essay *The Origin of Neurotic Disposition*,[87] Adler lists four personality descriptions: the oldest child, the second child, the youngest child and the only child. The latter two do not closely resemble any of the four roles Wegscheider-Cruse articulates. The first two resemble her Hero and Scapegoat in almost every aspect except that her descriptions are considerably darker than his. The more ominous characterizations are understandable in light of the fact that Wegscheider-Cruse is writing about alcoholic families.

Whereas in Adler's oldest child "we find individuals who develop a striving to protect others and help them;"[88] Wegscheider-Cruse's Hero or "Little Enabler" grows up "catering to other people's needs and wishes."[89] What Adler's older child reveres in authority and the law, the Hero suffers as a driving need, as control.

The second child and the Scapegoat share a defining sense of competitiveness and rebelliousness, both personalities shaped in reaction to the firstborn. When it comes to interpreting the effects of this reaction on the second child's personality, Adler and Wegscheider-Cruse contrast starkly. Her Scapegoat mirrors his second child in almost every respect, only her typology reads like an alter ego of his—a negative emphasis in place of his positives, an evil twin.

"The second child is often more talented and successful

than the first," Adler writes. "If he goes ahead faster, it is because he trained more. Even when he is grown up and outside the family circle, he often still makes use of a pace-maker by comparing himself with someone whom he thinks more advantageously placed, and tries to go beyond him."[90] Adler provides an example from the Old Testament, in which Jacob overtakes his older brother Esau.[91]

There is a dark side to the second child (and to Jacob) as well, which Adler likens to envy and the potential for setting unattainable goals: "This was well expressed by a little boy of four, who cried out, weeping, 'I am so un-happy because I can *never* be as old as my brother.' "[92] But overall, Adler seems to emphasize strengths, even when discussing the second child's dislike for authority:

> In his later life, the second child is rarely able to endure the strict leadership of others or to accept the idea of eternal laws. He will be much more inclined to believe, rightly or wrongly, that there is no power in the world which cannot be overthrown. Beware of his revolu-tionary subtleties![93]

This flavor of grandfatherly amusement toward the sec-ond born is absent in Wegscheider-Cruse's counterpart. "If one looks only at his facade," she writes, "the Scapegoat is not a very appealing client, but the more perceptive counse-lor can see in him a tragic picture of low self-worth."[94]

Gone too, is Adler's emphasis on the second born as "often more talented and successful than the first."[95] After discussing the second child's underachievement in school, Wegscheider-Cruse writes, "A bright child who finds him-self in the Scapegoat position is more likely to use his mental abilities to become a leader of his peer group or to devise schemes that eventually end up in juvenile court."[96]

As is normally the case between any two therapists, there may be philosophical and stylistic differences between Wegscheider-Cruse and Adler, even within the same stylistic subgroupings of mental health. Besides the concept of personality traits related to birth order, the most similar characteristics noted by Adler and Wegscheider-Cruse are the rule orientation of the oldest, and the rebelliousness and envy of the second oldest.

Despite these similarities, Alfred Adler's name does not appear in *Another Chance*, either in its original 1981 edition or in its second edition in 1989.

A Codependent Society

The fortunes of HCI and the beginnings of the broader recovery movement were defined by one book more than any other. *Adult Children of Alcoholics* was a slim book about a comprehensive issue that a generation of self-seekers approaching mid-life were ready to confront. It gave birth to the organization, ACoA, which resulted in ACoA meetings within AA. Bill Wilson's wife, Lois Wilson, developed the Al-Anon program for family members of alcoholics, . In 1987, sales of *Adult Children of Alcoholics* peaked, four years after the book was published. It remained on the *New York Times* best-seller list for 48 weeks. This was a remarkable publishing feat considering HCI did not purchase advertising for the book other than through its own publications.

More stunning, *Adult Children of Alcoholics* was only the third book published by HCI. Its author, a former schoolteacher named Janet Woititz, while earning a doctorate in education, had taken a special interest in family problems caused by alcoholism. As a therapist, Woititz observed patterns in children of alcoholics, who were forced into coping with chaotic and unpredictable home lives. Examples of the 28 "characteristics"[97] she compiled were that adult children of alcoholics can only "guess at what normal is,"[98] they have difficulty entering or maintaining intimate relationships,[99] "lie when it would be just as easy to tell the truth,"[100] are unable to complete projects and have trouble at work. Woititz referred to her list of characteristics as "clinical observations."[101]

Apart from finding value in these descriptions, people seemed to experience an emotional lift from reading the book. Its style was simple, to the point, clear and compelling. Woititz had given America permission to breathe a little easier. It was now "okay" to have an alcoholic relative, or to bare the scars of a hurtful childhood in selected public places determined by an evolving recovery subculture. A kind of Bluebeard's door had been opened a crack. The answer to other problems might also lurk behind that door.

Codependent No More by Melody Beattie has sold more than 3 million copies since it first appeared in 1987. Beattie's book became standard reading list material for treatment center outpatients. Drawing upon research by Dennis Wholey, author of *The Courage to Change*, Beattie concludes that 80 million people (nearly a third of the U.S. population), "are chemically dependent or in a relationship with someone who is. They are probably codependent."[102] For definitions, she offers a checklist of 241 traits under categories such as "Caretaking, Obsession and Low Self-Worth." Codependents may "feel sad because they spend their whole lives giving to other people and nobody gives to them," or they tend to "have a lot of 'shoulds,'" or "expect themselves to do everything perfectly."[103]

The popularity of Beattie's book helped launch codependency as a popular disease. Despite the lack of a clear definition and a broad range of symptoms, treatment centers for alcoholism and drug addiction began expanding their services to treat codependency.

"Many codependents feel very scared, hurt and angry,"[104] Beattie advises, and "have strong sexual fantasies about other people," they "get confused,"[105] "become withdrawn and isolated"[106] or "feel controlled by events and people."[107]

"You may be reading this book for yourself; you may be codependent," Beattie writes. "Or, you may be reading this book to help someone else; if so, you probably are codependent."[108] Anyone not covered thus far could fall into the "denial" category, in which codependents "tend to pretend circumstances aren't as bad as they are."[109]

The Basics of Co-Dependence, a 1983 tape by Minneapolis alcoholism counselor Earnie Larsen, echoed Beattie's theme. Larsen estimated that between 10 and 15 million alcoholics existed in the United States, and that each alcoholic adversely affected between 20 and 30 people.[110] Assuming that alcoholics create codependents, a ceiling of 465 million alcoholics and codependents could easily swallow up the U.S. population and still allow for overlap.

In 1984, HCI released a collection of articles entitled *Co-Dependency*. Using the terms "co-alcoholism, para-alcoholism, near-alcoholism" and "co-dependence" in a similar vein, physician Charles Whitfield summed up the scope of the problem: "(Codependence) affects not only individuals, but families, communities, businesses and other institutions and states and countries."[111]

In the same book, Sharon Wegscheider-Cruse first revealed a now widely cited estimate: 96% of the public can be classified in some way as codependent.[112] Although the basis of this figure is unknown, it would be repeated into the 1990s, notably by John Bradshaw who interpreted it to mean that 96% of American families are dysfunctional. In fact, Wegscheider-Cruse had said something slightly different, but of similar import. The following is her definition of codependents:

> All persons who: (1) are in a love or marriage relationship with an alcoholic, (2) have one or more alcoholic parents *or grandparents*, or (3) grew up in an emotionally repressive family.[113]

Wegscheider-Cruse then concluded, reasonably enough, that these parameters would extend to 28 million people. In *Codependence: Misunderstood, Mistreated*, Anne Wilson Schaef lists some of the following "characteristics of the disease":

External Referenting
   Relationship Addiction
   Cling-Clung Relationships
   Lack of Boundaries
   Not trusting Your Own Perceptions
Caretaking
   Making Yourself Indispensable
   Being a Martyr
Physical Illness:
Codependents work hard. They are so intent on taking care of others, keeping things going, and surviving that they often develop stress-related functional or psychosomatic diseases. They develop headaches; backaches; respiratory, heart, and gastrointestinal

problems; and hypertension. Even cancer has been linked to the disease.[114]

In 1987, Schaef tackled societal dysfunction in her book *When Society Becomes an Addict*. She cited Wegscheider-Cruse's 96%[115] figure and echoed *Road Less Traveled* author M. Scott Peck's theme of an impending social crisis. By then she realized that what she had called the White Male System in previous books and what she was now calling the Addictive System, were "one in the same."[116] In a 1990 book of meditations and recovery humor, Schaef wrote:

> This book is dedicated to laughter and those who laugh and those who don't.
>
> It is dedicated to those in recovery, those who aren't, those who refuse to be, those who know they need to be and aren't, and those who don't know they need to be.
>
> Have I left anyone out? [117]

As meanings and potential applications for addiction and recovery continued to expand, what were once considered vices—drunkenness, nymphomania, smoking, gambling, gluttony—were, depending on the theorist, redefined as neurotransmitter shortages, the result of bad upbringing or a search for spirit.

The late 1980s also marked a burgeoning of books for people from dysfunctional families. This terminology grew from "family systems;" a branch of psychology which sees families as organisms in themselves with their own sets of strengths and weaknesses—and most important, a survival instinct. In a dysfunctional family, the family must survive even at the expense of individuals. Alcoholic families were said to be oriented around the active alcoholism of one or both parents. A host of other types of dysfunctional families began appearing at addiction and recovery conferences. The chief characteristic among such families, it was said, was the desire to keep the family's unhealthy secrets hidden. Recovery consequently meant exposing secrets and discussing previously taboo subjects. As a result, some of the following phrases became popular: "enmeshment," "boundary violations," "shame," "surrogate mother or father," "covert incest" and the umbrella term "codependency."

Robert Subby, a Minnesota therapist and popular HCI author, defined codependency as "a disease of the intrapersonal system. Body, mind and spirit are divided from one another as a result of the dysfunctional rules."[118] Some of the learned family rules, Subby wrote in his book *Lost in the Shuffle*, include: "Do as I say . . . not as I do; It's not okay to talk about problems; Always be strong, always be good, always be perfect" and "It's not okay to play."[119]

In 1987, Keith Miller published *Sin: Overcoming the Ultimate Deadly Addiction*. Harper & Row, the book's publisher, was probably the first large New York publisher to get a foothold in the recovery market. Miller, a former oil executive, used medical books to arrive upon a definition for disease, noting that both sin and addiction have a "definable onset, symptoms" and a "predictable outcome."[120] Miller departs from the AMA text in declaring "Sin is apparently a spontaneous reaction to the holy and godlike."[121] He explains:

The symptoms of the disease of Sin are many: swollen self-importance, manipulation and using of people for our pleasure, all kinds of abuse, lying and denial of the truth about our selfishness, and the many symptoms surrounding and supporting our repression of the truth about our motives (e.g., compulsive and addictive behaviors such as addictions to work, intensity, sex, food, money, drugs, and alcohol). The predictable outcome of the disease is fear, isolation, paranoia, increasing compulsiveness, physical symptoms, "accidents," and death.[122]

Miller cites the 1984 edition of the *Encyclopedia of Psychology*:

The word "addicted" has become generalized and is no longer confined to the World Health Organization's definition . . . In common parlance addiction relates to any substance, activity or interaction.[123]

Certainly recovery had experienced a quantum leap in the 1980s after the relatively quiet decades following the birth of AA. For those watching parallel developments in political talk, legislation, media interest and a suddenly-booming treatment industry, these were exciting times. One could only wonder what further developments lay ahead. Sociologist Robert Ackerman's comment about the groundswell of interest in adult children of alcoholics and related subjects said it all: "You couldn't stop this thing now if you wanted to."[124]

CHAPTER TWO

Feeling Good About Feeling Bad

Change is an appealing word. Eulogized by T.S. Eliot in *The Waste Land*, mythologized by Persephone in her seasonal sojourns to Hades, change hints at the divine, of nature and of acting in harmony with nature. Bill Clinton used "change" as the key word in his successful campaign for the White House in 1992. And change, it is often said, is "what recovery is all about." *Changes* magazine, ambitiously launched by HCI in 1986 as the heart and soul of the recovery movement, strove to lead the way to a brighter future for millions of troubled adults.

It was a glorious vision. The sales from *Adult Children of Alcoholics* indicated *Changes* would be a sure winner. The compassion-oriented articles addressed readers who were reviewing previous painful events and patterns, some of which continued to influence them.

Changes began small, with press runs of 1,000 to 2,000 copies. It was never intended to generate large amounts of money. Like other trade magazines, the publication's primary purpose was to sell advertisers' goods and services.

Most of the advertising came from the owners, whose bread and butter was provided by book sales.

There was a touching simplicity in those early issues. Therapists wrote about the shaky and vulnerable periods that accompany growth. Rokelle Lerner, a former school-teacher and author of the popular *Daily Affirmations For Adult Children of Alcoholics*, wrote a *Changes* article about simply accepting the possibility that we are all valuable human beings. When we grow up hearing words such as, "You're worthless"—"You're just as stupid as your father"— or "You'll never succeed at anything!"[1] she says it's too easy to forget one's inner worth, if indeed we had ever found it.

The contrasts *Changes* presented on the magazine rack beside the slicker publications such as *Cosmopolitan*, *Men's Fitness* and *Gentleman's Quarterly* provided reasons for optimism. Their budgets were lavish in comparison to HCIs. Yet most (though certainly not all) of these mainstream lifestyle magazines suffered from terminal shallowness.

How many times had *Cosmo* enticed readers with cover blurbs on the order of "Dump that Loser!" or "Seven Sexual Secrets"? The men's magazines were not much different: "Are You in Shape—*Really?*" a typical headline challenged.

Changes was not like that, at least in the beginning. It told readers they could be fat, thin, in prison or out of work—and it was all "okay." It was possible to dream, at least, of a trend in the direction of greater honesty, of an acknowledgment that as human beings there can be dark-ness and uncertainty, that we can have within us a Hitler, a Dahmer, a Homer or Marge Simpson and possibly a Christ, and that sorting through these things is messy but we can do it; not because sorting it out will make us great but because it will make us human.

One 1987 *Changes* article by therapists Herbert Gravitz and Julie Bowden, discussed a six-stage internal progression from "Survival" to "Genesis," including the possibilities for appreciating each day and improving our impact on others. The authors also addressed the possible pitfalls of recovery, such as self-righteousness or assuming a cult-like mentality. They blamed these behaviors not on the recovery process but on people who try to skip stages.[2]

Most of the therapists mentioned spirituality, and some did so eloquently. They were always careful to distinguish spirituality from religion, including the latter as a subset of the former. Sometimes they referred to God or the universe as elemental to finding the new, caring parent within yourself. The notion of creating a "family of choice" was ushered in as an alternative to one's "family of origin," which if hopelessly dysfunctional could at least be reframed as a birth accident.

In the regular feature "Ask Jan," readers queried Janet Woititz on love and sex, self-esteem, confidence, struggles with self-help groups and family issues. In a 1987 issue, Larry from Washington writes:

> I am an ACoA, a recovering poly-abuser, and father of four clearly affected children. . . . However, I have worked through the hate, even achieving some measure of empathy, but I just can't (won't) forgive my father who has passed away, and have found no basis for liking or loving his memory. Consequently, I can't make peace with myself. We obviously can't negotiate a living peace between us. I am left with a lot of unresolved feelings for his widow and feel alone in dealing with my own kids.
>
> Where do I go from here?

Janet replies:

> It sounds as though you have done a lot of hard work and now are stuck. I agree that you need to close in order to be OK with yourself. You do not have to forgive, like or even love. You may have to give up the fantasy of having his love.
>
> Have you written him a letter and expressed all your feelings? Have you visited his grave and read it to him? Death, as strange as this sounds, does not mean that it is impossible for you and your family to achieve closure.
>
> If you are near Seattle, why not call Lori Dwinell or Jane Middelton-Moz (co-authors of *After the Tears*)? [3]

Changes kicked off its second year with a run in Waldenbooks stores. Though it never did particularly well on the newsstands, *Changes* did address a growing core of adults who identified themselves as being "in recovery," particularly those who were recovering from "secondary" afflictions. Secondary here refers to issues other than addiction. Alcoholic parentage was the first conceptual lure. It resonated with success. But it became clear early on that there was more here to be developed, explained and defined.

Meanwhile, an energized group of therapists, social workers, Ph.D. psychologists and an occasional M.D. pulled apart every aspect of addiction they could think of. It was almost magical how interest in this subject generated more interest on its own. Addiction had become the mother of all metaphors; so rich with demographic refinements and spin-off illnesses that its own questionable status as a set of scientific truths scarcely mattered.

In the publisher's statement in the January/February 1987 issue of *Changes*, Gary Seidler said that:

> [Last year was] one of enlightenment for countless thousands of children of alcoholics—children of all ages across the length and breadth of this country.
>
> And the year 1987 promises to be even better as we continue in our journey of recovery from many of the wounds of our childhood. Equally encouraging is the growing number of individuals who are identifying with the ACoA characteristics although they themselves are victims of other troubled backgrounds.[4]

The trend Seidler foresaw didn't take long to materialize. A 1988 *U.S. Journal* conference in Albany, New York "confronted such topics as compulsive overeating, intimacy, self-worth, addictive relationships, panic attacks, shame, women's issues, gay issues, medical and psychiatric aspects of co-dependency, sexual compulsivity, tobacco addiction and workaholism."[5] Max Schneider, one of the alcoholism field's long-time supporters among physicians, spoke about codependency, which he defined as the "impaired ability to freely think, feel, relate and act in a relationship with a chemically dependent person or other codependent."[6]

At the same conference, Sharon Wegscheider-Cruse said, "Children of loss, grief and emotional deprivation should learn to turn their losses into lessons"[7] and husband Joseph Cruse, advanced his theory of a codependency "medical model." "Scratch an alcoholic and you'll find a codependent"[8] Cruse asserted, blaming an alcoholic's relapse on untreated codependency. But another quote of his is perhaps more revealing: "It's time to obtain a consensus on what the disease of co-dependency is and pass this on to third-party payers and others."[9]

Such questions—what is codepency and how do we get others to pay for it?—could be asked simultaneously and without irony. It seemed only fair to give the authors a break, totally apart from the fact that as paid journalists/ promoters (an oxymoron if there ever was one) we had no choice. After all, it seemed that HCI's products and public opinions, which were inextricably tied to the authors and their pronouncements, were on to something big.

A Star Is Born

The mid-1980s had seen a number of minor poets on the growing recovery lecture circuit. Some were 12-step program members whose engaging speaking styles carried them beyond their immediate locales. Others were therapists who used appealing methods to package the concepts of alcoholic families, relapse, 12-step work and spirituality. Their venues were hotel ballrooms and junior college auditoriums. Their marketing was often limited to brochures.

John Bradshaw was one of the more promising names in circulation around this time. Though his message, like others, was rooted in AA, Bradshaw widened those themes considerably. Family therapy had given him entrée to discuss alcoholic family systems and the "toxic shame" they created. So, far from positing chemical dependency as a combination of biological heritage and environmental stress, Bradshaw was calling shame "the root and fuel of all compulsive/addictive behaviors."[10]

In 1987, HCI's outreach coordinator, Debbie Hazelton, heard Bradshaw speak in Pompano Beach, Florida on the first night of a two-night stay. She immediately urged HCI president Gary Seidler to attend Bradshaw's second speech. She told Seidler he simply had to hear this guy. The talk would not only be interesting but relevant to HCI's books and publications and to the direction in which the recovery field was headed.

Seidler went, and soon after invited Bradshaw to visit HCI and discuss a book contract. "There was an incredible electricity about him," Seidler recalled later. "I felt that he was saying some extremely important things, and in a way that anyone could relate to."[11]

My supervisor introduced me to Bradshaw, who he hoped would write a column for *Changes* magazine. I remember him as an energetic man with silvery-graying hair and a well-trimmed beard. He was wearing a blue and white striped dress shirt and a white tie. His smile was engaging. I had no strong impressions of him at the time.

As it turned out, Bradshaw took the weaknesses of the field—its propensity for sweeping diagnoses, its rampant spiritualism masquerading as hard fact—and, through his writing, turned them into strengths.

With high hopes, HCI published his first book *Bradshaw On: The Family* in 1988. Though not, strictly speaking, an original thinker, Bradshaw was a consummate popularizer, which is not necessarily an indictment (a lot of people said the same about Freud).

In the mid-to-late 1980s, around the time Bradshaw passed through South Florida on a speaking tour, people loaned recovery tapes to each other like avid readers exchanging books. There was a handful of people who came across particularly well on this audio medium—AA poet Bob Earll and Bradshaw were among them.

In one of his first cassettes, Bradshaw discussed the child within—that precious, helpless thing who did not deserve to be hurt, but probably was. It was curiously meditative and alluring. It was odd how this man could talk to an audience of strangers and make them feel as though he were reaching each person's heart. It was as if someone were acknowledging, for the first time, some vague burden they had been carrying for as long as they could remember.

The Conference Scene

Technology will never replace human contact, even for those who travel the "Information Superhighway." One of the best ways to maintain contact with large numbers of people was through the recovery lecture circuit. Causes brought people together and conferences created a fertile climate for ideas to grow.

During the years 1986 to 1993, HCI held approximately 100 conferences nationwide. Some were targeted exclusively toward the professional addictions audience, the majority, however, invited recovering people to attend; offering "dual-track" programming for professionals or others who were already acquainted with the current issues. Conventioneers were free to mingle between semi-academic and purely feel-good presentations. As many as half of the registrants at these conferences worked in the mental health field; but when asked for a show of hands of those who were attending for "professional and personal reasons," a solid two-thirds of the mental health hands went up.

No one worked an audience better than Woititz. Others seldom even attempted the improvisational "intimate dialogues" she'd mastered while searching conventioneers lined up at the microphones, ready to lay their deepest fears at her doorstep.

Janet Woititz's book, *Adult Children of Alcoholics*, had touched some kind of nerve. Woititz never claimed to offer proof of her 28 ACoA characteristics, only "clinical observations." Nor did she claim that these characteristics were exclusive to adult children of alcoholics. If you listened carefully, you might hear her say that the ACoA traits "generalize beyond the population."

Just how far the traits may have generalized didn't matter, and part of the reason it didn't matter was Woititz's charisma, wit, empathy and stage presence. Though feared at times for her quick temper and willingness to use the clout that accompanied success, Woititz became known as the godmother of the children-of-alcoholics movement.

At a 1987 *U.S. Journal* conference in Oakland, California, she hosted one of many part-lecture, part-sharing, part-confronting exercises for a ballroom filled with adult children. A woman approached the microphone asking how to become more assertive. She said she had been putting up with the upsetting behaviors of others for as long as she could remember. She had been to therapy, read books and had even practiced confronting people, but always "flaked out" at the last second. "I end up protecting their feelings," she admitted.

The exchange that followed was typical, vintage Woititz:

Woititz: What are you afraid is going to happen if you tell them?
Woman: *(no response)*
Woititz: What just went into your head? First thing that went into your head.
Woman: Well, that they're not going to like me.
Woititz: They're not gonna like you, and what's gonna happen if they don't like you?
Woman: They're gonna leave.
Woititz: They're gonna leave, and what's gonna happen if they leave?

Woman: Then I'll be alone.

Woititz: You'll be alone, what's gonna happen if you're alone?

Woman: Then it'll be just like I'm used to. (*Laughs self-consciously*).

Woititz: No, no, no, no, don't give me the right answer. What'll happen if you're alone?

Woman: (*Pause*)

Woititz: Quickly.

Woman: Then I'll have pain.

Woititz: You'll have pain, and what'll happen if you have that loneliness pain?

Woman: (*Pause*)

Woititz: First thing.

Woman: I don't know.

Woititz: Yes, you do. What's the fear?

Woman: (*Long pause*)

Woititz: If you have that terrible pain in the pit of your stomach and you're all alone, what's gonna happen to you?

Woman: Then I'm gonna . . . I want to check out.

Woititz: You're gonna "die!" (*Healthy pause.*) You see, for the child of an alcoholic, don't ever, ever, ever let anybody minimize what you experience in doing things that other people work on doing. Don't ever let them do that. Because you come up and you say, "This is not a big deal, I just want to know how . . . because I get flaky." Those are her words. "Flake-ey." Honey, this is not "flake-ey," Okay? Flaky is "silly," alright? For the child of an alcoholic, a lot of things that appear on the surface not to be a big deal, really are. So, in effect, what you are saying is, "I risk death if I confront you." That's a very big thing, that's not a flaky thing to work on, Okay? That's a big thing to overcome. What happened when there was anger in your family?

Woman: I don't remember.

Woititz: You blocked it out. Okay, so it was big enough that you have no memory of it. (*Pause*) What would happen to you if you got angry in your family?

Woman: I got ignored.

Woititz: You got ignored. Okay. So, you didn't exist! Alright, so she has a couple of options here. If she gets angry, she either dies from the loneliness, or she doesn't exist! So we're really talking more not existing here than dying. Alright? (*Laughs*) So, the worst thing that somebody can do to you is not respond to you. Alright? Alright, 'cause it brings you all the way back. So your fear is probably not that they'll get mad at you or that they won't understand, your fear is that they'll walk away and won't respond to you. Okay. But you can control that—now. 'Cause you can run after them and you can say, "You can't do that to me, nobody can ever do that to me again!" So, you know the "behavior."

Woman: (*Unintelligible*)

Woititz: You can breathe.

Woman: Thank you. (*Deep laughter from audience*)

Woititz: Thank you for working. Thank you.[12]

In opening remarks to conferences in Oakland, Albany and Orlando, Woititz paid tribute to AA and the alcoholism treatment model, crediting the alcoholism field for "giving us a model that works."[13]

In 1987, The 3rd Annual National Convention on Children of Alcoholics (CoA) in Orlando, Florida, attracted a record 1,300 registrants—up from the 250 at the first CoA conference three years earlier.

Seminar topics ranged from the traditional mental health system (which had yet to appreciate the uniqueness of CoAs), to breaking the cycle of abusive parenting, to money, spirituality and sexual abuse. Virtually all of the conference presenters worked as therapists. Although most employed a standard style of public speaking—this was not the Living Theatre—it was understood that hearing about abandonment, pain, grief and the like would probably "bring up issues." For this reason, HCI had designated a number of "roving therapists" to walk the corridors throughout the event. These rovers wore colored arm bands. If someone was feeling overwhelmed, a rover could be flagged down at any time.

Adults were observed sobbing in the "personal support room," flanked by women in Sunday school dresses. One man became completely catatonic, refusing to move or respond for several hours. One evening, a group of adults all wearing pajamas and carrying teddy bears were in the room where children normally met for daycare, to learn about alcoholic families.

Two of HCI's recovery stars, Barbara Naiditch and Rokelle Lerner, read bedtime stories to them aloud. They read *The Little Engine That Could* by Watty Piper and *The Velveteen Rabbit* by Margery Williams. Later, one of the participants said that after hearing *The Velveteen Rabbit*, she had cried long and hard. When this participant was a teenager her alcoholic father committed suicide. The family's response? "We set one less place at the dinner table," she said, a chill in her words.

The Velveteen Rabbit, she explained, was about someone who left you. No matter what you did it wasn't good enough because either way, you were going to be left. She did get something of value from the conference, but shortly thereafter, she felt that she had read all she cared to of adult-children's literature and was ready to move on.

In a packed ballroom one morning, Sharon Wegscheider-

Cruse led a meditation. She urged the group to "visualize the way in which *you will contribute to this movement.*"[14]

Claudia Black, another leader in the ACoA field, told her listeners to have empathy for the squashed children they might have been, for the inner children who had tugged at their sleeves to get to the conference. "ACoAs must address the past," she said, when "losing control meant violence, ridicule, embarrassment, now you need to let go of that."[15]

The sexual abuse presenter was a therapist named Linda Sanford. She discussed her work with children, some of them offenders. Sanford had a number of things to say about prevalent jargon, mostly negative. "Sexual abuse," she said, was a misnomer. The act it is meant to describe should simply be called "abuse of power." She also spoke out against the burgeoning notion that children of sexual abuse are "damaged goods and need to be fixed; that this is the worst thing that could have possibly ever happened to you in your whole life, and you will never be the same."[16]

Sanford advised the audience to prepare themselves for some type of emotional fallout during the discussion on sexual abuse.

It will be a normal part of the healing process if this raises new feelings for you. It will be a normal part of the healing process if you recover memories, if you have flashbacks as a result of being in this workshop.[17]

The audience, Sanford said, had "a right to get answers" to their questions about what had happened to them, and she hoped that by reaching out to one another they would get these answers.[18]

The following summarizes the material that was distributed during the conference. Adult children of alcoholics are "super-responsible or super-irresponsible"; they tend to hoard their money or spend it compulsively; they flit from job to job or stay in one place when they shouldn't; they show equally extreme patterns in their dependence relationship or avoidance relationship; they eat or exercise too much or too little and they have "rigid ego boundaries" or no boundaries at all.

Wayne Dyer: A Clash of Decades

In 1987, I interviewed Wayne Dyer, a local South Florida resident and self-help star from the 1970s, for *Changes* magazine. Reactions to Dyer's thoughts demonstrated just how much self-help had changed in the previous decade.

Dyer was an adult child of an alcoholic. But that's where the similarities between him and HCI readers ended. He said his childhood was "not a bad time at all."[19] He also said that running eight to 10 miles a day, every day for 12 years, was the biggest single accomplishment of his life—better than writing the most popular self-help book of the 1970s, *Your Erroneous Zones*, and other subsequent books. While Dyer praised AA and the recovery movement in general, he had misgivings about the disease concept of alcoholism because it says that I am imperfect, that there's this part of me that's flawed.[20]

He said that bad habits tend to drop off on their own, once people begin thinking and living in a way that is incompatible with the habit. He himself had stopped smoking, dropped 30 pounds, stopped eating red meat and putting salt on his food, "There's a lot I don't do now that I used to do that I never decided not to do."[21]

There was a significant reaction from readers. These people were more than angry—they seemed deeply hurt. The clash of world views between Dyer and these recovery readers—

who wrote about a dozen letters concerning the interview, seven of which were negative—reflected the enormous changes the self-help field had undergone during the past 10 years.

When *Newsweek* came to HCI's offices to interview staff about the adult children's field, I asked the correspondent how many letters of complaint *Newsweek* needed to receive on a particular article before taking the complaint seriously. He answered, "10 or 11" out of a circulation of 11 million. *Changes* had less than 1% of *Newsweek*'s circulation at the time, and had received at least a dozen letters plus several distraught phone calls in response to the Dyer article.

If It Helps People, It Must Be Good

Meanwhile, some of the private debates researchers had waged with one another on alcoholism were becoming public. After her husband Michael's unsuccessful run for the presidency in 1988, Kitty Dukakis checked into Edgehill-Newport, an upscale treatment center in Newport, Rhode Island. The odd thing was that few people had seen her drink heavily or much at all before the campaign began. When she later relapsed on wood alcohol, the headline of the *New York Post* cried, "Kitty, what happened?"

Stanton Peele attempted to answer that question in his book *Diseasing of America* by laying the blame squarely at the feet of Edgehill-Newport. Peele argued that the Edgehill staff had missed Dukakis's bipolar disorder (which she later acknowledged in an interview), and "taught" her to view herself as an alcoholic.[22]

Peele warned that one-size-fits-all "education" can lead many patients to believe they cannot control their drinking, then act on these beliefs once they do drink.[23] Alcoholism professionals on the other hand, claimed that people who do not have serious alcohol problems rarely get admitted for treatment. And since alcoholism is a "progressive disease," it is much more useful to teach necessary abstinence. For them, usefulness was next to godliness.

Usefulness also rated very highly with William James, whose *Varieties of Religious Experience* was a seminal influence on Bill Wilson. Among other interesting insights, James offers a theory that alcoholics are "frustrated mystics." They are just going about their spiritual search the wrong way.[24]

Many in the professional recovery field, from alcoholism outward, have long preferred the "whatever works" standard of truth over that which has been demonstrated to be true. The following discussion is not intended to "prove" this statement, only to provide an indication as to just how ubiquitous utility thinking can be.

The Uncertain Status of TIQs

Since the early 1970s, researchers have been unable to pin down what role, if any, substances called *tetrahydroisoquinolines* (TIQs) play in a drinker's craving for alcohol. Early studies showed promise in this regard.

Experiments with rats and monkeys indicated that oxidized alcohol products, or aldehydes, interact with certain neurotransmitters to form TIQs—which in turn may cause an irreversible preference for alcohol. "A variety of studies have tried to confirm reports that production of TIQs might be higher in alcoholics than non-alcoholics,"[25] hence contributing to alcohol withdrawal symptoms and alcohol-related brain damage.

Early studies seemed to confirm that suspicion, showing a

higher production of TIQ in the brains of rats who had consumed alcohol. A Swedish study showed the "presence of TIQs in the cerebro-spinal fluid of intoxicated alcoholics,"[26] said Michael Collins, a biochemist at Loyola University and leading researcher on TIQs, who disputed the conclusiveness of these results. Collins and his colleagues found that TIQs (and certain amino acids conducive to TIQ formation) can also be found in rat chow, the food laboratory rats commonly consume. When Collins substituted a liquid diet for rat chow, he was unable to replicate the earlier results.[27]

The Swedish study found similar levels of TIQs in non-alcoholics, casting doubt on the significance of the findings. During an interview with the *U.S. Journal*, Collins called the TIQ issue one with "a lot of open questions and no simple answers."[28]

This hasn't stopped certain treatment centers from using TIQs as compelling evidence for the disease of alcoholism. A treatment director for Glenbeigh Hospital in Miami, Florida, stated that putting a positive spin on TIQs makes a counselor's job easier. He reasoned:

> It's still a good enough find to be able to talk about as another valuable piece in the body of addiction knowledge. It shows that the brain can play tricks on an individual, that there are biochemical cues predisposing some people to greater vulnerability.[29]

Collins was surprised to learn that his own and others' tentative theories were being taught as fact. TIQ research remains largely unreplicated by other scientists. "I view it as almost a total distortion," Collins said of TIQs being taught as a definitive reason for a patient's drinking problem. "It's still very much a hypothesis."[30]

The Shakiness of Children-of-Alcoholics "Traits"

A personality study of 147 college students at the University of Wisconsin—River Falls by Richard Seefeldt and Mark Lyon, published in the *Journal of Counseling and Development*, measured applicability of 13 characteristics cited by Janet Woititz for adult children of alcoholics.[31] The traits included self-criticism, being overly loyal, poor impulse control, feelings of worthlessness, difficulty in having fun and "[lying] when it would be just as easy to tell the truth."[32]

Seefeldt and Lyon found no differences between children of alcoholics and those with non-alcoholic parents. Nor did they find differences between treated and untreated adult children of alcoholics. As a result, the authors surmised, "The proverbial cart has been placed before the horse by building treatment groups based on certain differences that may not exist."[33]

Woititz's response was that college students may not be the best population to test, as the traits of adult children of alcoholics' may not become apparent until later in adulthood. "It's a question of when the issues really impact on your life," she said. "More typically it's when they get out into the real world."[34]

This response seems to raise more questions than it answers. *Adult Children of Alcoholics* does not discuss the difference between "characteristics" and embedded personality traits, which are said to be formed within a child's first few years. One would think that the personality of a college student is fairly well-defined.

The Seefeldt article appeared on the front page of the *U.S. Journal* where it was read by thousands of people in the professional recovery field. Unfortunately, HCI's owners often required conciliatory words in the same issue when a controversy threatened to rock the boat. The treatment centers offering services for adult children of alcoholics, after all, were their advertisers.

"What are we to make of this report?" asked managing editor Jeffrey Laign in his editorial which accompanied the article. "Woititz's book helped me—and hundreds of thousands of others who grew up with alcoholic parents. The Wisconsin study in no way negates the value of that work."[35]

Laign's editorial ends with a plea for the ACoA field to "feed its undernourished body of research."[36] This is what people had been saying about the entire recovery field for years, yet very little solid information had been produced. Grants and other funding may have been difficult to come by, but a more likely reason is that studies are time-consuming and produce indirect profits at best.

"The Acid Test Is, 'This Helps People.' "[37]

Studies on alcoholics and children of alcoholics tended to be self-serving. At The 2nd National Conference on Sexual Compulsivity/Addiction held in Minneapolis, Minnesota in September 1988, Patrick Carnes, a psychologist and highly visible proponent of the concept of "sexual addiction," cited a study conducted through the now-defunct Golden Valley Behavioral Health Center in Minnesota. Carnes told conventioneers that preliminary results from a survey of 500 sex addicts in 12-Step groups showed that "42 percent also described themselves as chemically dependent. Thirty-eight percent said they suffered from eating disorders, and over a quarter of the respondents said they were either workaholics, compulsive spenders or both."[38]

Consequently, Carnes argued (as did many others seeking

recognition for the respective disorders of their trade) that sexual addiction is at the very least a cofactor in chemical dependency and other problems, and possibly an underlying cause. Accepting such a premise would make alcoholism counselors negligent if they did not check patients for a possible sexual addiction. Besides preventing relapse due to unaddressed "issues," the sex concepts were useful in themselves,[39] Carnes said.

The problem with the study sample was that it was only composed of patients at Golden Valley. It's more than likely they had already familiarized themselves with the concept of sexual addiction, as articulated in Carnes's book, *Out of the Shadows*, prior to seeking treatment at Golden Valley. Carnes acknowledged this possibility, but added, "The acid test is, 'This helps people.' "[40] He also rejected arguments of cultural relativism similar to critiques against the disease model of alcoholism.

Shortly before the conference, an article criticizing the concept of sexual addiction appeared in the *Journal of Sex Research*. In it, sociologists Martin Levine and Richard Troiden had correlated psychiatric diagnoses of various sexual problems with prevailing social mores as reflected in the *Diagnostic and Statistical Manual* (*DSM*) of the American Psychiatric Association.[41]

Psychiatrists in the conservative 1950s provided illnesses of "too much sex"[42] such as nymphomania and homosexuality, Levine and Troiden wrote. As the pendulum swung in the other direction during the 1960s, sexual abnormalities in the *DSM* shifted to frigidity, "anorgasmia" and impotence—or "not enough sex."[43] Levine and Troiden summed up the shift, saying:

The twin concepts of sexual addiction and sexual compulsion emerged in response to shifts in the wider sociosexual landscape. The health threats associated with genital herpes, hepatitis B, and AIDS, national concern about drug use, addiction, and teenage pregnancy, a renewed interest in committed relationships, and the rise of politically powerful right-wing religious groups altered the societal values surrounding non-relational sex. In response, some mental health professionals and members of sexual "self-help" groups came to regard people who engage in frequent sex, nonrelational sex, or sex in "inappropriate" settings as sex addicts or sexual compulsives.[44]

Levine and Troiden lamented what they called "the medicalizing of human problems" and "value judgments parading as therapeutic diagnoses."[45] They added that "the invention of sexual addiction and sexual compulsion as 'diseases' threatens the civil liberties of sexually variant peoples."[46]

Interestingly, Troiden had presented a summation of his criticisms at The 1st National Conference on Sexual Compulsivity the year before. Recovery conferences usually steer clear of controversy. But sexual addiction was a new field. This, apparently, was a learning experience for the conference planners. Troiden was not invited back the following year.

In 1988, Troiden discussed that first conference. "One woman had to be physically restrained,"[47] he said. The woman had been angered by Troiden's remarks on sexual addiction.

It felt like being in a revival tent. Right after my talk, I was surrounded by Carnes groupies. They said, "It's okay, Dr. Troiden. You can express your stifled anger here. You're among friends." It was as though by disagreeing with them, I had gone into the "sick" category.[48]

The remainder of the inaugural conference didn't go much better. One of the conventioneers tried to convince Troiden that sexual addiction was real because sometimes sex addicts vomited from "physiological withdrawal."

Without naming names, Carnes refuted sexual addiction critics (and possibly supporters who were intellectualizing too much) by saying, "The fact is, people are getting their needs met, and we who are wondering whether it's impulsivity or compulsion should look at that."[49]

Belief as a Confidence Booster

The following passage speaks for itself. In it, social worker Dene Stamas advises alcoholism counselors on how to regard controversy about the disease model itself.

No matter what a confident person says, he *believes* it to be true. There is no doubt. One of the ways you can be confident is to first *have* a belief about alcoholism. Believe that alcoholism *is* an illness; that alcoholics *can't* drink sociably; that alcoholism *is* a progressive illness and the alcoholic won't progress, until he stops drinking and starts changing. . . . Even the things you're not sure of, if presented as being true convincingly enough, will give you the appearance of confidence. Physically, you can show confidence by maintaining good eye contact and having your belief system down pat enough so that the words will flow without even having to think. . . .

Eventually, there will be no doubt to hold you back.[50]

The Ethical Seat Belt

As associate editor of two magazines (*Focus: Educating Professionals in Family Recovery* and the *U.S. Journal of Drug and Alcohol Dependence*) that both revolved around the legitimacy of the disease concept of alcoholism; and another magazine (*Changes*) that at one time described itself as being "For and About Adult Children of Alcoholics," I sometimes felt a schism between my private suspicions and the line of products that paid my salary. As a result, I gradually developed the mantra of wearing an ethical seat belt.

If I did my job and wrote reasonable stories, no matter how strange some of the recovery concepts seemed to me, that would be like wearing a seat belt. As I occasionally discovered, however, seat belts only help one survive collisions. They cannot prevent them.

A case in point: I had just finished interviewing Richard Seefeldt about his study that tested HCI author Janet Woititz's ACoA characteristics when he cheerfully asked: "So, Andrew, how do you do this?"

My questions must have indicated an internal conflict which was beginning to form within myself regarding the truth. If the existence of ACoA traits was at best controversial, was it not a form of misrepresentation to present them as fact? To the extent that the traits were not controversial, how much did they actually add to psychology? One could also ask, what characteristics are shared by children of plate throwers, knife throwers, snake handlers, etc.?

It is not difficult to understand that the inconsistency and sometimes malevolent behavior of an alcoholic parent could affect a child. But alcoholics do not hold a patent on inconsistency or on malevolence. It is also possible that certain alcoholics have made better parents than have certain teetotalers. And to the extent that they haven't, what important knowledge has been gained? The answer would seem to be, not very much. The body of literature on ACoAs supplies not information, but emotional support. While providing reassurance to people who have been damaged is a worthy activity, it is somewhat less than earth-shattering to learn that drunks often make bad parents. If I was to continue writing such revelations as news, the only solution would be to do so carefully and circumspectly, the ethical seat belt somewhere nearby.

The Little Thing that Became a Big Thing

In 1988 I covered a nicotine addiction conference in Minneapolis, shortly after the previously mentioned sexual addiction conference. The conference sponsor, the American Medical Society on Alcoholism and Other Drug Dependencies (now the American Society of Addiction Medicine), was known for presenting interesting and substantive meetings, and this was no exception.

One of the speakers was a psychologist named Judith Ockene of the University of Massachusetts. Her material on behavioral techniques to help people stop smoking seemed harmless and possibly helpful. It emphasized executing "contracts" with patients to quit or decrease the number of cigarettes they smoked each week. It was especially interesting because her presentation contained no "disease" language, she simply spoke about helping patients to quit smoking.

A psychologist in the audience realized this and interrupted Ockene to ask why she had not mentioned the 12 Steps of AA as it applied to smokers.

Ockene replied that the steps were not a part of her work, but added, "certainly the steps have helped many people."[51]

The psychologist in the audience continued to stress that the steps were essential to withdrawal from addiction. A companion next to him egged on the attack and arguments ensued among the audience members. The questioner had succeeded in disrupting the presentation. Someone pointed out that 30 million Americans had quit smoking on their own after the surgeon general firmly linked cigarettes to lung cancer in the late 1960s. The psychologist in the audience countered and asked how many more people would have quit, had the steps been a part of the government's anti-smoking message. Finally, a society senior statesman restored order to the room.

It was rather surprising to see that a meeting of physicians could be disrupted by a speaker's omission of the 12-step concept.

These events provoked an uncomfortable feeling. Perhaps the psychologist in the audience was just a crackpot and his friend a random clone. But what had empowered this person, what had given him the confidence to disrupt a professional meeting not because of something the speaker said, but for something she had not said, the allegiances she had dared to omit? How did two people put 40 professionals on the defensive and hold them at a standoff? Something happened in that room. In recovery parlance, it felt clammy and strange, uninviting and unwelcome.

Szasz: A Window

Famous for his critique of psychiatry and psychology in *Myth of Mental Illness* and through 20 other books, Thomas Szasz will be remembered long after the last recovery star has disappeared. Yet in a 1989 interview with the author, he showed little of the fatuous self-importance with which recovery experts gilded their pronouncements, their product lines and their very presence, at times.

Szasz emigrated from his native Budapest in 1938. In 1944, he graduated first in his class from the University of Cincinnati College of Medicine. Though he no longer practices psychiatry, he still maintains an office at the State University of New York at Syracuse where he taught for more than 30 years. Occasionally painted as a radical, Szasz sees himself as a sometimes lonely voice for traditional medicine. "I am really quite conservative,"[52] he said in the interview.

In his 1970 book, *The Manufacture of Madness*, Szasz devotes a chapter to Revolutionary War figure Benjamin Rush.[53] A cosigner of the Declaration of Independence and the nation's first Surgeon General (or "Physician General"), Rush can be viewed as an early precursor to the addiction treatment industry. It seems the man saw disease nearly everywhere he looked.

As he surveyed the boisterous, post-revolutionary mood of liberated colonists, Rush concluded that many of them suffered from an "excess of the passion for liberty . . . a form of insanity, which I shall take the liberty of distinguishing by the name of *anarchia*."[54]

Those who remained loyal to England suffered from "revolutiona," unless the loyalists were women, in which case the diagnosis was "hysteria." Liars suffered from the disease of lying ("Persons thus diseased cannot speak the truth upon any subject."); blasphemers suffered from "derangement in the principle of faith, or the believing faculty," exemplified by "persons who refuse to admit human testimony in favour of the truths of the Christian religion."[55]

Doubters of medicine and doctors also fell under this diagnosis.

Most revealingly, Rush decided that Negroes suffered from the disease of "Negritude,"[56] a form of multi-generational leprosy whose only remaining symptoms were broad lips, flat noses and skin pigmentation. Rush had little doubt that those suffering from Negritude would prefer to be white, and devoted much energy toward finding a "cure."

But Rush is most remembered for introducing the involuntary confinement of alcoholics in "sober houses." This represented a step up from jail or the asylum, and embodies the spirit of an AA slogan, "We are sick people getting well, not bad people getting good." Yet, as Szasz notes, "Rush did not *recognize* that drinking was a medical problem; he *defined* it as one."[57]

The following is an interview I conducted with Szasz for *Focus* magazine:

Focus: The addiction field has generally regarded calling addicts "sick" rather than "bad" as a liberating development. You seem to consider it an instrument of oppression.

Szasz: I think it is stupid to be boxed into that choice. We can simply say that what is called addiction is a particular form of behavior—which that person obviously prefers to any other, or else he would change it.

I would compare it to any other form of behavior—particularly religious behavior. Is the Ayatollah Khomeni bad? Or good? Or does he just have a religion which perhaps you and I don't have?

Focus: Do you recognize the scientific evidence regarding addictive processes in the brain?

Szasz: I neither recognize it nor deny it. I am not competent to judge that. But it's irrelevant to my view of addiction.

Focus: In other words, if the addict has an addictive nature, then it is that person's responsibility not to partake of the drug.

Szasz: Exactly. His susceptibility *enlarges* his responsibility, since he has a disposition to react unfavorably to that drug, much as the person with a fear of high places has to avoid being a construction worker on skyscrapers.

Focus: You have sanctioned voluntary therapy, but are opposed to coerced therapy of any kind, is that correct?

Szasz: Yes. I am entirely in favor of psychiatry or therapy between consenting adults. To me, that is analogous to freedom of religion. It doesn't mean that I necessarily think any particular therapy is good or bad. If a person wants to try out a form of therapy, that is that individual's choice—just like going to church or taking drugs is a choice.

Focus: Where do you draw the line between coercion and free choice?

Szasz: I draw it the most conventional way possible—at the use, or threatened use, of state-legitimized force. After all, that is the only kind of legitimized force there is. You can't force an addict to go to church, but you can force him to go into a treatment program.

Focus: Isn't it in some way still the addict's choice to cooperate?

Szasz: Yes, but in the face of coercion, choice becomes absurd. Most of us don't feel we have a choice whether to pay our income taxes or not.

Focus: Is it fair to say that you regard the language of addictions and mental health as skewed?

Szasz: I would like to be a little more precise about that. When it comes to addressing socially controversial behaviors—such as taking illegal drugs—it is virtually impossible to be morally neutral in one's language. So all of us are guilty of what I am pointing out. But to describe drinking too much, as in the case of Mrs. Ford, or supposedly, Mrs. Dukakis—as an illness—excuses the behavior to an absurd degree; just as calling such a person a lush or a sinner would be very condemnatory. I prefer simply to say, "They like to drink." And it's their business. It's certainly not the taxpayers' problem. Why should I care? Why should we, the American people, care?

Focus: We might be moved to care from the testimony of the addicts themselves—who say that, when they were drinking or using, their lives were out of control.

Szasz: I would give that no more credence than I would give Oral Roberts, when he says that he needs more money or otherwise God will call him home. Those are simply the quasi-religious, self-aggrandizing statements of nobodies who in this way get their 15 minutes in the limelight. Who are Mrs. Ford or Mrs. Dukakis in their own right, except for the fact that they are married to famous men? They are nobodies. So now their claim to fame is that they are reformed drug abusers and experts on alcoholism.

Focus: Most treatment professionals would deny that there is a theological dimension to their work.

Szasz: Given the theological nature of Alcoholics Anonymous, they can deny it as long as they want to. That's like denying that the U.S. Constitution is racist, when it specifically mentions "three-fifths persons" in Article II. I don't care what people claim. I want to know the truth. It's there in black and white.

Focus: But Alcoholics Anonymous says that one can come to a god "of one's understanding"—which theoretically could mean no god at all.

Szasz: I admit, they are not religious in a strictly denominational, sectarian sense—but in a sociological and existential sense, they are religious. The point is that what they do has to do with values. They claim that drinking is bad, and that is simply not true. Drinking in moderation is not bad. They say taking heroin is bad, and that is a lie: It's not bad if you have cancer and suffer from pain. In other words, they obscure the issue.

I insist that Nancy Reagan is a religious zealot. She says, "Say no to drugs!" What's wrong with taking penicillin if you have pneumonia? But she never qualifies her slogan.

Focus: Many in the treatment field say that they are getting away from putting values on addiction, that they are simply responding to scientific evidence.

Szasz: That's too funny for words. The ultimate moral cop-out is to say, "I base my morality on science." Because science is morally neutral. An oven can be scientifically sound for baking bread or for incinerating people in a concentration camp. Furthermore, a scientific explanation for the pharmacological effects of alcohol is not in contest. What is in contest is how the alcohol gets into the body. And that process can only occur in one of two ways: Either the person takes it himself or it is given to him forcibly. In the second case he has been poisoned; in the first case he may be poisoning himself or simply enjoying himself. Every one of these is a moral act.

Focus: But some say the evidence shows that some alcoholics cannot stop poisoning themselves on their own.

Szasz: I don't agree with that. But even if I did, it would not affect my argument that changing a person's behavior from drinking to not drinking is a moral act—or that coercing a person to change is a moral act.

We have come to a crucial issue. To endorse coerced therapy, and then say that what one is endorsing is not a moral act, is so radical a departure from what we normally mean by "moral" that at that point one cannot continue the dialogue. There is a profound human rupture: because it is an allegedly supra-moral justification of coercion.

Focus: Suppose we say that forcing treatment is a moral act—that it is sometimes good to protect the individual and society this way.

Szasz: Then we can have an intelligent discussion. One person can say it's good and another that it's bad. Just like people said about slavery, or killing witches or Jews, or putting Japanese-Americans in concentration camps.

Focus: Where is the demonstrable suffering in this treatment? After all, many outpatients from coerced treatment say it was beneficial for them.

Szasz: The answer is implicit in your question. In a free society, coercing a person, except as part of the judicial process, is *ipso facto* bad, a cause of suffering. It has nothing to do with the consequences. A person may be drafted into the Army, and that might turn out to be a very good experience for him. That wouldn't affect the fact that being involuntarily conscripted is a form of coercion that causes, at least for a period, suffering. After all, if a person wanted to be conscripted, he could voluntarily join the Army. The same goes for drug rehabilitation. What is bad about coercive drug programs is that they authenticate laws which diminish the self-control of every citizen. After all, there could be drug centers that, like the Army—or like fat farms—would promise to discipline you. Then those who wanted to be coerced in this way could volunteer to be so coerced. And every other law-abiding person would be left unmolested by the state.

Focus: We've heard a lot about prevention lately. If you could write curriculum for school children on drug education, what would it include?

Szasz: I can't address that issue, because as long as we have drug prohibition as a national policy, there cannot be anything educationally and morally reasonable taught in the schools. That context frames politically and morally illegitimate policies, as far as I'm concerned. It is not proper for the American government to prohibit an adult from putting whatever he wants into his mouth. And until that policy is reversed, it doesn't matter what is taught, because children quite correctly learn from the way things are—not from the way they are taught.

I have one other comment about schools. What we have in the schools is not drug "education," it is drug propaganda. "Education" implies telling students the truth. And they are not being told the truth about drugs.

Focus: Propaganda in that children are not being asked to make a choice?

Szasz: Correct. They are given the message, "Just say no to drugs." They are not told, "Just say no to murder"! That would be ludicrous. If drugs are so bad, why do we have "drug stores"? There's something silly about it.

Focus: So, in the wake of crack cocaine, for example—can no measures be taken to stop the loss of life?

Szasz: If we wanted to stop the loss of life we could legalize it.

Focus: How would that help?

Szasz: There would be no incentive for people to kill each other over crack.

Focus: What about the crack babies born to addicted mothers?

Szasz: They have the right to kill the baby in the uterus, don't they? Now I read that some women, who could have obtained legal abortions months earlier, are being prosecuted following the deaths of their addicted babies. So we have created a monstrous inconsistency and moral chaos that I can't sort out simply by addressing drugs. Now, obviously, if drugs were completely legal, with the popular state of mind being what it is, there would still be a great deal of chaos. That's why I don't expect it.

Focus: How does the terminology you use as a practicing psychiatrist differ from that of your colleagues?

Szasz: In one respect, my terminology is quite different, and in another respect not different at all. To put it somewhat grandiosely, I prefer the language of William Shakespeare and of the everyday man to the jargon of psychiatric—or the addictions—professionals. I use such words as "temptation," "craving," "desire," "want," "self-discipline." It's perfectly obvious that there are life events that in some ways induce people to take drugs and other life events that induce them to stop taking drugs.

Therefore I would like to emphasize that the language in which we have been addressing these problems is flawed. Instead of talking about "illness," "addiction," "prevention" and so on, we should be talking about "temptation," "desire," "want," and "self-control," "moderation" and "renunciation." We want things, we crave things. And we become civilized by denouncing them. If we need a lot of money we don't go around robbing banks and jewelry stores. If we crave sex we don't go around raping women. If we crave revenge on someone we don't go around shooting them. And if we crave drugs we should control ourselves—whether it's alcohol, tobacco, food or illegal drugs. It's as simple as that.

Focus: And everyone has the capacity to make these choices equally well.

Szasz: Not equally well, no. No more so than everyone has the capacity to box or write English equally well. The more a person lacks the capacity of self-control the harder he has to work to develop it. But everyone has that capacity, and must have it, if he is to enjoy the rights and liberties of living as an American citizen. Otherwise they become criminals; not because they take drugs, but because they then do something illegal.

Focus: What examples of self-directed addicts do you find?

Szasz: Well, consider that 30 to 40 million Americans have stopped smoking. How could this happen unless we allow that people do listen to input and can and do change their habits?

Focus: Are you saying that in no case does an addict lose power over his addiction?

Szasz: Right. It is always a matter of degree of motivation. Imagine approaching an impoverished cocaine addict in the slums of Washington or New York who supposedly can't stop and saying, "Look, Joe, you [stop] taking drugs, we will give you $100 or $1,000, $10,000 or $1 million? Does anyone believe that he wouldn't stop? He can stop. He just doesn't have enough reason to stop.

Focus: But many people say they have lost fortunes to drugs.

Szasz: So what? That, too, is a decision. And if they commit suicide, that is another decision. Whoever said life was a bowl of cherries? The point is that I personally do not see how one can look at the war on drugs as anything but a moral and religious crusade—no different, essentially, from the Ayatollah Khomeni's crusade against impure books.

Focus: Suppose we define addiction in terms of adjusting to life problems. Couldn't it be that treatment providers serve as effective role models for their clients—and that their example makes the interaction with clients useful?

Szasz: They're role models, all right, though in a somewhat different sense—of which I am, perhaps unfairly, rather contemptuous. They model the sinner who has fallen and has been redeemed. This almost childlike figure of religious mythology is more valued in religious tradition—especially today—than the man who has always gone straight. That is why many ex-drug addicts become drug counselors. It's a game of cops and robbers, in which the robbers have become cops.

Focus: I'm still a little puzzled by your description of "coercion." Sometimes you use the word "induce." How does that differ from coercion?

Szasz: To induce is to persuade, or to seduce. Two very important words.

Focus: Both of which are excluded in your definition of coercion as the threat of legal action. In the case of an intervention, when individuals manage to get someone into treatment by applying extreme social pressure—is that person still acting entirely on his own free will? Isn't there a fine line between persuasion and force?

Szasz: There is no fine line. It's a sharp line. But this has nothing to do with addiction. You are touching on an extremely important philosophical issue, which most professional philosophers, in my opinion, and most lawyers, for that matter, are confused about. You used a word I would never use when you said "I don't see how this is *entirely* his free will." Free will is never all-or-nothing. Of course it can be worn down.

Let's get away from drugs, let's talk about something which is less confused in America—namely sex. There is no question that when somebody is just minding his own business, he will not be induced to engage in sexual activity just out of the blue. But let's assume that he's exposed to pornography which has stimulated him, and now is exposed to a woman who's extremely seductive—certainly, his free will now to resist sex is reduced.

But assuming that in some ways he does not wish to engage in sex, he can make sure that he is not exposed to these things in the first place. Similarly, the free will of a priest who hears a woman repeatedly confessing to him: "I'm in love with you, I want to have sex with you," is somewhat more compromised than that of some old man who hardly ever sees the young woman. So the range of free will is enormously varied. Does the pope have free will not to be a Catholic?

Focus: I suppose he does.

Szasz: How much free will does he have to become Jewish tomorrow morning? I would think less free will than a cocaine addict to stop using cocaine. How much free will does the prime minister of Israel have to change his religion?

Focus: As the treatment industry mushrooms, are you skeptical that profit motives are clouding the way people talk about addiction?

Szasz: I am not skeptical, I know that is exactly the way things work. We are producing fewer and fewer useful things, and are engaged in more and more pseudo-activities, for which the government pays. If drug treatment is so useful—we hear of these long waiting lists—why have we never heard of someone mugging someone else to get into a treatment program? What is treatment worth, if no one but the government is willing to pay for it? If all third-party money—including insurance funds—were taken out of drug treatment programs, I think there would be no more than five drug counselors left in America, if that many.

Focus: They say they are underfunded.

Szasz: Of course. What do you expect them to say? This is a bottomless pit, like the War on Poverty or the war in Vietnam.

Focus: How do you define disease?

Szasz: I define disease the same way pathologists define it: as a demonstrable, anatomicopathological lesion—not as a form of behavior. In other words, cancer, high blood pressure, diabetes are diseases. Drinking is not a disease, despite what the American Psychiatric Association says. It may cause disease, just as boxing or skydiving may cause disease—but it is not a disease.

Focus: What is your reaction to the developing co-dependency field?

Szasz: It is another revealing, rather humorously revealing, example of wanting to expand the category of illness so that those in the therapy business get their hands on more and more government funds. It's sort of like enlarging the communist menace in order to get more defense funds. The bigger the menace, the more money you can get. Now we have a kind of open season on undesirable behaviors. Look at the great anti-smoking crusade. And then, there is the overeating person; the anorexic person; the irresponsible AIDS patient; the homeless, poor person; *ad infinitum.* The therapy racketeers can shoot as much game as they want, and the government pays them for every carcass, every pelt.

Focus: Should treatment for these behaviors—or diseases—be reimbursed, in your opinion?

Szasz: Of course not. I think the whole subject should be of much greater interest to industries and insurance companies than it is. They are the ones, after all, who have to pay the bills—which in the auto industry accounts for between $500 and $700 a car. Now out of that sum, a large amount—I don't know what the amount is, but it is substantial—goes towards treatment for these non-diseases. In that category I include all mental diseases, including schizophrenia and manic depression. Not to mention all the behavioral diagnoses such as addiction. So this is a sort of economic cancer.

Eventually, if we don't stop it, it will kill us.

Focus: But doesn't most of this fall under contractual agreements between consenting adults?

Szasz: No. In the first place, the employee usually has no control over the coverage he gets, or, therefore, the premiums the company deducts from his paycheck. Secondly, the company is not free to refuse offering coverage for so-called diseases–for example, mental illness and alcoholism. It is compelled by the state legislatures, it is mandated by the politicians, to provide coverage without "discrimination" as a condition of being permitted to do business. For example, years ago, Blue Cross/Blue Shield was mandated in Massachusetts to cover alcoholism. How can there be anything contractual about it if the whole business is permeated with government control and coercion?

Focus: Do doctors have the liberty to define disease as they see fit?

Szasz: Everyone has that liberty. The question is, who can impose his definition on others? Again, that is where the government comes in. It's worthwhile to remember that the American Medical Association was for many years, from the 1920s to well into my own adult lifetime, in the forefront of denouncing alcoholism as a disease.

Focus: You regard the subsequent developments as a step backwards?

Szasz: No! I regard it as a circus, as part of the human comedy. The thing to do is to think clearly about this–and whether we are taking a step forward or backward depends on our values. I mean, I don't think it's particularly nice to stigmatize people who drink or take drugs. I'm not in favor of calling them bad. There is a lot of middle ground between stigmatizing such individuals and glorifying or excusing them. And that is where I want to stand.[58]

CHAPTER THREE

Churches, Sects and Cults

T hough chemical dependency numbers were drop-ping, the broader recovery movement saw clear sailing throughout the late 1980s. Markets were friendly, addiction-and-recovery sections began appearing in bookstore chains, and a number of individuals opened stores that sold recovery books exclusively. Though the recovery movement drew occasional fire from conservative Christians (to whom recovery sounded similar to New Age thinking), reaction from churches was generally favorable. Publishers seeking to capitalize on an economically viable Christian market began dealing out such titles as *Twelve Steps for Christians* and similar appeals to those who would get recovery while maintaining ties to traditional worship.

The demographics of HCI's readership became apparent through surveys: baby boomers in their 30s and early 40s— 80% of whom were women with an above-average educa-tion and income, 57% of whom were divorced. They thrived on the swelling industry's T-shirts, coffee mugs, medallions, bumper stickers, jewelry and wallet-sized cards bearing inspirational messages. Therapists trotted out vanity press books, audio cassettes and video tapes, urging potential customers to "Reclaim your right to have a happy childhood!" Vacationing yuppies boarded sober cruises with John Bradshaw, while the more adventurous went white-water rafting in Idaho.

As the movement grew in size and strength, the amount of possible offenses became greater. Try to cheer someone up, and you might be denying them their grief. Allow them their grief, but with a pat or two on the back, and you might be patronizing them. Admit to running or reading or windsurfing too much and you might be trying to escape your feelings. Better to lie low and talk a good emotional game.

Granberg and Other Court Challenges

Sending a drunk driver to AA might ultimately help that person come to terms with the serious consequences of his drinking. On that basis alone, and with little apparent forethought, states have been requiring AA attendance of Driving Under the Influence (DUI) probationers for quite some time. This could change as First Amendment challenges continue to mount, arguing that forced AA attendance violates constitutional guarantees separating church and state.

In the most famous case to date, John Norfolk, a committed atheist, was sentenced by a Maryland judge in 1988 to 20 days in jail for failing to regularly attend AA, a condition of his probation.

Norfolk went to a few meetings, but said, "They were praying and talking about God about half the time at the meetings I went to."[1]

Attorney Jeremy Garber of the American Jewish Congress,

which submitted a friend-of-the-court brief on Norfolk's behalf, argued:

> The outrage would be instantaneous if, as a condition of probation, Maryland required probationers to attend meetings of an organization that urged its members to reject all belief in the existence of any power greater than oneself. Nor would the coercive nature of the atheistic recovery program be negated by the claim that the steps were merely "suggestions."[2]

American Civil Liberties Union attorney Ellen Luff, who represented Norfolk, said that elements such as metaphysical claims, together with "a total system and attitude" of seeing the world and oneself, [3] pushes an organization in the direction of being called or considered a religion, regardless of how the organization views itself.

"I think everyone agrees that no matter what test you use for a religion, AA meets it,"[4] Luff said.

Similar reasoning prevailed in a 1979 case in which the group Transcendental Meditation (TM) was classified as a religion, over TM's strenuous objections.[5]

Norfolk lost his first round with the courts, but won on appeal. Circuit Judge John Sause of Queen Anne's County District Court in Maryland announced a change in his sentencing policy, allowing probationers to design their own, non-religious, self-help programs if they so desired. Defendants would be given several weeks to design their programs.[6] Later, the probation department would review the case to see if the defendant complied with the probation program of his or her own design. District courts in Alaska and Colorado have also made rulings forbidding coerced attendance of AA meetings or treatment programs built around AA.

"People all over the country are challenging this," said Luff, explaining that the majority of criminal defendants who fight forced AA attendance on religious grounds win, and that similar lawsuits don't even make it to court "because the case that it is a religion is so strong."[7]

"Some states are trying to accommodate probationers who object to what they consider AA's religious flavor."[8] For example, a class-action lawsuit in the state of Washington asked the state to restrict funding for AA treatment programs on the grounds that it violated a person's rights under the First Amendment. And in 1991, Maryland's legislature passed a bill requiring the availability of non-spiritual alternatives to mainstream treatment.

The first important case occurred in 1984, when Norman Granberg, convicted of driving under the influence, filed a federal civil rights suit against three Wisconsin counties and two county social services boards. Granberg claimed his civil rights had been violated when he was forced into an inpatient alcohol rehabilitation center containing religious elements.[9]

A staffer at AA's General Service Office in New York confirmed that some groups object to court-ordered visitors.[10] She added, "The general feeling I've gotten, though, is that, as a fellowship, we're not concerned about how people get to us. Our duty is to make them feel welcome once they arrive."[11]

On the other hand, Lucy G., an AA veteran with more than 40 years of sobriety, refuses to sign the probationers' required attendance slips. "I'm not going to inform on someone and say that he was there," Lucy said. "That is a total violation of anonymity as far as I'm concerned, which is the foundation of the program."[12]

Some authorities maintained that court orders were often

the only way to get an alcoholic to face his or her problem and accept help. And there is evidence that some forced interventions can be effective.

"Psychologist Kathleen O'Connell of Capitola, Calif., said studies have shown that 'extrinsic motivators,' such as the threat of losing one's driver's license, can benefit some people, 'if they eventually make the shift to internal motivation.' " [13]

Spirituality as Salvation

Part of the reason for the trend favoring convicted DUI plaintiffs who sue the state over religious rights violations is that the meaning of religion has broadened during the latter half of the 20th century. Again, legal definitions play an important role.

World War II triggered a wave of individuals seeking conscientious objector (CO) status. Members of mainline denominations fared best in receiving it, followed by members of groups whose beliefs were more difficult to define, such as Quakers and Unitarians. Extending CO status to these latter organizations confirmed the courts recognition of them as religious institutions, despite the fact that they did not worship a specific deity. While this did not include pure humanists or members of organizations such as the Ethical Culture Society, it was nonetheless an important shift.

Theologian Paul Tillich made important inroads in modern theology by blurring the lines between denominational religion and individual quests for meaning. Central to this redefinition was the concept of "ultimate concern." Since everyone has an ultimate concern, everyone is in a sense religious. For Tillich, ultimate concerns usually revolved around something concrete, such as another person or group, rather than something purely metaphysical.[14]

Yet these concrete objects of worship symbolize the ultimate for the individual, and everything which defines the individual. It is this inner life, this striving for union with some objective reference point outside of the self, that makes up religion, far more than organizations of people with similar attitudes.

People's ultimate concerns vary enormously and many of these are not religious in any conventional sense. To entertain Tillich's idea of ultimate concern as religious in character, perhaps religion could be defined as a group of people organized around an ultimate concern, as suggested by Keith Irwin, a retired philosophy professor at Eckerd College. Irwin comments on where AA might fit in a Tillichean framework for religions:

> Once you have an organized group of people around an ultimate concern that has any kind of formalized life, then you are moving in the direction of what could be called a religion.
>
> Organizations such as AA, which are not denominations in any traditional sense but do subscribe to something and have a program that you follow, would fit into 20th century definitions of religion. Once you move out of organized churches, groups that are organized and have programs with even a vague appeal to a supreme being, as in AA, are now included.[15]

If these types of acknowledgments were common in the recovery field, lay or professional, discussion over the years would have been far less frustrating. Instead, counselors, employee assistance managers, treatment directors and recovering men and women seemed to regard the separation between religion and spirituality as a point of information to be conveyed rather than as a position to be argued.

Instead, the addiction experts relied on the most literal, Yellow Pages definitions of religion available, perhaps as a way of whitewashing strong emotional elements of their science.

As a popular 12-step cliché has it, "Religion says you've got to; spirituality says you get to." AA, and by extension the scores of organizations modeled after AA, place the given life problems—drinking, overeating, gambling, drug addiction, recovery from sexual abuse—as the fulcrum of a transformed identity. This transformation and the vocabulary used to describe are enough to move AA into religious territory. Not to mention (as many atheists in the program do) that six of the Twelve Steps mention God. Yet many people within these secular groups deify the disease concept of alcoholism as a kind of higher power, and approach their particular secular cures in the same manner a priest approaches an altar.

Therefore, assurances that these references refer to "a God of one's understanding" miss the point. Nor is the issue clarified when therapists who have an explicit spiritual orientation define addiction as a "quest for the divine," ignoring religion. The present habit of addressing the two concepts as fundamentally different must be improved.

However, allowing that AA may be a religion unto itself does not necessarily mean that the body of believers in AA should be referred to as a church. A church, as described in an influential definition by theologian Benton Johnson, is "a religious group that accepts the social environment in which it exists."[16]

A sect, according to theologian H. Richard Niebuhr, can be viewed as an unstable organization which has split off from a church, often because church members felt that the larger body was not meeting their needs.[17]

A cult, on the other hand, need never have belonged to a religious body. Churches start out as cults. A key difference between churches and cults, according to Stark and Bainbridge in *The Future of Religion*, is that the latter has no necessary connection to any religious body. To a point, the ideas of a cult are often hostile to the society mainline that churches have accepted. This friction can be quite subtle. "Unless an outsider gets into a religious discussion with members," Stark and Bainbridge write, "no indication of their religious deviance is likely to be evident."[18]

Promises and Compensators

John Wallace, executive director of the upscale treatment center Edgehill-Newport in Newport, Rhode Island, and Stanton Peele frequently cited each other's work in a pejorative manner in a series of published papers during the late 1980s. In his 1987 article for *Professional Counselor*, Wallace responded to an argument made by Peele, who compared AA-style sobriety to evangelical religion.

> One wonders how an empirical scientist like Dr. Peele has managed to get his observations of AA so dreadfully confused by religious metaphor. Having attended several thousand AA meetings, I have never heard anybody stand up and preach a doctrine of redemption (salvation from sin through the atonement of Christ). Moreover, considering the day-at-a-time program that AA actually is, Dr. Peele's assertion that AA people preach "teetotaling forever" has a strange, almost resentful ring.[19]

Around this same period of time, a monthly recovery

tabloid called *Sober Times* printed a review by John Wallace of Peele's book, *Diseasing of America*. Similar to asking Marcia Clark to review a book by O.J. Simpson, the headline—"Reviewer Completely Refutes Author's Ideas, Opinions"—left no doubt regarding *Sober Times*' position.

In Wallace's *Writings*, his chapter entitled "The Attack of the 'Anti-Traditionalist' Lobby" states that "basically, this lobby is opposed to the disease concept of alcoholism and would like to see most alcoholics trying to drink rather than trying to stay sober."[20]

Stark and Bainbridge define religion as "human organizations primarily engaged in providing general compensators based on supernatural assumptions."[21] There need be no specific deity or object of worship. Stark and Bainbridge explain:

> [A compensator] is the belief that a reward will be obtained in the distant future or in some other context which cannot be immediately verified. Compensators are a form of IOU. They promise that, in return for value surrendered now, the desired rewards will be obtained eventually. Often people must make regular payments to keep a compensator valid, which makes it possible to bind them to long-term involvement in an organization that serves as a source of compensators. Put another way, humans will often exchange rewards of considerable value over a long period of time in the hope that a reward of immense value will be forthcoming in return.[22]

The manual for spiritual compensation in recovery is *Alcoholics Anonymous*, more frequently referred to as the *Big Book*, an anthology of personal stories, descriptions of alcoholism and AA's model for recovery by working the 12 Steps. The steps describe an evolution of personal change starting with an admission of "powerlessness" over drinking; finding and establishing a relationship with a higher power; taking moral inventory of one's character traits; making amends to those one has harmed; and maintaining a vigilance throughout life for helping others to stay sober.

The *Big Book* also maps out the terrain for how the organization of AA is to be maintained. Twelve organizing principles, or "traditions," ensure that AA (and other 12-step organizations modeled after AA) will, among other things, maintain confidentiality for all of its members and have no financial ties to outside institutions.

In return for working the steps, AA members eventually achieve a state of mind characterized by words such as "serenity" or phrases such as "quality sobriety," "working a good program," or "walking the walk and talking the talk."[23]

Despite the third tradition—"The only requirement for membership is a desire to stop drinking"[24]—the criteria are somewhat more demanding for those who wish to be members in good standing, or to gain the spiritual compensators commonly known as the "Promises of the Program." Some of the promised compensators are:

We are going to know a new freedom and a new happiness.

We will not regret the past nor wish to shut the door on it.

We will comprehend the word serenity and we will know peace.

Self-seeking will slip away.

Our whole attitude and outlook upon life will change.

We will suddenly realize that God is doing for us

what we could not do for ourselves.[25]

The power a group can exercise over individuals, propelling them toward the emotional and sometimes physical destruction of all concerned, is simultaneously fascinating and horrifying. Destructive cults have certain characteristics that separate them from benign cults and everyday groups and organizations which may contain cult-like aspects.

Psychiatrist Robert J. Lifton, who studied Chinese prisoners of war in *The Future of Immortality and Other Essays for a Nuclear Age,* coined and summarized these aspects:

● Milieu control. Members live at prescribed residences, every aspect of which is tailored to reinforce the group's ideology. Outsiders are generally distrusted.

● Mystical manipulation. Seemingly spiritual experiences are manufactured by the group. This "planned spontaneity" is sometimes achieved through selective interpretation of events, sometimes through overt trickery.

● The demand for purity. Perfectionistic standard not only for action, but for thought and feeling.

● The cult of confession. Members in the destructive cult habitually empty their consciences to others, disclosing not only past wrongs but ongoing perceptions, thoughts and fantasies deemed unacceptable to themselves or to the group standard.

● Doctrine over person. The beliefs of the group are paramount, and all human experience must work to support the group doctrine.

● Loading the language. Lifton writes: "Totalist language, then, is repetitiously centered on an all-encompassing jargon, prematurely abstract, highly categorical, and relentlessly judging, and to anyone but its most devoted advocate, deadly dull: in Lionel Trilling's phrase, 'the language of nonthought. . . . It is in part an expression of unity and exclusiveness.' " The most prominent feature of loading the language is the presence of "thought-terminating cliches."

• Dispensing of existence. Individuals and their defining ideas within the group or society are either in or out. Deviants are expelled rather than killed. But after expulsion, it is as if the departed members are dead.

• A sacred science. More accurately, many cults build up pseudosciences around them. This enables them to accuse unbelievers or members who are tempted to stray as not only heretical, but unscientific. Anyone who leaves the group is doomed, not only as punishment for heresy but scientifically determined to fail.[26]

Treatments based on AA are often strident in their insistence that addicts and alcoholics adopt a "higher power." Yet accounts from early members of AA clearly state that the phraseology of "Power greater than ourselves" and "God as we understood him" were the result of arguments between the more and less early religious AA members. It was, in other words, a political concession, a theological average or mean.

In *Lois Remembers*, AA founder Bill Wilson's wife recalls a lengthy period of negotiation between different groups of AA members prior to the final draft of the *Big Book*.

The pros and cons were mostly about the tone of the book. Some wanted it slanted more toward the Christian religion; others, less. Many alcoholics were agnostics or atheists. Then there were those of the Jewish faith and, around the world, of other religions. Shouldn't the book be written so it would appeal to them also? Finally it was agreed that the book should present a universal spiritual program, not a specific religious one, since all drunks were not Christian.[27]

The solution then was to draft the book in language that Christians, atheists and other religious people could live with. It does not follow, nor need it be inferred, that atheists should "become" more spiritual, or that evangelical Christians should tone down their personal religious beliefs in order to stay sober.

Yet today many alcohol counselors and educators are intent on ensuring that atheists acknowledge some higher power, because in their rigid understanding it is necessary for recovery. This priority leads to such absurdities as, "Your higher power can be a chair." Atheists do not want to pray to a chair or anything else for that matter. So the concept of a "higher power" tends to get scrapped, but not without enduring a certain amount of stigma from mainstream members.

The Sustaining Sermon

Young churchgoers are often taught to look for and value the "good" sermon; the intellectually pleasing yet uplifting sermon that combines the past and the present and elevates the abstract to the concrete and mundane.

John Bradshaw could deliver that sermon, or its therapeutic equivalent. He had been trained in homiletics—the art of preaching—during nine years of training as a Jesuit monk. He also had enormous enthusiasm for his subject matter, which was essentially reducing every known human malady to unfortunate or painful aspects of childhood. His Texas twang, his knowledge of philosophy and theology (which easily exceeded most therapists, on or off the lecture circuit), his liberal and eclectic use of other's observations, his righteous anger over the "soul murder" of children by adults and his self-deprecating humor all blended together into a single, gyrating performance of uncontainable fury.

As writer Mark Pendergrast eloquently stated in his book, *Victims of Memory: Incest Accusations and Shattered Lives*:

> He speaks in staccato cadences, with the urgent intensity of Billy Graham in his glory years. The words spill forth, the italics and exclamation points practically visible in the air. He repeats the same key buzzwords, the same phrases—*shame, dysfunctional family, abandonment, abuse*—hammering them hypnotically home. . . . Everything Bradshaw says seems to be *terribly* important. [28]

Long before Bradshaw's audience reached into the millions, these talents were visible. One particular meditation—in which you go back to see and comfort your emotionally or physically battered "child," then either take him or her away with you, or just say au revoir—was already in wide circulation. Despite the fact that every therapist was using it, Bradshaw's unique style added something no one else could duplicate.

In the meantime, HCI was grossing $1 million a month in book sales, a figure that peaked at $2 million a month by 1990.

In 1988, at HCI's 5th Annual ACoA Conference in San Francisco, Bradshaw spoke to an audience of about a dozen people. He imparted his standard speech about toxic shame and the tragic flaw in Western civilization (that we favor thinking over emotion, which he blames on Descartes). It didn't take long for Bradshaw to be discovered. Before the conference was over a thousand people showed up, including 200 walk-ins, for a special Bradshaw night.

Argument by Diagnosis

As recovery spread through books and conferences, self-help tapes and word of mouth, a countermovement was afoot. This movement was inspired by disaffected AA members who wanted to provide alternative routes toward curing substance abuse. Founders such as Jack Trimpey of Rational Recovery (RR), Jim Christopher of Secular Organizations for Sobriety (SOS), and Jean Kirkpatrick of Women for Sobriety sought attention for these alternative support groups in response to a treatment industry still dominated philosophically by AA concepts.

In 1989, Trimpey and Seattle attorney John Meyer raised the challenge to a new level, attempting to drum up support for a class-action lawsuit that would force treatment centers to provide "secular alternatives" in handling court referrals such as DUI cases or lose their state funding.[29] Yet a mass mailing to attorneys in all 50 states failed to produce a single response.[30]

The differences between AA and RR are mostly in their language—which is a powerful difference. RR replaced the often-ominous "disease" lingo with a set of practical tools. Instead of concentrating only on alcohol problems, Trimpey had attempted to widen the field of rehabilitation. RR does not require its members to believe in a higher power. Nor does RR incorporate AA's custom of sponsorship, which is a tutorial relationship with someone who has been in the program longer than you. There is no pressure to attend twice- or thrice-weekly meetings to discuss these issues. On the contrary, RR encourages members to "graduate" after exposure to the group's philosophy for an average of a year and a half.

False Validators and Meaningless Qualifiers

Perhaps the average therapist is far more aware these

days of the potential for these (unnecessary and decidedly non-therapeutic) conflicts in 12-step groups and has at hand pertinent names and phone numbers for nearby meetings of RR, Women for Sobriety or SOS. Hopefully this is the case, but it seems that only therapists with few professional or personal ties to 12-step groups are capable of these insights or can be relied on to supply relevant information.

While at HCI, I often expressed my concerns to addiction and recovery therapists regarding AA's pervasive rigidity and intolerance.

"You must have had a bad experience," many of them would say. After hearing this response on numerous occasions, I finally gave it a name: The False Validator (FV). There is no doubt that these individuals meant well, nor can I say that these conversations ended before reaching a useful conclusion. On the contrary, it was sometimes possible to make further progress and find areas of agreement and understanding. But those experiences only became possible after I recognized the False Validator as an ideological blockade and learned how to circumvent it.

The False Validator is not a question but a declarative statement. As a weapon against dissent, it accomplishes three objectives:

• The False Validator isolates the dissenter from any hypothetical others. You, and only you, must have had a bad experience.
• The False Validator shrinks the implied time frame—hence the significance—of the observation. Whatever frustrations you may have had did not accumulate through repetition over months and years; you merely had "an experience."
• The False Validator establishes control: the FV dispenser assumes the role of care giver. That which was offered up as

analysis is translated into a cry for help, the sharing of a "bad experience." Traditional recovery therapists, needless to say, love the False Validator.

The most common response to criticism of the ideology or social structure of AA and similar programs was qualified validation for complaints, coupled with qualified endorsement of 12-step programs. Occasionally this support has appeared in blunt, unqualified form ("You misunderstand: AA is a spiritual program; it has nothing to do with religion"). More frequently, therapists who are simply looking for ways to send people to 12-step groups offer inducements far more subtle.

• Reduction of problems to individuals or groups: "Some people" (or particular meetings) within the program can be full of rigidity, but (this part needn't be stated explicitly) most people and most meetings are not.

• Appeals to sophistry: "The group" or "a chair," (or, in some cases, "the therapist") can be your higher power. Liberal theologians often go to great pains to prove that Jesus was not a fundamentalist. The Presbyterian church in which I grew up has a number of theological liberals who give very generous interpretations for various authoritarian-sounding remarks attributed to Jesus ("I am the way, the truth and the life; no one cometh unto the Father but by me").

Similarly, AA theologians often show great dexterity in attempting to bend program "suggestions" to suit their tastes. Their qualified interpretations are as much in keeping with AA (what it is or what it has become) as are the more literal, charismatic pronouncements and *Big Book* re-enactments one encounters in meetings every day. This is sophistry, at least to the extent that unambiguous intentions are subverted to possible twists in the meanings of words and phrases.

Seeing one's higher power as "a chair" is a helpful ruse—a "training deity"—until one develops the intestinal fortitude to utter "the G-word." But it is (almost) equally sophistic to say, "The group can be your higher power," since the strongest selling point of this idea is that the group is not God. Yet, as those who offer this suggestion realize on some level, the flow of the group's ideas runs directly to God. "Turning it over" to the group (most groups, at least) is equivalent to entering the river a few miles upstream and floating effortlessly downstream to God. Besides when people say, "Your higher power can be anything," they don't really mean "anything." It is theoretically possible but unlikely, for example, that one would hear, "Your higher power can be a group of atheists" or "Your higher power can be a stack of virulent anti-recovery books."

Even the innocuous, disembodied chair has its symbolic function. Chairs are visually striking when clustered together in rows or circles before meetings, dominating the architecture of the room. More potently, a newcomer is likely to spend many more minutes a day among chairs that are occupied by fellow AA members than unoccupied ones.

Therapy and Treatment Cults

The wire services relayed the unforgettable photos—more than 800 bodies littering the ground; victims of a mass suicide at Jonestown, Guyana, in 1978. Like many other cults, Jonestown began as a mission with noble goals. Gradually, through isolation and the forcefulness of one personality, the People's Temple deteriorated into a paranoid circle hiding in the jungle from a hostile world.

Yet the huge scope of Jonestown proved almost a disservice to the cause of cult awareness. It magnified the scale of damage to an outlandish extreme, causing the practices of hundreds of smaller destructive cults to pale by comparison. It also perhaps sent a false signal to the public that destructive groups are easy to recognize—there is nothing ambiguous about 800 dead bodies.

Cult experts say that Jonestown made it harder, not easier, to enjoin the public to recognize the dangerous aspects of cults and cult-like groups—that is, those employing methods of "coercive persuasion" designed to break down a person's will to resist the group and its totalizing ideology. At the same time, there has been much attention paid to the existence of so-called satanic cults proliferating in the United States and their alleged atrocities. Networks of highly organized, well-connected citizens are said to be holding secret rituals involving animal and human sacrifice, and impregnating brainwashed female "breeders" for this purpose.

It is difficult to speculate as to why the public became so sensitized to satanic cults whose existence is unproven, while at the same time becoming desensitized to the very common existence of groups and organizations employing mind-control techniques. This is a hugely complicated issue.

After conducting interviews with former members of groups such as the Boston Church of Christ or the Unification Church, people who often spent years in anguished mental and emotional enslavement, reporters are often asked:

But couldn't any group be called a cult? Aren't you just talking about the way people behave in groups? And as for those people who become zombies and renounce their families (because the families sense a personality change for the worse and won't embrace the cult's vision); sleep five to a room (in order to save money which will be donated to the group); or stay up 19 and 20 hours a day (often working at low-paying or underemployed positions, plus hours in Bible studies, witnessing for hoped-for recruits, de-briefing with appointed supervisors, endlessly 'processing' their feelings, or squeezing out every last drop of energy to sell flowers on street corners)—aren't they just crazy?

The answer, emphatically, is no, or at least "not necessarily." New York University psychiatrist Marc Galanter echoes the views of other cult experts when he writes, "The behavior of individuals, which may appear pathological, may reflect no more than responses induced in the group to assure its integrity."[31] As an example, Galanter notes correlations he has observed between increased suspiciousness of outsiders (of non-members of the Divine Light Mission, in this case), and an improvement in neurotic distress. Rather than paranoia, the suspiciousness could be interpreted as an example of a group protecting itself from influences that might undermine its integrity. For insofar as members have joined truly cult-like groups, they become like gears in a machine, learning to equate the group's best interests with their own and to identify potential enemies of the group as their enemies.[32]

"Similarly," Galanter writes, "a cult may implicitly suggest that members close themselves off from any outsider's influence. Because of this, some members may even manifest behavior something like dissociative phenomena when they feel that they are vulnerable."[33]

In Chapter Eight of this book, parents discuss losing

contact with their adult children after failing to "admit" to having molested these children years or even decades ago. Of the dozens of families interviewed, all spoke of an early phase in their adult child's estrangement, during which time he or she seemed preoccupied, unusually distant and evasive. This is often the phase during which the children make repeated inquiries about their pasts—asking for details about vacations, changes of address and so on. They often want to go through family albums and study photographs of themselves as children.

Groups can cause people to behave in strange ways. In extensive studies on the Unification Church, or the "Moonies," Galanter found that new members tend to experience relief of psychiatric symptoms upon joining the group, and a slow increase in stress and neurosis once the reality of church life sets in. However, there remains a minority of members who do not experience the symptoms in any measurable way and continue in the church indefinitely.[34]

Galanter's paper, "Cults and Other Zealous Self-Help Movements: A Psychiatric Perspective," appeared in the May 1990 issue of the *American Journal of Psychiatry*. For thematic purposes, Galanter seems to soften some of the more recognizable features of coercion and escape the aversive reaction often brought on by the term "cult" by creating a model of the charismatic group.

> The model of the charismatic group can be used generically to describe modern cults and zealous self-help movements. Such a group is characterized by 1) a high level of social cohesiveness, 2) an intensely held belief system, and 3) a profound influence on its members' behavior. It is "charismatic" because of the commitment of members to a fervently espoused,

transcendent goal; indeed, this goal is frequently articulated by a charismatic leader or ascribed to the progenitor of the group. Charismatic groups can relieve certain symptoms associated with psychopathology, but they can precipitate psychiatric symptoms as well.[35]

Galanter's discussion of AA in this context focuses on Bill Wilson.

[Bill Wilson] was experiencing great despair when he had a revelatory experience that was clearly religious in nature: "All at once I found myself crying out, 'If there is a God, let Him show Himself!' Suddenly the room lit up with a great white light. . . . It seemed to me in my mind's eye that I was on a mountain and that a wind, not of air, but of spirit was blowing." Bill went on from this experience to preach to other alcoholics and, as with cultic groups described above, the forces of shared belief and group cohesiveness have become central in the engagement process of AA. Furthermore, the program's evolution from these early origins to a large organization parallels the development of rituals and bureaucracy described by [legendary sociologist] Max Weber for charismatic religions.[36]

Being a charismatic group, or a cult for that matter, is not necessarily a bad thing, say Galanter and other experts, who tend to define "cult" in terms of clusters of characteristics on a continuum rather than by black-or-white criteria. For example, Galanter considers AA a "benign cult" as opposed to a "destructive cult." [37]

Arthur Deikman, a psychiatrist at the University of California at San Francisco, in his book *The Wrong Way Home: Uncovering the Patterns of Cult Behavior in American Society*, relates a common fantasy he calls "the dependency dream."[38] Unlike the myth-making, talk-show magnification of collective fears, Deikman zeros in on everyday life. Yet, far from saying we should not be concerned at the ubiquity of cult patterns—in our jobs, our civic clubs, our religious organizations—he stresses awareness of subtle appeals many of these groups make to that universal longing for a beneficent authority.[39]

Deikman's central metaphor is a *Peanuts* cartoon, in which Charlie Brown and Patty are sitting back to back against a tree. Their dialogue is worth reviewing:

> **Patty:** Lately everything seems to bother me.
> **Charlie Brown:** How do you mean?
> **Patty:** What do you think security is, Chuck?
> **Charlie Brown:** Security? Security is sleeping in the back seat of the car . . . when you're a little kid, and you've been somewhere with your mom and dad, and it's night, and you're riding home in the car, you can sleep in the back seat. You don't have to worry about anything . . . your mom and dad are in the front seat and they do all the worrying. They take care of everything.
> **Patty:** That's real neat!
> **Charlie Brown:** But it doesn't last! Suddenly, you're grown up, and it can never be that way again! Suddenly, it's over, and you'll never get to sleep in the back seat again! Never!
> **Patty:** Never?
> **Charlie Brown:** Absolutely never!
> **Patty:** Hold my hand, Chuck!![40] *

*Text from *Peanuts* cartoon strip reprinted by permission of United Feature Syndicate, Inc.

Deikman says:

> The wish to ride in the back seat of the car—the depen-
> dency dream—has great strength and tenacity. It should
> be recognized as a permanent part of the human psyche
> even though in adults it ceases to be as visible as it is in
> childhood. This dream is dangerous because in its
> most extreme form it generates cults, makes people
> vulnerable to exploitation, regression, and even vio-
> lence. Even in the less intense, less obvious manifesta-
> tions which occur in everyday society, the dependency
> dream may impair our ability to think realistically. If
> we recognize our dependent wishes for what they are
> we can make appropriate corrections in thought and
> behavior, but usually we do not. Rather, we engage in
> thinking and behavior more subtle than that of the
> People's Temple but qualitatively similar. The back
> seat of the car does not carry us home.[41]

There is something universal, almost touching in this
longing. And it's possible one could go completely in the
opposite direction, refusing to become vulnerable and avoiding any situation that some "big person" might capture
one's mind. Part of Deikman's message seems to be that we
cannot live in society and not be vulnerable to group pressures, which can often produce beneficial results.

And as said before, "surrender" to "something greater
than ourselves" is considered an indispensable element (in
varying degrees) in both 12-step groups and most forms of
Christianity. Most likely every adherent has a truth to tell.
But the essence of the struggle is to maintain some balance
between committed group participation and cult engulf-
ment, between learning new programs and overwriting

previously stored programs. Balance, here, suggests an average between poles of hermetic skepticism on the one hand, and cult-like suggestibility on the other.

It seems plausible that most human beings approach extremes of suspicion and belief on a frequent basis, perhaps every day or several times a day. But overall, a reasonably independent person can sort through conflicting feelings, re-evaluate belief systems and step up or scale back commitments to various organizations at will. It also seems that this sense of balance was favored by founding influences in both AA and Christianity.

Bill Wilson writes, "I see 'humility for today' as a safe and secure stance midway between violent emotional extremes;"[42] and elsewhere, "Nobody can cause more needless grief than a power driver who thinks he has got it straight from God."[43]

Yet both AA and the Christian church have attracted and inspired many dangerous individuals and groups. The same can be said for the military, non-Christian churches and most political parties. But the ubiquity of coercive group dynamics is not a reason to ignore them. And there are some excellent reasons for singling out the destructive potential within certain AA groups and AA ideology itself—one reason being the almost total exemption AA has heretofore enjoyed from any type of critical, meaningful analysis.

Instead, 12-step groups have been allowed to maintain an underdog status dating back to contemporary alcoholism as a fledgling concept, a status AA has long since outgrown. Therapist cheerleaders rally around the underdog—little grassroots AA against the big, bad medical establishment—as if no one over the last 30 years has noticed that AA has become the medical establishment, in the sense that disease and abstinence ideology thoroughly pervades hospital-based treatment and most other treatments available in the United States. There are few therapists and fewer AA members who have been willing to bring issues of group dynamics before the public.

Scapegoat Rituals

In the ancient Hebrew religion, two goats were offered on Yom Kippur as atonement for the sins of Israel. The priest, having purified himself before God, drew lots to determine which goat would be sacrificed and which would be banished into the wilderness. The remains of the sacrificed goat were burned outside the village—they were considered unclean.[44]

The "wandering goat" was exiled, carrying the sins of the community with him. It was "sent" to the rebel angel, Azazel, who has been variously translated as "the goat that departs"[45] and "strong one of God."[46] This was not always the case. Azazel was at one time a goat god for herdsmen. Yet by having the sins of mankind bestowed upon him, he came to symbolize the rejected aspects of humanity.

As modern religions began to form, creating sharp distinctions between good and evil entities, Azazel increasingly became identified with the shadow side of Yahweh himself. According to Jewish legend, Azazel asked God why he did not destroy the people of Israel who had disappointed Him, instead of showing mercy toward them. "And God replied, 'If thou wouldst be among them thou wouldst also sin.' Whereupon Azazel requested to be tested and descended to live among men. An evil impulse overcame him."[47]

In her book *The Scapegoat Complex*, Jungian psychoanalyst Sylvia Brinton Perera beautifully recounts the legend and its aftermath in which Azazel is exiled into the wilderness as a warning to those who would find fault with their peers.

> Azazel came then to stand, psychologically, for the arrogantly pure, condemning, supercritical judge who would hold men to a standard of behavior he cannot live by himself, for the instinctive impulse erupts through his brittle discipline. His is a standard that takes no account of the facts of life and the embeddedness of man in nature. It implies contemptuously that, by arrogance and will alone, one can withstand the tests of life.[48]

Individuals Perera calls "scapegoat-identified," internalize society's codes as:

> A heightened but oversimplified morality which stands for collective virtues, and hence against instinctual life; yet it has the impersonal and compelling force of an instinct. It is perceived as an automatic sneer or accusation, a black and white judgment, an evaluation before even the facts are noted.[49]

This is true even for those who see themselves as scapegoat victims. Such individuals go through life with their best instincts—their sexuality, spontaneity and creative drives—absorbed and held hostage in the black hole of societal judgment. Perera writes that the return of creativity is one of the signs that a person is improving.[50]

What is useful about this construct is its applicability to certain types of group behaviors. For it is not only the so-called evil characteristics that make up a scapegoat; people can be singled out because of their singular beauty, strength or talent. Accusers need canvasses upon which to project—and banish—qualities they fear in themselves.

Moreover, there is a fusion between accusers and the accused in that both are cut off from life. One exile is self-inflicted, the other imposed by society. The accuser Azazel became the banished one by virtue of choosing to embrace a sterile code of conduct at the expense of humanity. That which has been identified with the destructive cult—an atmosphere of continual accusation, self-recrimination and the threat of exile—lives like algae in the waters of our social lives. There is nothing necessarily wrong or bad about having ethical standards, and there are at least plausible arguments for punishments ranging all the way to execution. We as a society come to accept the inevitability of injustices that will result from mistakes. No system is perfect.

But under the right conditions, the urges toward self-improvement, justice, community and an absolute blanket against life's uncertainties can form a cult; much like the algae blooms can form the red tide, and the fish die.

Nowhere are the ancient dynamics of the scapegoat more evident than in the supposed healing rituals of group therapy. In almost any group, designed around any particular system, it doesn't take long for a scapegoat to be selected. I have seen it happen within the first 15 minutes.

Those who are old enough may remember the no-holds-barred "encounter groups" of the 1960s, which promised a deep emotional closeness with relative strangers in 48 hours or less. But these encounter groups had their share of casualties, which may be the reason they fell from favor. Sometimes the rough, confrontational therapies still in place today remind me of the story "The Lottery," in which the good, solid citizens of a small town drew marbles one day a year to see which of them would be stoned to death.

Harsh confrontation often referred to as "ego stripping," was the linchpin of the therapy at Synanon, a California treatment center which reached the height of its acclaim in the early 1970s. Founder and leader Charles Dederich, a reformed heroin addict, prided himself in his ability to dish out "emotional haircuts" to Synanon residents at the slightest hint of rebellion. The haircut analogy was also employed literally in the military-style buzz cuts the residents had to maintain.

At one time Synanon enjoyed national recognition as the nation's first "therapeutic community." Its style of harsh confrontation won nationwide praise, and no one seemed to be questioning Synanon's ambitious claim of a 90% cure rate. Prominent political figures flew in to meet Dederich and get a nickel tour of the grounds. But gradually word leaked that Dederich had changed. There were reports of a paramilitary goon squad watching his back at all times. He began to arrange the sexual partnering of specific male and female residents. When a weekly newspaper, aided by Berkeley psychologist and cult expert Richard Ofshe, began to investigate Synanon, Dederich fought back by having a rattlesnake placed in their attorney's mailbox. Dederich was convicted of attempted murder and sent to prison. The newspaper editors and Ofshe shared a Pulitzer Prize for their work.[51]

It may be that Ofshe's investigation into Synanon was more than an effort to bring down a violent man. It was based on a recognition that in cult-like situations there are patterns of interaction. Cults choke a person's sense of individuality, liberty and connection with those in their past. Having a drug addict's past can be a wonderful excuse to employ the worst coercive methods available short of physical torture. It is also an excuse that is met with sympathy in the hospitalization and treatment of adolescents against their will, a practice made easier by the drug war and the temperance culture.

Who can say what it is about drugs that brings down society's scapegoating instinct? Perhaps it is a harsh counter-reaction to the 1960s, along with the prevalent rationale at the time that taking drugs could "expand consciousness." The political implications of this idea were that by exploring alternative lifestyles we might create alternative cultures with alternative policies of government regulation and exchange. It is clear, however, that alcohol, drugs and politics have been intertwined in our culture for a long time.

When the Eighteenth Amendment to the U.S. Constitution, prohibiting alcoholic beverages went into effect on January 17, 1920, the Anti-Saloon League launched a negative enforcement campaign using the drunken and rioting Bolsheviks as an example. "Bolshevism flourishes in wet soil," a campaign poster warned. "Failure to enforce Prohibition in Russia was followed by Bolshevism. Failure to enforce Prohibition HERE will encourage disrespect for law and INVITE INDUSTRIAL DISASTER."[52]

John Kobler documents these heady days in *Ardent Spirits: The Rise and Fall of Prohibition*. The following passage demonstrates alcohol's banishment into the wilderness.

Through the streets of Norfolk, Virginia, 20 pallbearers escorted a horse-drawn hearse containing an effigy of John Barleycorn. Behind it walked a masquerader dressed as Satan, feigning hysterical grief. The cortege entered Billy Sunday's tabernacle. "Good-bye, John!" roared the evangelist from the tabernacle door. "You were God's worst enemy. You were hell's best friend. I hate you with a perfect hatred. I love to hate you," and he promised his spellbound congregation of 10,000: "The reign of tears is over. The slums will soon be a memory. We will turn our prisons into factories and our jails into storehouses and corncribs. Men will walk upright now, women will smile and the children will laugh. Hell will be forever for rent."[53]

But John Barleycorn did not die. He would continue to terrorize millions, so long as there were willing consumers of legal or illegal alcoholic beverages. The end of Prohibition marked the beginning of a long, tortuous road leading to what is now called the Recovery Movement, which extends the split between blame and personal responsibility from alcohol to almost any problem a person might encounter in life. Early AA members recognized the need for individual action, but at the same time never lost their sense of mystifying reverence for alcohol itself—an enemy "cunning, baffling, powerful," whose defeat required nothing short of divine intervention.

As the move to treat alcoholics became more aggressive, and psychology began borrowing from alcoholism, the stigma of skid row came full circle. True, enlightened society no longer looked upon alcoholics as simply irresponsible people, but as people with a disease. In a climate of creeping neo-temperance, however, disease defined the person. Just as moral condemnation once erased the notion of worthy individuals who drank too much, the battle against an insidious disease force erases any individuality or dignity for people who cannot or choose not to embrace the cure which has been extended to them. Nonperson status then links the drunkard of the 1930s with the unrecovered addict of the 1980s and 1990s.

In some ways the drunkard was better off. For whatever

his measure of neglect, he at least received credit for having made a choice in order to arrive at his predicament. The unrecovered addict receives no such credit. And society, in order to combat the disease of the addict, has marshalled the forces of church and state and cult.

The goal of this campaign against addictions and dysfunctions is to rescue individuals by obliterating (or "arresting") their disease. Yet individuals are defined, measured and engulfed—by others—in terms of their diseases, both before, after and in spite of their "recoveries."

CHAPTER FOUR

Acceptance and Defiance

In *I'm Dysfunctional, You're Dysfunctional*, Wendy Kaminer notes the recovery movement's penchant for using testimonials as a substitute for thinking. "People love to talk about themselves," she says. Even experts indulge in this pleasant activity as a means of enhancing their believability.[1]

In *Memory and Abuse*, author Charles Whitfield provides a table entitled "Levels of Statements that May be Made about Emotionally Charged Experiences and Issues."[2] The five levels rank degrees of "directness" on an ascending scale beginning with the most "indirect" styles. They include:

1) Media, Public Speeches, etc.
2) "Scientific" or Academically Oriented Writing or Talks
3) Answers Under Oath
4) Beliefs Underlying the Above
5) Experiences from the Heart[3]

"When a person speaks from their heart, their authentic

experience, they tend to be the most direct,"[4] Whitfield assures us. "People in recovery tend to be able to speak and write this way more easily than those who are not."[5]

Whitfield believes healing occurs when one expunges his or her joys and sorrows. "Research is showing," he writes in *A Gift to Myself*, "that writing these things down is not only **enlivening** and **increases** our **self-awareness**, but it also **strengthens** our body's **immune system**."[6]

The following is an attempt to answer questions Whitfield, Bradshaw or Anne Wilson Schaef might ask regarding my thoughts and motives. Recovery people—members of 12-step groups, "wounded-healer" therapists and passionate, naive observers—always hold the cards when it comes to expressing their narrative truths. While Wendy Kaminer may be on target with her criticisms on the validity of the recovery movement's jump from narrative truths to global axioms, it is more a matter of transitions than starting points. One can interpret Kaminer's complaint as one of "emotional realities" in place of coherent thought or political action. Yet everyone has a story, a personal "truth" to tell.

The following passage is an excerpt from Jean-Paul Sartre's "Portrait of the Anti-Semite" as it appeared in Walter Kaufmann's *Existenstialism from Dostoevsky to Sartre*, which articulates some of my own "experiences of the heart."

> The rational man seeks the truth gropingly, he knows that his reasoning is only probable, that other considerations will arise to make it doubtful; he never knows too well where he's going, he is "open," he may even appear hesitant. But there are people who are attracted by the durability of stone. They want to be massive and impenetrable, they do not want to change: where would

change lead them? This is an original fear of oneself and a fear of truth. And what frightens them is not the content of truth which they do not even suspect, but the very form of the true—that thing of indefinite approximation. It is as if their very existence were perpetually in suspension. They want to exist all at once and right away. They do not want acquired opinions, they want them to be innate; since they are afraid of reasoning, they want to adopt a mode of life in which reasoning and research play but a subordinate role, in which one never seeks but that which one has already found, in which one never becomes other than what one already was. Only passion can produce this. Nothing but a strong emotional bias can give instant certitude, it alone can hold reasoning within limits, it alone can remain impervious to experience and last an entire lifetime.[7]

The ultimate objective of the broader recovery movement is probably to lead people into emotional certainties about their lives, and to elevate those feeling states to the realm of fact.

The Coffeepot

The intent here is to establish that there is such an entity as recovery, which although not formally structured, nonetheless imparts expectations to those who participate and draw nourishment from it. *Changes* magazine, conferences and informal dialogue expressed several ideals that were offered up as definitive of "what recovery is all about." Therefore, the recovery entity existed, albeit socially constructed and jointly defined. Recovery touched on a number of shared interests, and more importantly, shared values.

Some of the shared interests included: addiction, eating disorders, sexual abuse, sexuality, communication, the family, relationships, parenting, 12-step groups, therapy and spirituality.

Some of the shared values included: honesty, integrity, unconditional love, "original pain," working on your issues, being "okay" with yourself as a precondition of being of some benefit to anyone else, staying clean and sober, keeping up with recovery literature, correcting your relationship with your family and "moving on" or trying to move on with the rest of your life.

One of recovery's penultimate values is the intrinsic merit in "sharing one's story." M. Scott Peck, psychiatrist and author of *The Road Less Traveled*, who I interviewed in 1988 for *Changes* magazine, regarded story-sharing as the root metaphor behind AA, which he considered "the single most impressive community in the nation, perhaps even in the world."[8] Two alcoholics in the grip of a devastating compulsion overcame it simply by sharing with one another.

AA history eulogizes the old-fashioned coffeepot at Bill and Lois Wilson's house in Akron, Ohio that warmed the earliest members who had escaped frigid weather to sit at their kitchen table and "share their experience, strength and hope."[9] By the 1950s, coffeepots had become treatment centers; by the 1980s, conferences, scores of different 12-step groups and self-help books had replaced the coffeepot.

Throughout the years, the element of storytelling remained central, although the stories themselves were affected by the increasing size and organization of the broader recovery movement. They became more streamlined; unified by the expectation of common experience. Seminar and conference audiences ranging from 50 to several thousand did not possess the same flexibility as those early AA members sitting around the coffeepot. How could they? Like everything else in our society, recovery became mass-produced.

I have heard speakers at conferences unhesitatingly tell hundreds of people they had never seen before about the "ways in which you were shamed." The same analogies were repeated from conference to conference and book to book. Here are just a few of the most common, quoting a compositely-drawn "recovery speaker":

On the confusion of being a child of an alcoholic: "If you asked your mom why your dad was passed out in the front yard and your mom replied, 'Oh, Daddy's sleeping,' that is very damaging to a child's reality."

On achievement as a cover-up for feelings of inadequacy: "I was a human doing, not a human being. I had to do it better than you, better than anyone else so that I could keep my job. I worked 80-hour weeks restructuring the whole company. And still I felt like a fraud."

On loneliness: "I know a lot of adult children who were raised by pets."

On shame versus guilt: "Guilt says you made a mistake; shame says you are a mistake."

On the ambiguities of the disease concept: "I just call it 'dis-ease.' "

On the joke about the drowning codependent: "Someone else's life flashes before her eyes."

On the process of recovering memories of abuse: "Usually it doesn't begin to happen until people are strong enough in their recoveries for the memories to begin to surface. The triggers can be something like having a child who reaches the age you were when you were abused. Or it may be a facial expression (such as a suggestive look), or the scent of cologne."

These statements were repeated often before large audiences, year after year. Thus, little by little, a "composite recovering person" was drawn in the social world and was shared by people in recovery. A consequent norming process seriously watered down the integrity of "telling our stories" as a healing exercise and the credibility of the stories themselves. This process was unstoppable. Like many of the recovery movement's key axioms, "storytelling" has acquired a self-justifying cachet of legitamacy.

For quite a few years now, various writers and critics have argued that recovery was profoundly apolitical—meaning it supported the status quo. The admonition, Kaminer reported at an HCI conference on women's issues, that "You can't work on the world until you work on yourself,"[10] is one I have heard hundreds of times. Work on yourself, work on the world. Do one now, another later. Yet because recovery is an exercise in relentless self-questioning, and experts have given their followers so much grist for doubt, one could spend lifetimes processing the events of a single day.

Being able to tell a story about oneself first meant having a self that was separate from the group identity and group reality. "Individuation" (a Jungian term meaning "the act of forming a distinct entity")[11] was supposed to be one of those things that "recovery is all about." But that distinct identity was exactly what the audiences left at home when they attended HCI's and other recovery conferences.

So when people talked about telling their stories and sharing their narrative truths in a recovery context, one has to wonder where the stories originated. As an AA member from 1981 to 1989, I sometimes felt myself saying things I did not mean and did not believe. I would prepare to make a point in which I did believe and found myself saying some-thing like, "Well, you know, before I got into the program all I did was drink."

Somewhere within, I'd hear the sound of screeching brakes: "What?!" It was a ridiculous statement. I had worked full-time (never missed a day because of drinking), acted in dozens of theatrical productions, written articles and short stories, dated, took vacations, read books, played basket-ball—all during the time I was supposedly laid up drunk. Yet for a long time it was very difficult not to practice this reverse denial.

Obviously, drinking had been a serious enough problem for me to go to AA and to accept abstinence as the best policy for me personally. But if I said that I used to drink all the time, and I didn't drink all the time, then I was telling a lie. There were other statements I made that were not entirely true, or that were technically true but whose shad-ings and implicit meanings had been pushed into a mouth of group description. For example:

● How I "knew" I had to go to lots of meetings (and not write or go to my karate class during those times).
● How sure I was that one drink would inevitably lead to dysfunctional drinking.
● How the hours and hours at meetings were always well-spent because there was at least one gem to take away from every meeting, one thought that I had "needed to hear" at that time.

These partial truths were designed to justify my priorities and to maintain the social ties I had established at these meetings. Despite my controversial views, I felt a sufficient need for approval by fellow members, so much so that I compromised my story to more closely match theirs. I felt the sprain of it every time, the tearing of some internal truth ligament.

In their well-known book, *The Social Construction of Reality*, Peter Berger and Thomas Luckmann link political indoctrination and aspects of psychotherapy with religious conversion. The irreplaceable aspect of their work is their argument that this conversion psychology need not be explicitly religious, but can apply to any significant lifestyle change which involves entering a new environment or joining a new group. In extreme cases, they write, an individual "switches worlds,"[12] joins a religious community, and through socialization, discovers the "plausibility structures" that make the new world coherent, fully tangible and fully believable.

As an individual blends into a religious community, or an equally potent community espousing a kind of political or therapeutic transformation, he redefines his past in terms of the new present. The formula for reinterpretation of the past is, "Then I *thought* . . . now I *know*."[13] Moreover, Berger and Luckmann write:

> Prealternation biography is typically nihilated *in toto* by subsuming it under a negative category occupying a strategic position in the new legitimating apparatus: "When I was still living a life of sin," "When I was still caught in bourgeois consciousness," "When I was still motivated by these unconscious neurotic needs." The biographical rupture is thus identified with a cognitive separation of darkness and light.[14]

Similar to AA, the social reality of recovery is unwritten, though it is the subject of many books. But as with other large groups and organizations, its unwritten codes are more influential than any steps or traditions the group may espouse.

Dysfunctional families do not have their dysfunctional "rules" posted on the refrigerator:

<u>Need</u>
bread
butter
dill weed

<u>Also</u>
Don't talk
Don't trust
Don't feel

Likewise, AA and Narcotics Anonymous (NA) programs, or the assemblies of people in wider recovery groups, networks, retreats, treatment programs or computer bulletin boards, do not exhibit their more repressive aspects in their newcomer literature or hospital-based promotional packages.

So there is a difference between the "rigorous honesty" exalted in AA literature, and the "narrative bending" that is expected in the social reality of the AA program. The coercion can be gentle and loving, or it can be harsh and upbraiding. But it is there; shaping descriptions, "suggesting" vocabularies, "ever reminding us to place principles (theirs) before personalities (our own)."

"Principles before personalities"[15] is the final and crowning phrase of the Twelve Traditions. The traditions are organizational principles designed to maintain AA as pure and self-sufficient. Similar to the 12 Steps, the traditions have also been adopted by other 12-step groups. But "recovery,"

"AA" and "the program," just like "traditions," can also connote a network of unwritten laws. In the cases of "anonymity"[16] (Tradition Twelve) and "expressing no opinion on outside controversial issues"[17] (Tradition Ten), the unwritten can at times surpass the written in the scope of its power, to the point of the former trivializing the latter. The "organization" is fundamentally anonymous; it is not to be engaged in or subjected to the vagaries of commerce.

In the journal *Family Medicine*, University of Oklahoma medical anthropologist Howard Stein argues that addiction has replaced communism as the focusing, external enemy our culture seems to need and onto which we project our anxieties. As such, there is an ongoing interconnection between individual addicts and alcoholics and the culture at large. Stein writes, "Alcoholism and drug abuse treatment are a morality play in which few are at any given moment on stage, and for which American mass society constitutes the audience."[18]

Since the late 1970s, recovery has encompassed far more than individual men and women sharing experiences around the coffeepot. There has been a "war" in progress—a war not only on drugs but on the climate of social permissiveness that once excused their use. It has been a public war, a seedling of electoral campaigns carried out through the passage of draconian sentencing laws that have placed nonviolent 20-year-olds in prison for the rest of their natural lives. It has been a private war attempting to overthrow the identifying traits of "addictive personalities," substituting these for "old ideas" of excruciating self-awareness.

The distinction between public and private "supply- and demand-side" drug policies is a vague one. Therapeutic emissaries of the private war deplore televised drug busts, "zero-tolerance" rhetoric and Naval interdiction for a variety of reasons—one of which is that gung-ho militarism portrays them in a curved mirror with distorted reflections of their own hypervigilance and messianic zeal.

At the same time, both the public and the private drug wars contain elements of compassion. It is better to have safe streets than streets controlled by crack dealers. It is better to be abstinent or reasonably functional than to drown one's sorrows, cut oneself with a razor blade or overdose on heroin.

But stabilization, however necessary in times of crisis, holds no particular appeal as a lifestyle. And having "no opinion" on outside issues is no protection from the profound influence of the therapeutic drug war and the Neo-Temperance culture. It is comforting to think of recovery as one big "community," a modern media village of shared experience not qualitatively different from those early meetings around the coffeepot. Such sentimentality ignores the burgeoning treatment industry of the 1980s, which has survived into the 1990s, and which provides the most direct example of outside issues infiltrating supposedly autonomous groups.

I have seen more than one enthusiastic reference by treatment directors regarding outpatients as inadvertent "recruits" for treatment centers. Since these institutions employed the Minnesota-Model, 12-step groups would be the most natural place for outpatients to influence others. Addicts and alcoholics have relapses, so it is only natural that after abstinence has failed (a couple of times), someone might move from 12-step support to inpatient treatment. The names of local treatment centers were readily accessible at most 12-step meetings, together with usually positive, qualitative evaluations.

This huge accessibility between treatment and self-help

and vice versa did not diminish when insurance companies began shortening lengths of stay. This development only enlarged the scope of "issues" recovering people needed to address, as treatment chains scrambled for new ways to fill hospital beds. This expansion of needs was not necessarily or altogether cynical; codependency and underlying abuse seemed like natural extensions of addiction. But the recovering men and women who tended to staff these treatment centers and who by virtue of their recovery had been discouraged from "fixing the world" or participating in outside issues, did not seem to notice the economic undercurrents contributing to this expansion.

Instead, they brought into meetings and their social groups an evolving rhetoric of family systems, "trauma," and more recently, the importance of "uncovering" the past in order to heal the present. It could not be helped if to do so meant throwing their usual range of interests into a sudden stall, cutting off contact with family members while they "worked on their issues," "divorcing" their parents or even taking them to court. As Howard Stein notes, "In internal as well as external war, after all, acts are condoned and sanctioned that at other times would be held to be reprehensible."[19]

There exists a certain pressure gradient upon one's free will. Fortunately, the will is never completely worn down. If the will reached a point of total exhaustion, it would not be possible to take that "first step" to attend an AA meeting, to end an abusive relationship or to stop assaulting one's body with binge-purge rituals. Whatever spiritual forces may take credit, it was will (or choice) that first admitted "powerlessness" (Step One)[20] that "came to believe"[21] help was available (Step Two) and that "made a decision"[22] to turn the will over to a higher power (Step Three).

"Rational-emotive" psychologist Albert Ellis has gone

further, arguing that it is an act of will to create this God in the first place, or to invest "Him" with powers—a view that angers some but empowers others.[23]

The Recovery Channel

John Bradshaw's *Family Secrets: What You Don't Know Can Hurt You* opens with a parable called "The Secret History of Dorothy": "On a stormy winter night ravaged by high winds, a beautiful little girl was born in a small town in Kansas."[24] Bradshaw narrates the secret shame—and ultimate redemption—of an adopted orphan, who grew up thinking she was damaged goods: her only joy being a little dog named Toto; her share of miseries unfathomable. The imagery is at once flat and vaguely titillating, the narration a blend of compassion and lurid enthrallment. See the neglected waif rummaging through family albums, searching for the mother she never knew! Hear the evil Uncle Henry who "scrutinized Dorothy's every move, scolding and shaming her terribly if she made a mistake!"[25] Feel the sparkling ruby red dress on the good witch Glinda, who "looked just like the picture of her mother in the album."[26]

" 'Mother, take me home, take me home!' Dorothy cried. But Glinda did not gather Dorothy into her arms, as the little girl hoped. She was kind, but she firmly told Dorothy that the journey home was difficult and that she would meet many obstacles along the way."[27]

Bradshaw writes how he has always loved Frank Baum's story and wonders whether this is due to Judy Garland's performance in the movie version, or whether (and more likely) "it is because the story embodies something that is unconsciously shared by everyone."[28] He also notes that *The Wizard of Oz* has withstood the test of time [29] (although his condescending allegory may not).

If everyone has their narrative truth to tell, then shouldn't that privilege extend to Bradshaw—as well as to his multitude of broadcast listeners on the Recovery Channel, that mega-network (that super-station) in the sky?

Of course it does. The problem with the Recovery Channel was that it invited paying subscribers to find their truths, then beamed endless hours of programming at them telling them what their truths might be. The charismatic recovery stars who hosted these programs became attractions unto themselves, not unlike the secular self-help stars on other channels who offered themselves as proof of their inspirational books and tapes guaranteed to change your life: Tony Robbins on awakening your inner giant; the guy in the Hawaiian shirt on buying foreclosures with no money down; or the kid who swears greatness can literally be phoned in, once you set up your 1-900 line.

Secular self-help is straightforward; it is about gaining money and accomplishments. Christian programming is also straightforward; it is about gaining and developing a relationship with Jesus Christ. Both systems sell things, and from time to time, both may exaggerate their claims.

Compared to secular self-help and Christian programming, the Recovery Channel was the least straightforward. Its charismatic stars claimed to represent psychology, but often delivered only one-part established psychology to every four- or five-parts of nomadic venturing and watered-down religion. They wanted to establish that you "needed" help, that you were not God, that you could purge your original pain through family reconstruction and reparenting, two-day grieving seminars and ocean cruise training. The idea that you could function without their help struck many of them as sadly delusional.

The Recovery Channel offered pieces of metaphor woven

into jointly-shared stories of dysfunction. This type of "sharing" is like an AIDS quilt sewn by a single sewing machine, onto which mass-produced patterns of narrative have been stitched. The interchangeable details of persons come last, their content a prisoner of someone else's form.

Labels such as "alcoholic," "codependent" and "survivor" are mass-produced descriptions implying certain personality traits. The resulting sameness that often characterizes the self-descriptions of people in recovery stands in marked contrast with recovery's avowed priority of "honoring uniqueness."

Loss of Definitions

There simply are no hard and fast definitions for addiction. In order to be definitions, they would have to apply in every case. Certainly "loss of control" in a literal sense cannot be part of the definition for alcoholism if some alcoholics can be paid in the laboratory to moderate their drinking. Even heroin—originally marketed as a nonaddictive substitute for morphine[30]—was used with impunity by former heroin addicts, after those individuals returned from their tours of duty in Vietnam.

Stanton Peele describes how Lee Robins, John Helzer and their colleagues, who studied heroin addiction, found that half of a sample of veterans "who were addicted to heroin in Vietnam used heroin when they returned to the United States—*yet only one in eight (or 12 per cent)*" of these returned to "addictive" use of the drug.[31]

"Even when heroin was used frequently, that is, more than once a week for a considerable period of time, only one-half of those who used it frequently became re-addicted,"[32] the study determined.

Before leaping to any conclusions about "advocacy research" or the accuracy of self-reports, it is important to consider that Helzer's 1985 study was championed by the treatment industry as positive proof that alcoholics could not drink safely again.

Of all the drug problems, the addictiveness of heroin is one of the easiest to visualize. If the disease of heroin addiction can be avoided despite continued use of the drug, it is difficult to apply the accepted medical standards for addiction—loss of control, an escalation over time, a craving when the substance is absent—to heroin users, let alone to alcoholics whose withdrawal, however uncomfortable, is nothing like the wrenching withdrawal faced by heroin addicts.

There are softer and more interpretive definitions that the field has tried to capture through "biopsychosocial" descriptions for addictive disease. A clumsy term, the evolution of "biopsychosocial" marked the academic death of "naive disease theory," from which the addiction field's more prestigious members had been distancing themselves for some time.

Three Tiers of Addictions Knowledge

By 1989, Houghton Mifflin had released Stanton Peele's *Diseasing of America*. Just as Howard Cosell's *I Never Played the Game* can change a person's perception of professional sports, *Diseasing of America* was a beginning look beneath the surface of this country's multibillion-dollar addiction industry.

Peele has often quipped that he "created a monster" when he wrote *Love and Addiction* in 1975. In that book, Peele and co-author Archie Brodsky argued that addiction is not a medical disease "since it has the same compulsive profile as many behaviors we regard as quite ordinary and nonbiological, like love affairs."[33]

My aim there was turned on its head when subsequent writers agreed that compulsive love and sex were like drug addictions; therefore, they *also* were diseases. Second, *Love and Addiction* was a social commentary on how our society defines and patterns intimate relationships. But all of this social dimension has been removed, and the attention to love addiction has been channeled in the direction of regarding it as an individual, treatable psychopathology.[34]

In day-to-day practice, there remained a gulf between the ambivalent findings of academic researchers on alcoholism and the teachings of alcoholism counselors in hospital settings; and another gulf between AA, where naive disease theory flourished, and alcoholism counselors into whose rooms these hospital patients would be sent and whose allegiance the industry needed as a source of referrals.

Thus these three tiers—research, treatment and self-help—presented the truths of alcoholism in a descending order of academic completeness; yet with ascending influence. Researchers consumed the most reliable information both in quantity and quality. Ambiguities tantamount to heresy elsewhere were common knowledge to them.

Treatment clients were taught information that was somewhat reliable but often tainted by economic interests; better to "err on the safe side" and justify their costs by presenting only the research that would help patients understand the seriousness of their problem. Consequently the dubious TIQ data was often trotted out as a crown jewel. So was Father Martin's "Chalk Talk" film in which a Catholic priest describes alcoholism as a "progressive disease"—so progressive that a person's alcoholism continues to worsen inside them even when the alcoholic is abstaining for months or years. No research exists to justify this statement; it is nothing more than a hypothesis.

Competition entails pressure. It is easy to imagine that in the competitive environment of declining insurance revenues and rival treatment centers, employees would become more rigidly attached to those ideas which would justify the economic mission of the treatment center. Naturally, the most strongly-worded claims would justify treatment for the most people.

In a July 1989 opinion piece for the *U.S. Journal*, psychologist Jeffrey Schaler, who was then working on his Ph.D., complained of "medical fundamentalism" in the professional addictions field.

> The politics of genetics is beginning to smell like eugenics. Treatment specialists and recovering addicts alike defend an invalid theory of behavior by waving a book of holy science at heretics who dare to question the sacred doctrine. . . . A neo-nazi standard of "do you believe?" is operational in the field today.[35]

The lowest, widest and most influential of the knowledge tiers are AA and other 12-step groups. Treatment industry defenders have taken pains to align their middle tier more closely with research than with AA. In a compilation of his published writings, John Wallace states:

> A.A. talk cannot be understood on the level of ordinary talk, but must be approached as a complex symbolic system that at times defies conventional and literal interpretations. "Folk talk" and "science talk" obey radically different rule systems, proceed from differing

assumptions, and serve different purposes.[36]

Instead of simply claiming the high ground for themselves and sending patients directly into the arms of AA, perhaps it would have helped if alcoholism educators had provided their patients with some sort of cross-referencing dictionary: Science Talk/Folk Talk and Folk Talk/Science Talk.

Professionals organized by industry credentials would be inclined to hold similar views on the causes of alcoholism and its best course of treatment. These views would be consistent with whatever generated the most revenue for the industry in the short-term without destroying its long-term credibility, while incorporating new information to its commercial advantage.

For example, if alcohol runs in families and if family members are affected by one person's alcoholism, then bring all the family members into treatment. If eating disorders might be caused by prior sexual abuse, then extend the therapy of eating-disordered patients to cover that as well. The fact that controlled and uncontrolled studies attempting to document this linkage may be seriously flawed by the misinterpretation of results (as was argued in the April 1992 *American Journal of Psychiatry*) does not change a thing. The linkage between eating disorders and sexual abuse could be there, and treating patients as if the link were there "seems to help them." The "safe side" is usually in the direction of more treatment, not less treatment. And although one could make similar accusations against other branches of medicine and psychology, it does not change this circumstance.

As defenders of mainstream treatment will no doubt point out, commercial success in no way invalidates a set of findings. In the 21st century, according to a 1995 issue of *Scientific American*, technologies will be available to help diabetics monitor their glucose levels with a wristwatch device that supplies insulin through the skin as needed. Microchip implants placed in the back of the eye may one day be able to restore sight to people with damaged retinas. Genetic engineering has already produced "universal gene pools" for use in artificial organs and even "smart" artificial limbs constructed of biodegradable plastic. All of these developments will be quite profitable for manufacturers, hospitals and physicians. Parties who profit by these discoveries will, however, be able to prove the efficacy of their devices, which is something mental health professionals cannot say with the same degree of certainty.

Consequently, mental health will continue to be more ripe for abuses than bodily health, and more likely to be accused of being "driven" by profit potentials, as opposed to merely being inspired by them. Unfortunately, the relative lack of testability in mental health may at times lead to unfair or undeserved suspicions about competent professionals.

In a *Seattle Post-Intelligencer* article, James E. Royce, a Catholic priest and long-time defender of Minnesota-Model treatment, made the following claim: "Most research fails to adequately separate true alcoholics from alcohol abusers or problem drinkers, which makes reports of success misleading."[37]

He continued, citing a study done 10 years earlier in 1985, which showed that 1.6% of 1,289 diagnosed and treated alcoholics proved to be successful moderate drinkers.[38] Though Royce's effort was to minimize or eliminate even this percentage, it is worth noting that the study conducted by psychiatrist John Helzer of Washington University at St. Louis, required an extremely selective interpretation of its data to produce the 1.6% figure. To qualify as moderate drinkers, each month subjects were required to engage in some drinking but not consume more than six drinks on any given day.[39] Subjects could retain "moderate" status even if they exceeded six drinks—so long as it happened no more than three times in one month, without incurring measurable consequences such as drunk driving arrests, job loss, domestic disturbances and so on.[40]

During the three years of the study, another 4.6% of the sample drank within the specified moderation guidelines for 30 months out of 36. But because they did not drink every month, they were ruled out as being moderate.[41] As John Wallace wrote:

> 4.6 percent were mostly abstinent with occasional drinking. The investigators point out that the subjects were, however, likely to have been advised to stop drinking rather than to moderate their drinking. Helzer et al. concluded that the evolution to stable moderate drinking appears to be a rare outcome among alcoholics treated at medical or psychiatric facilities.[42]

Wallace neglected to discuss why the decision to go against medical advice should be considered a failure. Suppose—in a purely hypothetical, stingy and somewhat suspicious fashion—that the Helzer study was produced in response to a pair of highly publicized reports (1976 and 1980) by the Rand Corporation, which found that 18% of 14,000 alcoholism patients were able to practice sustained normal drinking.[43]

The Rand Report resulted in almost as much controversy as that of the Sobells. According to Peele, "the National Council on Alcoholism attempted to suppress the [Rand] report before publication and viciously attacked it in the press after it appeared."[44]

If real or imagined pressures from the traditionalist majority in any way influenced the commission or interpretation of this study, it might be helpful to reexamine these numbers. This is what formed the basis for Royce's conclusion: "In any case, it would be unethical to suggest to any patient a goal with a failure rate of 98.4 percent."[45] If those 4.6% of patients who drank some, but not enough to qualify as moderate under the study guidelines are added to the 1.6%, it means that 6.2% of this sample practiced moderation over three years.

Another 12% did exceed the guidelines, consuming seven drinks or more a day, on four or more occasions in one month. But these 12% incurred no measurable consequences for their actions.[46] As Peele notes:

> The investigators were very careful to scrutinize any claims by patients that they had drunk without problems—the researchers questioned those who knew such patients and checked hospital and police records. Nonetheless, despite the absence of information to contradict these former patients' claims, the investigators decided that they were denying their continued alcoholic drinking.[47]

Peele adds the following commentary:

> Consider the overall results of the Helzer et al. study: 6 percent of treated alcoholics never got drunk but drank lightly over the previous three years; another 12 percent sometimes drank heavily but reported no dependence symptoms and were not discovered to have

alcohol problems. Yet the researchers indicated that moderate drinking by former alcoholics was next to impossible to attain. Clearly, one might give these data a different cast. One could say that 18 percent of those hospitalized alcoholism patients drank sometimes but were no longer drinking alcoholically (compared with the 15 percent who abstained).[48]

Although it is unclear if the entire 6.2% (1.6% who drank moderately and 4.6% who drank at below-moderate levels) "never got drunk," it is interesting to consider the similarities Peele points out between the Rand Report and the Helzer study which supposedly refutes it.[49] If the 12% of non-problematic heavy drinkers are added to the above-mentioned 6.2%, the result is 18%—the same figure for moderation produced by the vilified Rand Report!

Yet instead of addressing these computations, Royce's 1995 article began with the 1.6% said to be drinking successfully in the Helzer study and attempts to whittle it down further. He does so by citing other studies favorable to his position and recounting the heroism of Mary Pendery and Irving Maltzman for "exposing the failure of the Sobell work."[50]

As for those ex-patients who have unequivocally shown an ability to moderate their alcohol intake, Royce theorizes that they were either in the "early" stages of their disease ("Monday's cold is flu on Wednesday and pneumonia on Friday"); or were never "true alcoholics"[51] to begin with.

To both possibilities, one must remember that all the patients documented in these studies had been treated for alcoholism. Warnings about "stages" of chronic drinking were always potentially correct, in that some alcoholics might drink in a cyclical pattern, followed by more cutbacks and more abuse.

It is not hard to imagine that someone could admit himself for treatment after a particularly frightening episode, abstain for a time, then drink in moderation for an even longer period—all prior to a shortening of the cycles and continued escalation until his drinking has become unquestionably chronic and problematic, regardless of whatever abstinence he may be able to eke out between binges. But Royce does not seem to prove that this escalation will occur; he only guesses that it might. Thus his ability to discount reports of successful moderation among formerly heavy drinkers[52] resembles the eternal "yets" AA members dangle over their own heads like a sword suspended by a single hair.

But it is his second dismissal—that those who manage to moderate their drinking were probably not "true alcoholics"[53] to begin with—that most exemplifies front-end loading. It seems that alcoholism professionals have two sets of definitions for "alcoholic," one is to be applied before treatment, the other after treatment is completed.

The pre-treatment definition is very broad and similar to the question, "Has alcohol ever caused a problem in your life?" It is useful for hospital admission. The post-treatment definition is exceedingly narrow, approaching the Bowery-bum stereotype, which the field's leadership worked so hard to overcome. Its usefulness lies in minimizing the success of former alcoholism patients who continue to drink non-problematically. (The shakiness of self-reports cuts both ways; for just as some ex-patients may tell a follow-up interviewer that they are drinking less than they actually are, others may report total abstinence when in fact they have been drinking moderately).

In light of the baleful warnings drummed into them dur-

ing treatment, it is amazing that so many former patients
have achieved moderation at all. Despite the negative predictions from their former counselors, experts and peers,
they have done so in the absence of a formal support group.

But if Royce is right, and the 1.6% (or 6.2%) of ex-patients
who drank lightly and with some regularity over time were
"not really alcoholics,"[54] then concerns regarding overdiagnosis and insurance gouging would not apply to true
alcoholics. It would only apply to the millions of people
who have been admitted (or forced) under questionable
pretenses into alcoholism treatment or presumed to be
alcoholic because they once attended an AA meeting.

Between 1985 and 1995, what percentage of the total
take from Veterans benefits, Medicare and private insurance
did these millions represent? This information is unknown.
(Although an estimate by the Sobells, published in a 1987
issue of *Drugs and Society*, contends that " 'problem drinkers' outnumber severely dependent drinkers by a *minimum*
ratio of 3:1."[55] If criteria for "alcohol problems" are expanded, the ratio jumps to 7:1.)[56] In *Ethics for Addiction
Professionals*, a 1987 book published by the Hazelden Foundation, Royce and physician LeClair Bissell write:

> Given the present state of our knowledge, is it ethi-
> cal to risk continued exposure to a life-threatening
> drug? The consensus in the alcoholism field is that the
> evidence does not warrant it and that abstinence is the
> only legitimate treatment goal.
>
> Even if some might continue to drink without major
> adverse consequences, their numbers are few and they
> cannot be identified in advance. Research may continue
> with those whose alcoholism remains in doubt, or for
> whom all other forms of treatment have failed, and who

really do reject abstinence as a treatment goal. Perhaps for some this is the only way they can learn for themselves what they have been unable to learn from others; that, for almost all, this approach will eventually fail.[57]

This sounds both reasonable and compassionate, until one considers the impoverishment of existing success rates and the field's own penchant for overdiagnosis. Bissell and Royce seem to imply they are only discussing a minute percentage of treatment patients "whose alcoholism remains in doubt,"[58] for whom "all other forms of treatment have failed," and "who really do reject abstinence as a treatment goal."[59]

Apart from these ethical standards, the cultish principle of making ultimate demands to gain converts and extract commitments is an equally powerful (though largely unspoken) influence on Minnesota-Model recruiting. Robert Jay Lifton called this principle "the demand for purity."[60]

Liberal underwriting practices during the 1980s reinforced the industry's greed, encouraging more diagnoses of anyone who had ever abused alcohol or drugs or consumed either with much regularity. Adolescents caught drinking at a football game became candidates for lifelong personality reform to the extent of their parents' insurance coverage. That some of these teens may have actually had chemical dependency problems was often accidental. Despite being "free" to do as they wished after treatment, entire treatment populations were warned of failure and predictions of doom if they should ever so much as drink a beer, smoke a joint or take a sip of communion wine. One can only wonder how many of these prophesies turned out to be self-fulfilling.

The result was a treatment system scrupulously self-aware of the ethics mandating its prevailing policies, but only dimly aware of the economic and religious undercurrents that helped shape these policies. Because it was the right thing to do, insurers out to endorse the individual's search for spirit and the treatment center's search for insurance dollars combined in a worthy cause. And in either search, economic or religious, the "usefulness" of giving (or being given) a diagnosis counted for more than its accuracy.

The flip side of this seeming compassion was obduracy toward the exceptions, toward anyone who did not accept the self-descriptions being offered or the prescribed advice. The ethos of the Minnesota-Model treatment was its representation of the sick and suffering, people who would die if not for the services found among its hospital chains. Yet this evangelism quickly turned to indifference once those patients left the fold, walked out of treatment, returned to drinking or using—as the majority eventually would.

For these patients the field left only two options: Either reinterpret a disagreeable package to more agreeable ways or face one's difficulties alone. The schoolmarmish rebuke of Bissell and Royce—"Perhaps for some this is the only way they can learn for themselves what they have been unable to learn from others."[61]—with its sing-songy, Bill Wilson "Preamble" rhythms, trails after the remorseful and the rebellious; after everyone who has entered a Minnesota-Model program and relapsed, regardless of the validity of the original diagnosis or the consequences of acting it out. Lifton's phrase for this was "doctrine over person."[62]

The very dialogue of AA, with its rhetoric of "terminal uniqueness," militates against the individual even as sophisticated apologists strive to improve client-to-treatment matching. As long as this "matching" remains bent on promoting a 12-step world view to the exclusion of all others, it remains hollow.

In sum, the chemical-dependency field of the 1980s was

in part a legitimate response to need. Its science, though indeterminate of necessity, made dramatic improvements in both depth and detail. But it is the greed and narcissism of its healers that may be remembered the longest. Greed deemed one model the easiest to mass-produce and sell, and propelled it forward. Avarice and short-sightedness placed profits over experimentation and research, resulting in a fiscal fault line that shifted at the mere request for proof. Narcissism encouraged the endless manufacture of copycat diseases based on a flawed model; replacing what began as concern for children of alcoholics with a tone-deaf medicalization of deviance.

Ultimately, nothing was safe from recovery or its cloying, patronizing notions of "healing" through groupthink and emotional pyrotechnics. Like Escher's ant on the Mobius strip, recovery stars did not see their perspective as inverted, even after they had thoroughly pathologized the normal. Instead, they set out to heal humanity.

A Word About "Religiosity"

An essentially religious character exists in most secular groups both inside and outside 12-step circles. Instead of God or a Higher Power or a 12-step program being deified, most secular groups tend to elevate the disease concept of addiction into an ultimate truth. As Berger and Luckmann wrote:

> The plausibility structures of religious conversion have been imitated by secular agencies of alternation. The best examples are in the areas of political indoctrination and psychotherapy.[63]

Times have changed since 1966 when their book *The Social Construction of Reality* was published. The best conversion psychology examples of today, as co-opted by secular agencies, are in recovery groups for alcoholism, drug addiction, eating disorders, codependency, sexual compulsivity and incest survivorship. In both secular and spiritual recovery (the latter also being secular in a sense, since it is not officially religious), regular attendance and long-term abstinence confer status similar to the pillars of a church community.

For in all three types of organizations—secular recovery, 12-step recovery and organized religious churches—something useful was being attained by participating regularly. The groups were kept alive by those who attended AA, NA, SOS or RR regularly while also abstaining. People could earn status in recovery groups simply by attending meetings over a long period of time.

The much-maligned church member, who was considered to be part of a system that was unfashionably religious as opposed to spiritual or atheistic, often did a lot more hands-on work for less credit and less status than was routinely bestowed upon those individuals who were exalted simply for showing up at recovery meetings over a number of years and saying things that "made sense."

"All in all the religious system has been a major source of toxic shame for many people,"[64] John Bradshaw writes in his book *Healing the Shame That Binds You*. He goes on to say:

> Religious perfectionism teaches us a kind of behavioral righteousness. . . These standards dictate how to talk (there is a proper God voice), how to dress, walk and behave in almost every situation. Departure from this standard is deemed sinful.[65]

Recovery literature is full of similar observations. In *Find-*

ing Balance: 12 Priorities for Interdependence and Joyful Living, Terry Kellogg and Marvel Harrison devote a chapter to spirituality, which they distinguish from religion.[66] In so doing, the authors say several times that church communities can serve as conduits for genuine spirituality.[67] This qualifier is like a low fence. Hop over it, and you will discover a preponderance of this kind of statement:

> Religion is a support system for spirituality. Unfortunately where there is little or no true spirituality, religion is similar to an empty shell—form and ritual but no substance. Spirituality feeds and frees the spirit.[68]

And this kind of statement:

> In spiritual recovery one of the most effective guidance systems we know of is the 12-Step program of Alcoholics Anonymous and other similar groups. A wonderful aspect of 12-Step programs is that they are available virtually anywhere. It is a secure feeling to know we can venture into groups and find support wherever we travel or wherever we live.[69]

And this:

> The 12-Step program is not a religion and has disavowed any formal connection with organized religion, although it is supportive of people using other spiritual support systems.[70]

To Anne Wilson Schaef, the differences between 12-step spirituality and religion are obvious. Her interpretation of

Step Twelve in her book *Escape From Intimacy* reads:

> Having had a spiritual awakening as a result of these
> steps, we tried to carry this message to alcoholics, and
> to practice these principles in all our affairs. . . .
>
> Of course, this is not evangelism. This step is giving
> information and being present as a clear, sober person
> in touch with my whole being. I can do that. It feels
> good, and others even seem to benefit from this proc-
> ess. Whoopee![71]

The message here was that clear, sober people presenting
recovery information that pertained to their whole beings
were not at all like clear, sober people presenting religious
information that also pertained to their whole beings.

Most recovery literature failed to address its own implied
codes of "behavioral righteousness"[72] and its inherent ten-
dencies toward perfectionism and judgment beyond the
most threadbare qualifiers about how one can become "rigid"
in recovery. When these qualifiers appeared at all, they
were usually buried in the back of the book. And even if
people who had read these qualifiers said to themselves,
"The recovery star is correct, it is possible to be rigid in our
recoveries—so let's not do that!"—certain social realities cannot be wished away.

In all types of recovery groups there is certainly a proper
healing, feeling voice; a proper brass-tacks-stick-to-the-facts
voice; a proper tremor to affect when a newcomer might be
confused by a dangerous idea; a persistently meaningful
hug; and a cliche to terminate every thought.

It is not uncommon for members of chemical dependency recovery groups to seek advice from other members
as to whether they should go on a trip, visit relatives or

attend a social function; or to be given such advice even when they don't seek it. The sum total of this oft-repeated advice sets a standard for the recovering person who wishes to "make sense," or be perceived as having achieved "quality sobriety." Departure from this standard is treated very much like sin.

The following represents a composite argument as to why people maintain their close ties to 12-step groups—that is, how they overcome their own awareness that these groups are often intensely religious (although not conventionally so) and coercive.

"I am aware of the social rituals of the program, and a tendency toward its own kind of religiosity." This statement explains why the speaker attended recovery meetings every week, or more likely several times a week, even after a decade or more of being clean and sober. Many people who were active in church harbored an inward skepticism about the religious doctrines and were also aware of social rituals connected with religious membership that at times might have struck them as arbitrary. And no one had a problem suggesting that their active church lives were an essential part of their active religious lives.

"The reason I continue to attend and am willing to 'talk the talk,' to some extent, is not so much that I will be considered virtuous or holy by other members, as that I continue to be alive." It was reasonable enough to connect the avoidance of life-damaging behaviors with remaining alive, and the seeking out of group support with the avoidance of those life-damaging behaviors.

Ceasing one's attendance at meetings or even resuming drinking or drug habits would not necessarily result in death. To imply that it would approached not just religion, but the totalistic belief system of the destructive cult. People who described their motivation to maintain group ties in terms as represented above would generally have no trouble rephrasing the statement to, "I improved my chances of remaining alive by attending meetings." This seemed more acceptable.

When, on the other hand, people insisted on a necessary connection between leaving the group and dying—or even between drinking again and dying—it became more difficult to believe them when they characterized their motivation as "not so much that I would be considered virtuous or holy by other members." All this really meant was that sobriety was more important to these people than anything else—that the only life worth living was a sober life. Rather than seeking communion with God through religious organizations, they sought sobriety and clean time through recovery organizations. It is this search that has been elevated to the level of ultimate concern.

It is amazing when recovery authors who have isolated spirituality as the *sine qua non* of a meaningful existence can then claim that this attribute is more likely to be found in their organizations than in the Roman Catholic Church—which predates modern recovery groups by two millennia and will almost certainly outlast them all.

"For none of this wonderful intellectual freedom you talk about can occur unless we are, after all, alive." This is true, but there is a point at which a life without intellectual freedom is not so wonderful. In order to avoid getting to that point, it is helpful to regard the free flow of ideas as good in itself. It is also helpful to remember the difference between political and philosophical freedom. As long as one has a tongue, a brain and vocal cords, one is free to speak. If there is a gun to one's head, they are not politically free.

Joining any group which had a "primary purpose" other

than that of playing with ideas entailed risks which could not be minimized or altogether escaped. The mass suicide at Jonestown is the most recent, striking example. Once doubt was suspended in order to "try on" an idea, there existed the possibility of never regaining it. If a group used certain techniques—love bombing, harsh confrontation, ritual confessions, "thought-terminating cliches;" or made certain demands—constant self-monitoring of every impulse or feeling, not associating with family or others who did not share the group's beliefs—an escalating commitment to some ideal that would heal society increased the risk of being subjected to mind control. When doubt itself was demonized (except as a "normal" way in which one "used to feel" before coming around), that risk escalated.

Radical doubt is the foundation of our intellectual heritage. To the extent that its impulses are followed, radical doubt is what prevents innocent people from going to jail. Because of recent disregard, many people have been wrongly imprisoned.

Consider the emotional revolution of Mary Meehan, a staff writer for the *Orlando Sentinel*, from alcoholism recovery to a new definition of her childhood:

> I began to read books on incest, and came to know others who told me I had the classic signs of an incest survivor: Low self-esteem, lack of trust, blank spaces in my past. . . . Without fully accepting it, and without any complete memories, I began to act as if I were an incest survivor. I went on the assumption that it was true and tried to work toward a solution. . . . I would compare notes with other survivors and say, "*I think that happened to me.*" There was relief when there were no screams or shudders, but simple nods of empathy.[73]

Meehan did not address the possibility that going "on the assumption that it was true" might have created a problem worse than any she was trying to solve. It was safe to assume that the supportive people around her, along with many suggestions, promised certain things if she would "do the work." These promises most likely rested on certain assumptions, including:

- That there was a single "cause" for her drinking, low self-esteem, etc., and that finding that cause would greatly improve her well-being.
- That suffering leads to redemption, and the greater the suffering, the greater the redemption. Consequently, grislier memories implied a deeper spiritual growth and were reinforced accordingly.
- That once this "work" was done, certain things would unfold. These are similar to AA's first three Promises:

1) We are going to know a new freedom and a new happiness.
2) We will not regret the past nor wish to shut the door on it.
3) We will comprehend the word serenity and we will know peace.[74]

Bill Wilson, who presumably had a hand in writing the Promises, came to recovery through a great white light that appeared to him in Towns Hospital.[75] For the most part, this profound experience seems to have benefitted society and himself. There are, however, equally powerful experiences leading to very different outcomes. The dream of transcendence, while beckoning to life's highest possibilities, has often steered men and women toward humanity's darkest nightmares.

Albert Speer was a young architect when he first heard Hitler speak. As a boy he had seen the ranks of demoralized soldiers returning home after World War I. Deeply saddened, he felt that Germany had been in mourning ever since. Robert Jay Lifton, who interviewed Speer, describes the experience of that lecture in *The Nazi Doctors*:

> Now Hitler appeared, addressing a university audience in measured tones with the simple message that "all can be changed": Germany could become great again, and individual Germans could divest themselves of guilt and loss by embracing this glorious future. Speer was moved to the point of rapture, felt himself to be "drunk" or in an altered state of consciousness, and needed to go off by himself to walk in the woods outside Berlin in order to "absorb" what was happening to him. He was describing a classical experience of transcendence, an ecstatic state of feeling outside oneself and swept up by a larger force that could connect or reconnect one with ultimate spiritual principles. From that day on, he belonged to Hitler.[76]

Speer didn't even give himself a chance to "try on" this vision—it tried him on and declared a perfect fit. Not only was the fit comfortable, it was "right!" This was not the result of months or years of influence by a persuasive, coercive group. This was one speech.

One of the unethical things about pre-war Germany was its enforced totalistic belief system in Germany's special situation and its glorified future. This belief system was what justified mass slaughter. Some of the earmarks of repressive groups are, "This will save society;" "You can be re-made;"

"You can come home;" and especially, "Get rid of your doubt."

A more benign example than the Holocaust of the dangers in believing the above messages can be found in a description of a revival which drew 20,000 people in 1801, in Cane Ridge, Kentucky. Elias Canetti narrates from his *Crowds and Power*:

> An eyewitness who kept a precise journal reports that, in the course of this meeting, which lasted for several days, 3,000 people fell helpless to the ground—nearly one sixth of those present. Those who fell were carried to the meeting house nearby. At no time was the floor less than half covered with people lying there. Some lay quiet, unable to speak, or move. At times they would come to themselves for a few moments, then a deep groan, a piercing shout or a fervent prayer for mercy would show that they were alive. "Some talked but could not move. Some beat the floor with their heels. Some, shrieking in agony, bounded about like a fish out of water. Many lay down and rolled over and over for hours at a time. Others rushed wildly over stumps and benches and plunged shouting, 'Lost! Lost!' into the forest."

> When the fallen came to themselves they were changed people. They rose and shouted "Salvation!" They were "new-born" and ready to begin a good and pure life; their old sinful existence was left behind them. But the conversion could only be believed in if a kind of death had preceded it.

> There were also phenomena of a less extreme nature which tended to the same end. A whole meeting would suddenly break out weeping: many people were seized with irresistible jerks. Others, usually in groups

of four or five, started barking like dogs. After a few years, when the excitement had begun to take milder forms, people would burst out, first singly and then in chorus together, into a "holy laugh".

But everything that happened, happened within a crowd, crowds more highly-charged and excited than almost any others we know of.[77]

CHAPTER FIVE

Treatment

The following is a taped interview with a woman who spent five weeks in a particularly harsh treatment environment. The details of her story (and its unsuccessful outcome) illustrate what happens when zealous reformism, conjoined with the scapegoating of addiction itself and of addicts, is forcibly applied to human beings. The word "forcibly" is used here because the treatment center was an alternative to prison. She could have lost custody of her two children had she not accepted the treatment. This fact alone removes any element of meaningful patient "choice" as the term is understood in civilized societies.

Like many hopeful people in recovery, Laney seemed to have left the difficult days of addiction behind. Tall, glamorous and socially adept, she was more strategically assertive than confident. She attended a particular Narcotics Anonymous (NA) group that was known for the atheists and agnostics who gathered there.

Her interactions with the regulars was double-edged. People enjoyed Laney's friendliness and sense of humor, but there was a diciness to the arrangement. Even when she took the initiative to speak she seemed to be protecting something, which made her appear aloof.

Laney couldn't have cared less about the disease model but the God issue was another matter. She didn't believe talents were "gifts" as much as they were the result of will and vision. This was no doubt an issue of importance, for Laney had an abundance of talent. On the way to a Masters degree in art, she had a deepened respect for nature as expressed in the thoughtful landscapes of Brueghel.

Five weeks after being court-ordered to attend the Village South, a Miami, Florida treatment center known for its willingness to take on tough cases, Laney was back before the same judge. The treatment center had expelled her for rule infractions. The judge sent her to CareUnit, a subset of the Comprehensive Care Corporation hospital chain, where she completed her time and was allowed to return home.

Despite her seeming independence, Laney seemed to possess a passive authoritarian, "scapegoat-identified" streak. This combination of conformity and defiance, of breaking the tiniest of rules yet secretly believing the authorities were right to condemn her, could make an uncomfortable situation worse.

The required homework at Village South consisting of checklists and essay questions was extremely time consuming. One checklist, entitled "Powerlessness!", directed patients to check aspects of powerlessness that applied to themselves, including but not limited to:

- Failing to do household chores.
- "Compulsivity (*sic*) finishing household chores so you will be free to use."
- Not having a proper diet.

- Not exercising enough.
- Exercising compulsively.
- Not having a savings account.
- Failing to plan adequately for retirement.

The list continued for three pages. The introductory packet included a "letter from God," containing spiritual assurances and signed, "Your Friend, God."

The following is an excerpt of my interview with Laney (Laney's two children and other patients are presented with first-name initials).

AM: How many people did Village South house?

Laney: Maybe 80 to 100, maybe 70, but it's somewhere around there.

AM: How many counselors were there?

Laney: Counselors come and go. While I was there, my first counselor stayed for the first four weeks and then was fired.

AM: Why do you think there was a high degree of turnover?

Laney: Burnout. High burnout. Also, the system at this particular place was particularly difficult for women. There was a very small women's component. The majority of the patients were men, the majority of the counselors were men.

AM: How did they structure the time?

Laney: Very structured. You wake up at 7:00. Breakfast is served at 7:30. At 8:00 or 8:15, you have what's called house meeting—in which three books are read, a page from each book. A daily prayer, a daily message, the thought for the day, and something from NA, or AA, is read. People say good morning—it's a brief meeting, about 30 minutes. After that there's a half-an-hour break, and then another meeting begins.

AM: And the meetings?

Laney: The second meeting is broken up, it's the women's component and about four or five groups of men. It is basically for business at hand, if you need to make a phone call, if you need permission slips signed, if you need a pass to leave the facility for some legal purpose, very often it turns into a therapy session.

AM: Is there an orientation?

Laney: Not at this particular place, you just go right into the program. The first day in they give you what's called a big sister or a big brother. And that person is supposed to take you where you're supposed to go and he or she is someone who'll be in your group.

AM: Is that another patient?

Laney: Yes, another patient.

AM: Of the same sex?

Laney: Of the same sex. Women are only permitted to talk to women, men are only permitted to talk to men. And no interaction with the opposite sex.

AM: Was that true of CareUnit?

Laney: No.

AM: How many meetings would you have a day?

Laney: There was the morning meeting, which was like the wake-up meeting. That's the half-an-hour meeting where they read the prayer–they also do something that's called motivation in the morning, where you get in a circle and everybody claps their hands, and you sort of do this "chant."

AM: What is the chant?

Laney: (*laughs*) You say, "I've got the fever, I've got the fever, It's in my head . . ." It's just a whole chant, and every-body forms a circle, one person gets in the circle, and every-body claps and then they go through this chant. And then they pick someone else, and then that person gets in the circle and they do the chant. And, if that's not done, then usually we do the hokie-pokie–put your right foot in, put your . . . or, we do something that's called image breakers. Image breakers are: you get up and act like an idiot, basically. You walk like a chicken, you jump like a frog or—stuff like that. One of those three things is done in the morning.

AM: Was that done at CareUnit?

Laney: No. You have to participate.

AM: What happens if you don't?

Laney: If you don't? You get consequences.

AM: What are consequences?

Laney: Any number of things. The first consequence is you're asked to write a 2,000-word essay on why I have to participate or why I can't break the rules—why breaking the rules will ruin my life, why breaking the rules will do something terrible to me.

If you don't participate after that, you usually get a second consequence, whatever privileges you do have will be taken away. And you will either be forced to wash dishes at night, or clean the facility—pick up leaves, sweep around the pool area. If that doesn't work and you still don't participate, you go on contract, which means all your privileges are taken away for 21 days, you have no free time at all, you are forced to write papers and clean.

AM: But you still have to participate in image breakers and so forth?

Laney: Sure. Absolutely.

AM: Did you feel scapegoated, I mean right from the beginning?

Laney: I did.

AM: What kind of things made you feel uncomfortable?

Laney: Well, initially it was the fact that I couldn't say that I was an atheist.

AM: Right from the beginning?

Laney: [Yes]. The first week I had said it, I was called up on it the following Monday.

AM: Somebody called you up to their office or something?

Laney: No, it was actually one of the patients, who said that they thought I was setting myself apart and they didn't like hearing the word "atheist". Then staff brought it to my attention shortly after that.

AM: And if you had continued, would that have led to consequences?

Laney: For sure. Even after I stopped saying it and stopped any reference to atheism, God, lack of God—I was still constantly singled out and told that I couldn't recover because I didn't believe in God.

AM: Both counselors and staff told you this?

Laney: Not all patients, but many of the patients.

AM: But counselors also?

Laney: Counselors, it was counselors who told me that I couldn't recover without God.

AM: They told you—you just wouldn't make it.

Laney: I wouldn't make it.

AM: So what did you tell them, I assume you told them you knew people who had done it.

Laney: They said I hadn't and it didn't matter.

AM: You hadn't?

Laney: They said I hadn't made it yet.

AM: Oh, you hadn't made it yet.

Laney: I had continued to relapse, and that I'd better find God. I was forced to get on my knees and yell out for God.

AM: How many weeks had you been in the program at that point?

Laney: That was about a week before I left.

AM: Whose idea was that?

Laney: My counselor's. This was right before she left, she was having a breakdown. It was very, very obvious. She was coming into group and crying hysterically and flipping out. Just absolutely flipping out.

At the beginning, I was just disoriented to the whole place, I tried really hard to fit in. Early on I got what's called a "jacket." In other words, they said I set myself apart from the group, by the way I looked; also by the things I said, such as, that I'm an atheist. I was told that I was making myself unique, and basically they told me I had a jacket. A jacket is an image. And once you have it, it's hard to shake. In other words, if you get the reputation as being a trouble-maker—they watch you because they think you're a trouble-maker! If you get the reputation of somebody that's very good and who follows rules, you get the jacket of someone who fits in and does well.

Early on, my therapist said, "You have a jacket, and it's gonna be hard for you to get rid of it. And your jacket is that you set yourself apart from other people." Later on, she told me that my jacket was also that I was "defiant." And that I was very manipulating.

AM: She heard this when the counselors get together and talk about how the patients were doing?

Laney: Yes.

AM: Every day?

Laney: Every day. They have a meeting everyday after lunch. It's about an hour-and-a-half meeting. And everything you do is written down. You're observed "all the time." On your free time there is what's called a "milieu staff." And they rotate. There's usually two milieu staff on duty. Their job is to document who you talk to, if you "isolate," if you act out; your general behavior.

You're only allowed to smoke under the canopy they have. And usually people sit under the canopy during free time and smoke cigarettes. And you're documented while you're doing that–again, who you talk to, your general behavior. If you sit under the canopy, if you go into your room and isolate, if you read, what you read, it's all documented.

AM: What you read?

Laney: Yes.

AM: You're allowed to bring your own books?

Laney: No. You're not allowed to bring your own books.

AM: What books are you allowed to read?

Laney: Recovery literature only. When I first came in, I had been reading a book that I was almost finished with, they gave me permission to finish it–that book, in my room at night.

AM: How would you describe the interactions between patients and staff? Was anyone else defiant, for example?

Laney: Yeah, there were a few people who left while I was there–got kicked out or left. One guy, whose brother was dying of AIDS–he had already lost one brother to AIDS– and this other brother was in the hospital, on a respirator and they didn't give him more than two weeks [to live]. He had a pass coming, and you have to tell them where you're going on your pass. And he wanted to see his brother, and they felt that would be detrimental to his recovery, that it might cause him to relapse or use. They said that his being there or not being there wasn't going to make his brother live or die.

His parents came and said, "Listen, his brother's gonna be dead. If he doesn't come and see him, he's never gonna get to see him."

They wouldn't approve him to go–he actually left the place. He just said, "Screw you, I'm gonna go see my brother." He was there two and a half months. He had another two weeks to go. So he just left.

AM: What are some other things they said about you?

Laney: Well, one guy said I seemed to have a bad attitude. He had never said a word to me. He was a young kid, and he'd been living out on the street, and he rolled fags. He would beat up fags and take their money. He had a rough life. He confronted me—he said, "I sense that you have a street mentality and that you parade around."

Then someone else said that I was too intellectual, that I functioned from my head and I didn't show any feeling. It wasn't said in a kind and loving way, it was said in a really hurtful, nasty way. The purpose of this was to help you see yourself as others see you. Ten people could be confronted in one session. It was random. It was run by the milieu staff. The milieu staff was beneath the counselor. They are the ones who give the lectures. They don't run groups, except when it's confrontation. They were the ones who ran this confrontation, the movies at night and the lectures.

There was one milieu staff member who didn't seem to like me. He told me, "I sense that you have no humility, that you have an attitude that you're better than everybody." I'd never really spoken to this person, it was just his impression of me. But it wasn't just me, he told a lot of people that they had bad attitudes.

You couldn't say, "I think you're a really nice person, but I think that you aren't considerate in the dining room, you cut in line, or you're always the last one up in the morning." You couldn't start out by saying anything nice. And if you were gentle about it, the staff would say, "No, no. Give it to 'em straight." Usually the comments were things like, "I think you're basically a f----' asshole and I think you have a bad attitude, and I think you ought to shut up and listen more."

They wanted you to be rough, they wanted you to be nasty. You weren't supposed to get carried away with it, but it was done. Some profanity was really acceptable in those situations.

You were not allowed to do anything but say thank you. One guy got upset while he was being confronted, and started answering back and the therapist said shut up and listen. They would always end it saying, "the people that confronted you are the people that 'love' you, they're the people that 'care,' they're the ones that care enough to not care if you love them. They're just trying to save your life." And we'd usually end saying something nice about the people that were confronted. "I really love you" or "I'm glad you're my friend"—you knew you couldn't Band-Aid what you had said before—"I think you're a caring person" or "I've seen a lot of growth in you over the past few weeks." Just something nice.

And then it would end with, "Pat the person on your right on the back. Pat the person on your left on the back. Pat yourself on the back."

And I realized it was my initial atheism that set it off. You know, setting myself apart as an atheist. And my counselor was such a *Big Book* thumper, a God person.

AM: I guess you're glad to be out.

Laney: Yep. It seems like forever that I was there. It seems like so long. The first week was really slow getting into the routine of it. And, your groups are from early in the morning. Your last group ends at 10:00 or 10:30. You're there all day, going at this, a little break here [and there].

AM: Seven days a week?

Laney: Not Saturday and Sunday. Saturday and Sunday, people got passes, or had visitors come on the facility for anywhere between an hour to four hours. Whenever my husband,

Jewell, visited me, we were observed by staff who took notes.

AM: Took notes?

Laney: Took notes. Took notes and submitted it to my therapist.

AM: They were near enough to hear you?

Laney: Sat right with us. One day they not only had the staff observe me but they asked that one of the the girls in my group document our relationship.

AM: Yours and hers or yours and Jewell's?

Laney: Mine and Jewell's and the kids. Jewell and I had a little argument. D. was in the bathroom and he yelled out, "Mommy, come and help me."

And Jewell said I had to let him do things for himself, stop babying him so much, don't go running every time he calls you.

And it wasn't a fight. I said, "Jewell, listen, he doesn't sound okay, he's crying," and I got up and I went in.

She made this into a major fight. And after that, we were sitting and holding hands, and talking and playing with the kids. I played Simon Says—the only thing that she documented was that Jewell and I had a fight about D. and that there were bad feelings between us.

AM: What about people who talked the talk and were following the rules, did they go through this kind of stuff?

Laney: Everybody got confronted. Everybody. Not every single week, but over the weeks I was there everybody got confronted on one thing or another. If you were working a good program they would say, "You seem to want to be Mister Program. Why don't you get real and show some of your vulnerability?" or "You talk a good program but I don't really see it." There was no winning.

AM: So some people got it worse than others, or was it pretty much equal?

Laney: I think basically what happened was there would be one or two people, usually one person from each group, who was sort of like the staff pet. Like the girl in my group who was my counselor's pet was a real rough, tough girl, she had been in jail, she'd been in many, many mental institutions. I think she'd spent a total of five years in mental institutions—on medication, in straight-jackets. She'd been in there before a few times. She was a very streetwise kind of girl. Her occupation was a thief, that's what she did. And, she was given a lot more liberties than other people. And it came to my attention that she had done something—she was accused of going off of the facility and taking her car. And she denied it and one of the staff members said they saw her do it and asked me if I knew anything about it, and I said I saw that the car was gone and that L. was gone, I didn't know that L. took the car.

Actually, I really did think L. took the car but I wasn't sure—L. denied it, my counselor believed her, the staff member that accused her was reprimanded. Later, [someone] told that they knew that L. did take the car, and in fact did leave the facility without permission, and she was confronted and that someone said, "I know you did this and you've been lying about it." She admitted that she did do it, and the staff member said to her, "I saw the snake in her, but I didn't see the snake in you." The evil in you. That was L., the girl who had taken the car.

AM: Who was the "her"?

Laney: The girl who [turned her in].

BREAK IN TAPING

Laney: [There was this guy who] was constantly sticking his tongue out [at me], it was really gross. I never said anything, I figured, just ignore him and he'll stop. Well, one day I walked into the dining room and the men were lined up–the long-term men who are there for two years.

AM: Two years?

Laney: They would go to work during the day and eat their meals there. They would work on the facility.

Laney: [They weren't] there for crimes, some of them just went in. It's a government-run program, it's free. I think a lot of it is people who just need a bed. But I think a lot of them really did need treatment. Anyway, every time I'd walk in the dining room, [this guy would] bother me. I was ignoring him and [as] I walked through the line this guy grabs me! You know, grabs my ass.

I turned around [and] looked at him, I didn't say anything, my mouth [dropped open] and he stepped away, and I walked through, got my coffee and walked out. I said to my girlfriend "That guy just–" and she said, "I saw. I saw what happened."

I said, "He's been bugging me now for weeks. Now he's getting really brazen!"

She said, "You better report it to staff."

I said, "I'm in enough crap with staff, I don't want to report it."

She said, "Well, if somebody else saw what happened, and you don't report it, it'll be documented that you're encouraging it because you're not reporting it. And he'll do it again. Next time, he might catch you alone by the washing machine and you know, this guy's been in and out of jails and he's a real loser, he was hassling me when I first came here."

So I said, alright, I'll go report it to staff. I told this guy J.

He said to me, "Show me what happened."

I said, "He grabbed my ass."

He says, "Do it to me, show me what happened."

So I walked up to him and I grabbed his ass!

He says, "Okay, just wait here." And he gets my counselor and this guy's counselor from long-term.

They called him into the office without me. Five minutes later they call me back in.

They said, he admitted it. His therapist then took me in the office . . . sort of cornered me. [He's] big, a real street guy. He comes real close to me and says, "You're a sign that says, 'Abuse me, baby.'"

I'm looking at him, like "he's kidding me!"

And then he says, "But you and I know that you want it and you love it."

And I'm looking at him because I don't believe I'm hearing this.

Then he comes real close to me and says, "Tell me the truth. You love it, don't you, when you get that kind of attention?"

At this point I wanted to smack him.

He moved his arm away, and I said, "I can't believe you." And I turned around, and under my breath—I didn't say it to his face, though, I said, "F--- you." Because there's no winning. And I walked away. And that was the last I heard about it.

I knew this was a no-win situation for me, there was nothing I was gonna do. The guy admitted it, and they told me it was my fault. So at that point I knew that this was not just my imagination—the way he said it—his nasty attitude. He was really trying to degrade me, like I was some kind of slut who walked around trying to tease men.

BREAK IN TAPING

Laney: I didn't wear makeup, they had me wear my hair

slicked back, I had to wear it tight, rolled back in a bun. I wore no makeup, I mean, there was nothing I was doing that was provocative.

AM: Did they ever explain why they wanted you to wear your hair that way?

Laney: That was toward the end. I didn't have to wear it like that in the beginning. Toward the end my therapist said that she thought I hid behind my hair. "You hide behind your hair so I'm gonna take your hair away so you can't hide behind it." And they would have–if they could've they would've shaved it off. If I'd come out of my room in the morning and I didn't have my hair up, somebody would nail me–even the girls in my group, in my house–would say, "Put your hair up."

AM: So you felt scapegoated even inside the rooms with your friends.

Laney: Oh yeah, for sure.

AM: Did they talk to you casually? Chat about anything?

Laney: One girl, when she left, told me that I was a spider.

AM: When she left? That was her parting comment?

Laney: Yes. She said, "You're a spider. You're an evil spider." It had a lot to do with my atheism, I think.

AM: Did you hear much about the (Twelve) Steps?

Laney: This is the odd thing. The program itself is not supposed to focus on the steps. However, my counselor had us bring our *Big Books* to therapy and we were supposed to hide them–not let other staff members see that we were carrying the books. [We were] supposed to be inconspicuous about bringing our books. And she did the steps with us against the policy of the program.

And I did a 74-page First Step. She had a mimeographed sheet of questions that you have to answer, [for example], "sex with animals"–I mean, just unbelievable. And if you didn't answer it, said it doesn't pertain to me, she tended not to believe you.

AM: How were you holding up at this time?

Laney: Initially, I felt like I was having a nervous breakdown. When I went in there, I'd had a bladder infection, I was on medication. After I was there four weeks or so, I still felt like I wasn't at 100%, and I told my therapist I needed to see a physician, I had to go to a doctor, and she said no. She wouldn't let me.

Another time—see that little mark on my hand? That brown spot? I burned my hand on some hot coffee. And I went in the office and I asked them if they had some ointment to put on it and a Band-Aid. They told me to go put ice on it. And I had ice on it. And it really blistered [and] this was four months ago. I felt like I needed something. But it was like a get-tough attitude.

I was different from most of the women there. My therapist said, "How many of you have sold your body for drugs or given money for drugs?"

And everybody raised their hand except for me. She [the therapist] got out of her seat, and she came up to my face and she said to me, "You're a goddamn liar, you'll never get clean until you get honest."

And I said, "I've never sold my ass for drugs."

She said, "I don't believe you."

I said, "I don't care if you don't believe me." This was in the very beginning. And her attitude was that I did sell my ass for drugs and I didn't want to admit it. That I wanted to be better than the other girls.

My parents came up, and my mother spoke to my counselor—my parents thought they were wacko. Both my parents thought the place was just out of line. And my parents have never felt that way about a treatment center.

AM: And what are some examples of things they talked about when you were the subject of conversation?

Laney: My therapist said that she had just spoken to C. (Laney's daughter) on the phone, and that C. cried because she missed her mommy. She said it was her opinion that C. was being sexually abused by Jewell, that she herself had been sexually abused and knew the signs. She wanted a vote from the rest of the girls in the group.

Now, she had never actually met C., just spoken to her once on the phone. And never met Jewell at this time. She knew that Jewell and I had gone to a motel against regulations. (Laney and Jewell had gone to a motel with the children one weekend. A friend from the treatment center had watched the children at the pool so the couple could be alone.) Once that took place—that was like a turning point. They started in with the kids, with C. being molested, that I had a real sick relationship with Jewell.

AM: What was sick about it?

Laney: That we went to the motel, basically. They thought it was real sick. Real, real sick. I remember my therapist said to me, "You were servicing Jewell."

AM: Servicing?

Laney: She said I was doing it so that he would leave C. alone. She said, "You thought in your own way that you were protecting C. from him if you serviced him."

And there was no arguing with these people. You can't disagree, because if you disagree they tell you that you're closed-minded. "At least just be open-minded and listen."

AM: Just listen?

Laney: And say, maybe you're right. If you say, "You're not right or you're wrong, you're labeled as being closed-minded, as not willing to recover. You know, you're not okay. You have to be at least willing to say, "I'll have to take a look at that."

Which I did. I said to myself, "I'm in deep shit. I'm about to get thrown out of here." So I said, "Well, I'll take a look at that," and, "Maybe you're right," and, "I'll have to think about this," and everything. I went along with it. I didn't fight them.

AM: What was the vote to be?

Laney: The vote was that everybody agreed that C. was being sexually molested by Jewell.

AM: Everyone agreed?

Laney: Everyone agreed.

AM: And what were you supposed to do with this information?

Laney: I was supposed to think about it.

AM: Were you upset?

Laney: I thought they were crazy. And when I told them I didn't believe it, they told me I was closed-minded. See, at one point I said that I use as my higher power the group conscience. And so this was what they based it on, that if my higher power was the group conscience, then what the group said was true. And that I was supposed to believe this. She also made threats of calling HRS (Health and Rehabilitative Services) to have my kids taken away from Jewell.

They both did. The first counselor, but the second counselor was always in our group from day one. She was training with the first counselor. The second counselor had a second job, a volunteer job where she worked with abused children. She read us reports of little girls who were sexually abused, and she read us horrible reports. I think it was wonderful that she was involved in helping these kids. But I think she got carried away with it. Both therapists claimed to have been sexually abused and physically abused. Most of the girls in my group had been sexually abused or raped as children. And all agreed that C. was being abused by Jewell without ever meeting Jewell or C.

AM: Could you feel an increase in the stigma against you over time?

Laney: It was something I couldn't change. I tried to reverse it. I can't tell you how I tried to play myself down.

AM: What are some other examples?

Laney: [Often] I sketch and doodle. One day during my free time—I had done this sketch once before of the rock monster.

AM: The rock monster?

Laney: Yeah, the freebase monster. It's sort of an image of evil. I think I get really evil when I smoke. I'm real self-centered, and I don't give a shit about anybody. I want to keep getting high. And so I did this sketch, and I titled it "The Crack Monster" or "The Rock Monster." And I wrote, "This is what drugs do to me, this is what freebasing does to me." It was large and I really did it in detail, it was really good. And it was really scary.

My therapist saw it and she asked what it was.

I said, "It's a drawing of the rock monster. Would you like it?"

And she said, "Yeah," and took it.

The next day she called me up to her office and said she'd been having headaches all day, and she didn't sleep the night before. And that this thing on her wall—she can't stand it. It's haunting her. And she said, how did it happen that I drew this? And I said, I've sketched it before, it's an image that comes to me of the rock monster!

So she looked at me and said, "This is the devil."

I said, "Yeah, I guess you could say that."

She said, "Anyone who drew something like this would have to be sick—and evil. I can't imagine anybody putting this down on paper that wasn't tormented by Satan." She [asked if] I ever got into devil worship?

I said no.

She said, "Have you ever been in the occult?"

And I said no.

She said, "Have you ever been involved in sacrificial rites?"

I said, "No!"

She said, "This is the most sinister, evil thing, and I can't live with it. I want you to take it and destroy it."

So I took it and I brought it back to my room. Then I got scared. I [thought], what if I keep this thing and somebody finds it—they're gonna think I'm sitting in my room at night worshipping the devil. So I threw it away.

But after that—that incident in her office—she made references to me being into Satan worship.

AM: In front of the group?

Laney: Oh, in front of the group all the time! One afternoon I had on a black T-shirt and a pair of black jeans. We'd all just walked in and sat down. Nobody had said anything yet. She swung her chair around and right in my face said, "Look at you in black!" She started pounding, she said, "You are the devil. Look at you! You're Satan, you're evil!"

Well, needless to say, I wore pink from then on.

BREAK IN TAPING

Laney: There was an evening when I went up to the counter to get my food. And I sat down in the dining room and there were homemade cookies that the cook had made. I broke my cookie, I took a bite of it, and there was a piece of hair in the cookie. So I put the cookie down, and I took another cookie.

Well later, one of the men at the house meeting got up and accused me of stealing a cookie. So the milieu staff who was on duty–they stay in at these meetings–asked me to stand up and asked me, "Did you take another cookie?"

And I said, "Yes, but–"

He said, "No. Don't say another word. Anything you would say now could only be 'rational lies'."

AM: This is the treatment staff person?

Laney: This is the staff person.

"So I want you to get up, and tell this group what you are."

And I said, what's that? And he said, "Tell them that you're a thief, that you steal things, and you're not to be trusted."

So I was made to get up, and in front of the group say, "Hello, my name is Laney, I'm a drug addict, I'm a thief and I'm not to be trusted." And then I sat back down. I was not allowed to explain why I took the cookie. That's all I was allowed to say.

. . . Later, they made me lay down on a mattress in a room with eight people and kick my legs until my stomach hurt.

They said, "just kick your legs, just lay there and kick your legs."

I laid on this mattress and I kicked my legs and kicked my legs. I was doing this for 15 minutes. And finally my stomach was hurting and I said, "I can't do this anymore."

The guy jumped up and got right in my face and he screamed, "Keep kicking!"

Another time, we did something that was called a marathon. We were brought into this large meeting room, all the groups together. And we meditated for the first 45 minutes. We just closed our eyes and chanted.

AM: What kind of things were you chanting?

Laney: Just sounds. Whatever sounds you wanted to make.

Some people moaned and some people screamed. But no words. You're not allowed to use words. No words at all, just sounds.

And after that, they have mounds of pillows and mattresses. And people would get in the middle, sometimes one, sometimes two, sometimes three. And they would start pounding away at these pillows, and crying and screaming.

Then J. (he was one of the therapists) had us lay on the floor, all of us, and hold our genital areas. I'm telling the truth. [Then, he'd have us] call out—either to God, or to somebody—one time K. (my therapist) told me to get on my knees and just ask God for help. She said, "Get on your knees and start asking God for help."

AM: What are marathons?

Laney: We only had one. It was an all-day therapy group. Everybody, the men and women all sit together, and there's a bunch of mattresses and pillows and bats. And you just kick and beat and scream and hit and cry and yell.

K. told me to get in the middle—and you're surrounded by 60 people—to get in the middle on the floor, get on my knees and start asking God for help.

So I'm going, "God please help me, God please help me."

"Scream it out like you mean it! Beg him for help! Cry!"

AM: They told you to cry?

Laney: (*laughs*) They just said you better mean it. Start begging for help!

And I was on my knees, begging. "God, please help me! Please help me!"

AM: Were you able to generate some feeling for this?

Laney: Oh, I did the whole thing. It was like acting class. I put my heart and soul into it.

And it didn't do that much good.

My therapist said to me afterwards, "I think you're starting to take care of yourself a little bit."

AM: This is a group of women or a mixed group?

Laney: Mixed group. If you'd start to scream and J. didn't think you were screaming from your heart, J. would usually come up and grab your throat. And I mean grab your throat. J. had a way of doing it where he didn't actually hurt you—he would choke you! People had marks on their neck. Real marks.

AM: Did J. ever grab your throat?

Laney: Yeah, a few times. And then there were times when J. said that sometimes people didn't get in touch with their mental pain unless they felt physical pain. And that was the purpose of me kicking my legs. I would become worn down and exhausted. And sometimes he would bend your finger. And J. didn't really hurt you, but it [was] uncomfortable. He'd twist your finger until you'd scream enough so that he felt you were screaming from your heart.

BREAK IN TAPING

Laney: When I got out of there, I was so scared that I got thrown out. But I knew that I wasn't going to be able to stay. I knew that I wouldn't make it because I felt like I was going to have a nervous breakdown there. I felt like I was losing it. I was so afraid of everything and everybody.

I saw other people were functioning okay, I knew I wasn't. I was going to bed at night with my heart racing. I was waking up in the morning with this feeling of impending doom, like, "What's gonna happen today?" And I knew that I was not gonna make it the next 40 days.

AM: How did it come about that you left the program early?

Laney: After I took the cookie they told me that I had broken so many rules that they were taking my right to smoke cigarettes away. And I could no longer sit under the canopy—which is where everybody sits. So that meant I was isolated now from the whole group. I had to sit on the other side of the patio and I was not allowed to smoke cigarettes. And they told me, "If we catch you smoking, you'll be thrown out."

So I went about 24 hours, 26 hours without a cigarette. They took my carton of cigarettes away from me, but I'd snuck out a pack before I'd turned it over. And I snuck behind the washing machine and dryer and I had a cigarette. And one of the men whose dorm overlooked it—I didn't realize—had seen me smoke. And they called me—this was at night, right after snack.

They called me into the office and they said, "Have you been smoking cigarettes?"

I was terrified. So I said, "Why do you think I'm smoking cigarettes?"

And they got real irate. They said, "If you deny it, it's gonna be worse."

I said, "I'm not denying anything, what makes you think I'm smoking?" I didn't think anybody saw me.

They said, "If you admit it, it'll be easier on you, we know you're smoking cigarettes, admit it."

So I said, "Okay, I admit it."

They said, "But first you denied it!"

I said, "I didn't deny it."

They said, "Yes, you did deny it, you didn't admit it right away!"

I said, "Okay, well, I admit it."

They said okay, that's that, go ahead and leave. It would be discussed further tomorrow.

And [the next] morning I woke up knowing I was getting thrown out.

AM: Did you know that you were on your last chance?

Laney: Oh, yeah. I knew that. After the cookie and they took my right to smoke away, [telling] me if I smoked, that was it. I called Amy, my probation officer (P.O.), and said, "I want to get into another place."

She said, "I'm putting out a warrant, it'll be issued in eight days and then they'll come and take you away to jail for violation of probation."

I said, "Well, they'll have to take me to jail from a treatment center."

[I spoke to my lawyer], he said, "Get in a treatment center, because they're not gonna pull you out of there to bring you to jail. I'll arrange to have your hearing before the judge, before the warrant is issued, and then we'll take it from there."

The warrant [was] dropped.

When I spoke with my P.O., she said, "How are you doing?"

She liked me when I went in there.

She said, "I think that you're a good person, I think that you need another chance, and you seem like you're a good mother and you seem like a caring person and I like you."

After she spoke to them, her attitude was real different toward me. They told her I was real defiant, that I was breaking a lot of rules, that I was a real bad apple."

When I got on the phone with her she said, "What's going on? I want to hear your side of the story."

They wouldn't let me speak to her alone. I started crying, I said, "Amy, I can't take it here."

She said, "What's the problem? Can you talk to me?"

I said, "I can't."

She said, "Well, do you want to get out of there?"

I said, "Yes, I do."

She said, "Well, I don't know what to tell you."

And, then they said, "Hang up, you have to hang up, you have to hang up right now," and they grabbed the phone from me. They said, "She can't be on the phone now," and they hung up. [Then] they said, "What were you telling her, what was she saying to you?"

And I said, "I was just telling her that I can't take it here, that I'm miserable."

And they told me, my therapist told me as I was leaving, she said to me: "I will do whatever it takes to put in a report that Judge Korda sees that you belong behind bars."

BREAK IN TAPING

Laney: Things would happen—I'll give you an example—one therapist said to me, "Go find Jose and tell him I need for him to give me all the passes right away."

So I went to Jose and said, "Jose, Linda told me to come and get all the passes from you."

He said, "Well, tell Linda that as soon as I'm done I'll give her the passes."

So I went back to Linda who said, "Did you get the passes?"
I said no.

Then she said, "I told you to get the passes from Jose, go get them!"

I went back up and said, "Jose, Linda wants me—"

He said, "Do you want me to go to your counselor and tell her that you're bothering me? I don't want to be disturbed right now." Then he said, "If Linda wants the passes, tell her to come get them from me!"

She said, "Did you get the passes? Go get the passes!"
AM: It sounds intentional.
Laney: It sounds intentional to me too. It's crazy. I felt like,

"Can I make this work? I have to be here, and I have to make this work." But, you're put in a position where—one person doesn't know what the other person is saying, [one person is] telling you to do this, the other person is telling you to do that. And, you can't answer staff back—I felt like a kindergarten kid!

AM: What was different about the second place you went to, the CareUnit?

Laney: The CareUnit is just a regular treatment program. They told me at the CareUnit that my only option might be to go back to the Village South or to go to jail. And I told them I would go to jail. That would be my choice. I would much rather go to jail than to go back there.

Fortunately, my therapist had worked at the Village. She said, "That's the most dysfunctional place I've ever seen."

I was so lucky for that, because she knew what the place was like. She knew that it was a real sick place. And she had quit. So I had her sympathy or her understanding for what I had been through.

And her recommendation [to the judge] was that I continue with meetings and aftercare.

The period following Laney's release from treatment was a relatively good one. She was clean and painting again. In a paint-splattered workroom stood a half-formed creation suggestive of ear canals, or magnified neural photography, or blood and flowers racing over top of a small town.

The wildness had broken with form, away from the restrained and the meditative—such as the seascapes hanging in her spacious living room—to the bold and exuberant. A fresh spirit hovered, about to leap off the canvas. I didn't know what I was looking at or what it would become—I only knew that I loved it.

No one I know from our old group has heard from Laney in years. The last reports about her were not good, however. People say she had lost her home and her family, given it up for crack cocaine. I'm holding out hope that she's alive, that she's straight, that she's got her kids back and that she's painting. Alive and straight would be a decent start. It is possible to see in her story whatever one wants to see, depending on who one thinks deserves the lion's share of the blame. While I would not absolve any individual from ultimate responsibility for his or her actions, Laney's treatment is a far cry from society's best efforts to reach out to drug addicts.

Better treatment centers are, one would hope, the norm and were even in the late 1980s. Still, her experience at the Village South shows how indifferent courts, therapists and related social services can be toward the effects of the "help" they provide.

CHAPTER SIX

The Insurance Revolt:
Turning Losses into Lessons

Insurance coverage for substance abuse and all other mental health problems is dependent on the affordability of health care in general. In recent years, the challenges of health costs have been redefining American society. Consider the following:

- There were 56 million enrollees in health maintenance organizations (HMOs) in 1995, up from 19 million in 1985.[1]
- Of 33,634,000 people enrolled in Medicaid in 1994, 23.2% were in an HMO or other managed-care program, compared to 9.5% in 1991.[2]

When Bill Clinton looked for a way to expand health coverage to 37 million uninsured Americans, he turned to a familiar revenue source. "Sin taxes seemed like fair game,"[3] read a 1993 issue of *Newsweek*, "but the White House buckled under pressure from the beer, wine and spirits lobby. (Just to keep the pressure on, Anheuser-Busch is outfitting its trucks with placards urging Bud drinkers to dial

1-800-BEER-TAX.)"[4] Even with boosted cigarette costs bringing in an additional $70 billion over five years, Clinton's $441 billion health package fell woefully short of satisfying his conflicting goals of universal health coverage and balancing the federal budget.

According to the "Health Care Benefits Survey, 1989," cost-cutting tremors amounted to an undoing of a trend that had seen mental health costs per employee at large corporations rise by 50% between 1987 and 1989. The study, conducted by A. Foster Higgins & Co., found that much of these increased utilizations, (from an average of $163 per employee to $244) paid for spouses or dependents other than the employee, and covered anything from sexual abuse to codependency.[5]

As HMOs, preferred provider organizations (PPOs) and the like replaced traditional insurance carriers in hospitals and in the workplace, a new ethic prevailed. These managed care companies won their contracts through competitive bidding, then lived or died according to the accuracy of those bids. This system, known as "capitation," required managed care companies to estimate the cost of health services for thousands of future clients with unknown illnesses.

HMOs offer a variety of plans and pay doctors in different ways—some by capitation, some by fee-for-service, some by salaries. Whatever the method, HMOs must come under their lump-sum bids in order to survive. The capitation system allows HMOs to provide health care at lower rates than offered by traditional indemnity plans, which is why managed care has become the coverage of choice (or necessity) for the 1990s.

HMOs give coverage at a reduced cost to employers, who in turn must monitor their own costs stringently. The defeated Clinton health plan would have allotted about 30% of all health dollars to one form or another of mental health, reflecting the national trend. At a time of soaring health care costs, mental health billing (including chemical dependency) increased at twice the rate of other illnesses, accounting for about 15% of the total health care dollar. Most people in individual health plans rejected mental health and chemical dependency coverage. The bulk of reimbursements came from the group plans of large corporations and in states that mandated such coverage.

As John Goodman and Gerald Musgrave write in *Patient Power: Solving America's Health Care Crisis*:

> Where coverage is available, its cost tends to be quite high, especially since there are few objective standards for determining when an "illness" is present, when it has been "cured," and what treatment is "necessary." Small wonder that almost unlimited amounts of money can be spent.[6]

Many small businesses have rebelled against government proposals such as universal health insurance, saying that they cannot afford to provide it to their employees. Managed care became the dominant mode of reimbursement because it could provide insurance at a lower cost to employers. Some have argued that the very structure of managed care renders HMOs more loyal to the corporations who buy contracts than to the patients.

The consequences for addiction treatment providers have been devastating. Despite years of escalating complaints from insurers regarding a lack of documentation, the treatment community failed to provide solid research proving that traditional, 28-day inpatient treatment was more successful than other types of treatment, or no treatment at all.

"We're trying to channel treatment to less costly programs—usually toward outpatient,"[7] said Susan Flygare of Minnesota's Blue Cross in early 1990. At the time, the company's special accounts department was beginning to question a number of chemical dependency claims, particularly among adolescents.

"We've had and still have some incredible cases of inappropriate admissions," Flygare said. "Often the adolescent is acting out a family problem through alcohol or drugs or other strange behaviors. But instead of working with the family, they get zapped into treatment."[8]

At the same time, Brandeis University sociologist and health-care policy analyst Leonard Saxe said:

Hospitals have empty beds and have looked to psychiatric and substance-abuse treatment as a way to fill them. . . . We may lose the support of insurers and of society at large for hospitalizing so many people for psychiatric and substance abuse treatment at such a high cost, when so many kids who have problems get no treatment at all.[9]

By the early 1990s, the field's mood was bleak. Private rehabilitation centers were closing while waiting lists among indigent clients grew. Karst Besteman of the Alcohol and Drug Problems Association continued to complain about cuts in federal funding. Only by now, fewer politicians were even pretending to listen.

Parkside Medical Services, a major treatment chain, cut its services by half after a net loss of $82 million for their Fiscal Year ending June 1990. In December 1990, Parkside President Orville McElfrish told the *U.S. Journal* that his Christmas wish would be "a return to a healthy environment as far as reimbursement is concerned."[10]

While the cost-cutting mentality of managed care explained some of the downturn, treatment providers also had themselves to blame. In the late 1980s, the overwhelming odds were that a patient entering treatment for chemical dependency could expect to undergo Minnesota-Model therapy. The insurance cutbacks have drastically reduced the average lengths of stay insurers are willing to pay for.

The basic treatment philosophy remains the same, however. Originally intended for alcoholics, Minnesota-Model treatment was generalized for all addictions. The goal of treatment was almost always abstinence, plus successful affiliation with some type of 12-step group. Individual and group psychotherapy were combined with a number of educational activities such as writing, reading and lectures.

Unlike the longer-term and more highly-structured regimens at "therapeutic communities," Minnesota-Model treatment did not necessarily aim at a total transformation of body and soul. The average client at a 28-day facility such as Hazelden usually had a niche in society worth protecting; hence there was a diminished need to help patients deal with probation officers, restraining orders and unpaid traffic tickets. Release from treatment was usually followed by an extended aftercare program, which might have required meetings on a weekly, biweekly or monthly basis for several months.

But how effective was the Minnesota-Model treatment? No one really seems to know. A 1990 report by the Institute of Medicine (IOM), part of the federal Division of Health Care Services, noted a study of 83 individuals who selected a chemical dependency (CD) program for cocaine treatment—the patients could choose between a 28-day inpatient program, an outpatient program or a single education/information session followed by no treatment at all.

"The study found no significant differences between the CD and no-treatment groups eight months later,"[11] the IOM's authors remarked. The IOM report also called attention to the general lack of available data supporting the effectiveness of Minnesota-Model programs.

"The aggressive marketing deployed by many such programs has created suspicions about them in many quarters that cannot be allayed without investments in objective treatment research and evaluation."[12] Yet, as the authors observed:

> Only a few chemical dependency treatment providers have played positive roles in providing data and research opportunities for effectiveness studies. Many more need to do so to answer these questions: What is the effectiveness of chemical dependency treatment for drug-impaired clients of varying characteristics? Are there variations in program effectiveness—and if so, why? What are the actual costs and benefits of the most effective components of chemical dependency treatment?[13]

The information that did exist tended not to support the hefty reimbursement patterns of the past. A study by Glenbeigh Hospitals found no correlation between patients' length of stay and their ability to maintain abstinence.[14]

Another survey of 11,000 chemical dependency patients discharged between Oct. 15 and Dec. 1, 1986, found that both cost of treatment and length of stay were influenced more by who was paying than by the kind of treatment provided or place of treatment. This patient sample came from member facilities of the National Association of Addiction Treatment Providers, which commissioned the study.[15] For example, patients who billed through Medicaid were charged on average $4,511 per stay; while employees of self-insured companies needed treatment costing an average of $7,022.[16]

Treatment providers were aware of some of the abuses taking place in their own field. As Rick Esterly, chief executive officer for The Caron Foundation (a private alcoholism treatment fund), put it, "We have seen overdiagnosis, a lack of objective criteria, deferential assessment and some real shysters."[17] On the other side of the coin, some managed care companies were beginning to deny coverage for any alcoholism treatment on the grounds that it was a "preexisting condition."[18]

Debate ranged far and wide as to the reasons for the chemical dependency field's suffering. Some experts argued that they weren't getting enough help from the federal government and that the Drug War was only stigmatizing addicts anew. Mothers were getting lengthy probation, sometimes prison sentences and losing custody of their newborns for "delivering" drugs to their unborn infants. Judges were handing down stiffer sentences for drug offenses, a trend that helped to double our nation's prison population—from more than 500,000 inmates in 1980 to more than one million in 1994.[19] As the tougher laws took hold in 1989 and 1990, field leaders worried that addicts and alcoholics would be less likely to step forward and seek help.

Redefining the Trauma

The message for the treatment centers that wanted to remain in business was clear: Offer a range of services beyond alcohol and drug treatment and convince people that they need these services. If you want to sell hair coloring or skin cream, you try to convince people that they truly need these products–that, without them, they will somehow be incomplete. This tactic is no great mystery. It's observable on every television commercial.

Changes magazine's advertisers knew the principle well. They encouraged readers to "heal the pain" and "go beyond recovery to Personal Power." [20]

Many of the ads in *Changes* placed emphasis on various destructive behaviors, including difficulty with intimate relationships and weight control techniques.

"Eating disorders are a disease,"[21] an ad for the Rader Institute, an eating-disorder treatment chain, assured readers. "It's Not Your Fault . . . You're Not Alone."[22]

Glenbeigh Health Sources, a hospital chain, echoed the same sentiments: "If you do recognize these signs, recognize one more," their ad instructs: "YOU ARE A FOOD ADDICT–AND IT'S NOT YOUR FAULT!"[23]

To find out whose fault it might be, it's helpful to look at similar advertisements placed by Charter Hospitals, a large chain whose addiction-centered program declared bankruptcy in 1992. In an advertisement in *Changes* magazine, they asked:

- Was your childhood unhappy?
- Do you have difficulty in relationships and with intimacy, control, and trust?
- Are you terrified of abandonment or rejection?[24]

"If you or someone you care for has one or more of these characteristics" the advertisement says, "CO-DE-PENDENCY could be affecting your life." The reader is told that Charter will help them "change their lives for the better and trust themselves."[25]

Charter discovered that trauma survivors and codependents needed their services at the time its substance abuse bed count took a sharp decline. Substance abuse programs began aggressive marketing for psychiatric patients. Whether the new therapy was called codependency, eating disorder or sexual abuse recovery, it could be billed under existing diagnoses including major depression, panic disorder, generalized anxiety disorder, dysthymic disorder, adjustment reaction and Post-traumatic Stress Disorder.

Despite the insurance coverage cuts for mental health, from a baseline of 80% to a baseline of 50%,[26] many customers were well-employed and didn't seem to mind paying a little extra for anything from group therapy to psychiatric hospitalization. Insurers were still picking up a monstrous tab for these ancillary recovery services. Those clients who had to pay their own way were willing to do so, if they were told that they had buried trauma that had kept them from living a happy adult life.

The Paradigm Store

The enthusiasm of my few coworkers at HCI who had been in recovery diminished over the years, perhaps an inevitable result of seeing the grit behind the glory. Advertising salespersons were constantly hurling themselves against a wall of indifference. HCI's marketing department was pressing for tighter definitions of our target audience—by age, lifestyle, professional status and expectations. Although surveys supplied much of these data, the question regarding HCI's editorial content remained because of the fact that it was largely determined by book sale trends, which were constantly changing. Individual adult children of alcoholics (ACoAs) may have been hard to locate by demographics, but as a marketing concept it worked. Yet ACoAs, who had been the sole focus of the movement, were no longer the only clients. Hence the product line expanded accordingly.

But to what? Grandchildren of alcoholics? Adult daughters? People who are doormats? People who are ashamed? People who are caught in the crossfire, the shadow, the shuffle? Sexual abuse survivors? Spouses of sexual abuse survivors?

The answer changed by the time the question was phrased. And to think, this broader genre of self-help, now approaching self-hypnosis and mass hallucination, had been kicked off with a book published by HCI! *Adult Children of Alcoholics* had been the catalyst that sent hordes of seekers back to bookstores for more and other publishers on a scramble to cash in.

Yet neither HCI's authors nor anyone else truly knew how to answer the demand since they weren't even certain what the demand was. They developed stylized synthesizations of each other's work, which amounted to ornamental touches on a factory-made weathervane. The wind, however, was coming from the readers, not the authors; and it had shifted. What had started out as a way to reach out to family members of alcoholics turned into a 12-step call for society at large. Recovery authors were explaining their latest specialties as part of a "new paradigm." This was a term they and followers of fringe disciplines appropriated from Thomas Kuhn, an MIT philosopher who came to regret that he had ever uttered the word "paradigm."

Kuhn's 1962 best seller, *The Structure of Scientific Revolutions*, argues for the indeterminacy of science. It discusses how scientists tend to view things from the perspective of whatever paradigm happens to occupy center stage, doing "mop-up work" within the context of a given paradigm but not challenging the paradigm itself.[27]

Kuhn's book, which sold one million copies and was translated into 16 languages, did not say that because there is a certain arbitrariness and social dimension to the practice of science, one paradigm is as good as another and there is no such thing as knowledge. But that is how it was interpreted. Now, the few recovery stars who even knew what their critics were saying had a ready-made reply:

- "Our culture is experiencing massive *paradigm shifts*, which means that our view of the world is constantly changing,"[28] writes Patrick Carnes in *Don't Call it Love: Recovery from Sexual Addiction*.

- So aggressively has Anne Wilson Schaef seized on "paradigm," that the word has become foundational to her view of Western culture as an untreated addict. After receiving a stern letter in 1987 from an ethics panel of the American Psychological Association (APA) saying, "The committee. . . charges you to be careful in multiboundary endeavors and to carefully monitor your own needs,"[29] Schaef dropped her APA membership and declared herself a "recovering psychotherapist."[30]

  The committee met after a Michigan woman complained that Schaef had an affair with her husband while he was a client. Schaef claimed that the affair started six months after the man's therapy workshop ended.[31] In the 12-step paradigm of sharing, Schaef continues to lead intensives (not "workshops") in Montana. She is a "facilitator," not a leader.[32]

  As 75 people gathered to begin a year-long training in 1993, Schaef told a reporter for the *Montana*

Standard, "They aren't training to do anything. They are training to learn to make a paradigm shift, to learn to live another way in their lives, to live more fully."[33]

- In *Co-Dependence: Healing the Human Condition*, Charles Whitfield explains the shift: "The old paradigm rejected the spiritual because it could not be proven by its methods. The new paradigm experiences the spiritual and uses it constructively throughout all levels of existence."[34]

- A more coherent use of the term appears in Wegscheider-Cruse's *Another Chance*, in a foreword by physician James W. Keller: "The paradigm has shifted from focusing on the addicted person to focusing on the family system and each of its members individually."[35]

"I've often said I'm much fonder of my critics than my fans,"[36] Kuhn told reporter John Horgan in the May 1991, *Scientific American*. Kuhn noted that, among academics, psychologists and sociologists received the book with the most enthusiasm. He continued, "Some of them even said, 'Wow, now all we have to do is figure out what our paradigm is and enforce it.' "[37]

Idol Gossip

Almost overnight, John Bradshaw's demand as a speaker and talk show guest soared. He regressed audience members on *Oprah*. His tapes became a part of PBS fund-raising drives—usually reserved for the likes of Pavarotti concerts and Marlon Brando classics. After his second, equally successful book, *Healing the Shame That Binds You*, published by HCI, Bradshaw moved to Bantam, where two subsequent books cracked the best-seller list.

Other upstaged recovery stars grumbled about insights he had lifted without attribution. They saw Bradshaw as a popularizer and a showboat, whose primary concern was sales rather than individuals. In response, Bradshaw accused his critics of jealousy, especially male recovery stars, whom he called "the little princes" who did not like being dethroned or outdone.

In a very short time, Bradshaw's commercial success caught up to and passed those of therapists/authors Robert Subby, Robert Ackerman and Terry Kellogg—all of whom were extremely ambitious and concerned with their careers. Not only was Bradshaw receiving more speaking engagements, he was commanding up to $25,000 for a single day, as well as headlining recovery cruise packages in the Gulf of Mexico.

According to *Newsweek*, in 1990 Bradshaw earned $1 million.[38] He opened the John Bradshaw Treatment Center in Rosemead, California, and lent his name to numerous others. By 1991, *Bradshaw On: The Family* and *Healing the Shame That Binds You* had sold 1.3 million copies. His third book, *Homecoming* topped 700,000.[39] A speaking engagement in Boston drew 7,000 listeners and Steven Spielberg was encouraging him to launch a network talk show.

Celebrities in Recovery

As *Changes* began to appear on newsstands at Waldenbooks and B. Dalton chains, its mission was beset by growing pains. There was a well-defined target audience in ACoAs. Originally, everyone spoke merely of children of alcoholics. Then someone realized that children don't buy self-help books, and the label's first modification came about.

At the same time, the range of people who shared ACoA

"traits" stretched well beyond the label. More and more customers were "identifying with the issues," whether their parents had been alcoholics or not.

In a 1988 issue of *Changes*, Suzanne Somers, who was plugging a book about growing up in an alcoholic home, told her story.[40] It was a painful one and her message was one of compassion. In coming years she founded The Suzanne Somers Institute for the Effects of Addiction on Families, a professional training center in Palm Springs, California. For a time, there was also some discussion with the actress and her husband, producer Alan Hamell, about Somers hosting a *Changes* magazine recovery talk show on cable television.

The deal fell through. A separate proposal for hosting a conference also collapsed when Somers demanded $100,000 plus first-class air travel for herself and her personal assistant, limousine service and the best hotel suites.

Many other movie and television personalities–Louie Anderson, Steve Allen, Mariette Hartley, *Saturday Night Live's* Al Franken and others–fit themselves into the mold of the recovering celebrity.

Franken's contribution was most unique. An interview was actually carried out with Stuart Smalley, the *Saturday Night Live* character Franken created of an unlicensed therapist in recovery. When Franken was asked if "Stuart" was nearby, he went and got him. Then Stuart's voice could be heard in the background, repeating affirmations to himself about what a "great interview" he was going to give, because "I'm good enough, I'm smart enough, and, doggone it, people like me!" [41]

Although Al Franken appears to be sympathetic to the recovery movement, Stuart Smalley's satirical riffs added a new dimension, appealing to both people in recovery and the movement's most scornful critics. Perhaps Stuart's incessant self-analyzing, analyzing of others and his habit of speaking in clichés cracked a perceptual door open somewhere. It was a new experience to hear someone correcting himself on national television and making "immediate amends"— "I'm sorry, that was inappropriate"—as part of a comedic act. Franken attended an HCI conference for background research into the Stuart Smalley character.

Stuart Smalley's appearance—and the uproarious laughter from the audience each time he corrected himself—were indications of how much recovery had changed in a few short years and how much the culture was changing in response to recovery.

Achievement as Illness

Diagnosis for Disaster: The Devastating Truth About False Memory Syndrome and Its Impact on Accusers and Families is one of a growing list of rebuttals to a wave of incest-recovery literature published in the late 1980s. "I remember watching this movement develop,"[42] reflects author Claudette Wassil-Grimm, M.Ed. She went on to say:

> It began with meetings for Adult Children of Alcoholics (ACOAs), but many other baby boomers found that the "symptoms" of ACOAs also fit them.
>
> The original, genuine ACOAs were the lucky ones. They earned the right to everyone's admiration for surviving years in an alcoholic home where they were physically neglected, emotionally abandoned, and beaten. They had real battle scars to which they could point.[43]

Wassil-Grimm then summarizes the sideways slide of ACoA

symptoms to include anyone from a dysfunctional family, with the following observations:

> It was a new kind of midlife crisis. Baby boomers were coming up against the realization that their lives were half over, and they hadn't become great filmmakers, Nobel Prize winners, concert pianists, or astronauts and probably never would. Where former midlife sufferers had to come to terms with the fact that they weren't as bright or unique as they had once thought they were, baby boomers dodged that psychological crisis by telling themselves that they would have become President of the United States if only their potential hadn't been pulverized by the trauma of childhood sexual abuse.[44]

As it turns out, even being president can be a symptom of disease. For just as Wassil-Grimm's retrospective account was hitting the bookstores, so was another book by a psychologist who was advancing a markedly different perspective.

The Dysfunctional President: Inside the Mind of Bill Clinton, also identifies AA and ACoA as socially significant movements. The author, Paul M. Fick, Ph.D., considers President Clinton, whom he refers to in places as "the client," severely debilitated as a result of growing up with an alcoholic parent: "This client requires intensive, directive psychotherapy to break through the established walls of denial,"[45] Fick writes in a section titled "Recommendations and Treatment Plan":

> He should be under the care of a licensed clinician familiar with the concepts of ACOA treatment. Recom-

mendation is made for the therapist, at least initially, to be a male to defuse the potential for sexually acting out . . . This client has a strong need for approval, and the clinician may utilize that need to assist in the development of motivation.

The client, however, is a workaholic, and the therapist should be attentive to his potential of "working too hard" at his treatment.[46]

The "treatment plan" Fick recommended is outlined as follows:

1. Individual psychotherapy with a licensed clinician focused on the underlying ACOA issues.
2. Peer-group psychotherapy led by the client's clinician.
3. Twelve step ACOA self-help group.
4. Family therapy to address existing family systems problems.[47]

Fick had Clinton attend his therapy on an outpatient basis, fulfilling each of the above four components once a week. He added:

The treatment plan will be reviewed after six months. It is anticipated that treatment will take considerably longer than that period of time because of the client's level of denial and the duration of the problem.[48]

It is true that Clinton's childhood had its rocky moments, and may have been a rather dark period in his life. In a 1995 interview with *Good Housekeeping*, he recalled an incident in which his stepfather, Roger Clinton, fired a gun at his mother, Virginia Kelley. The bullet struck the wall beside where she was seated.

> I remember that incident vividly, like it was yesterday, That bullet could have ricocheted and done anything. It could have killed me. If anything had happened, Roger would never have gotten over it. Roger wasn't a bad man, and he didn't want to hurt anybody. He was just an alcoholic, full of self-loathing and anxiety, with no way to deal with it. He had problems before we ever came into his life.[49]

Twice the young Clinton had to intervene when Roger Clinton threatened to kill Kelley. He summarized the father-son relationship saying:

> There are two or three bad things that happened. Number one, I was deprived of a male role model. I grew up with this idealized version of my own father who died [in a car accident] before I was born. I loved my stepfather very much, but he was rarely—not never but rarely—engaged in my life. I can count, on one hand, the number of things we did together: the times he took me hunting or fishing; or into the woods to cut a Christmas tree; or to a baseball game in St. Louis. I tell you, I remember every one of them because they were so few.[50]

Clinton acknowledged the difficulty he faced emotionally going into a marriage of his own. "I wanted it desperately, but did not know if I could do it,"[51] he said.

> The third thing that happens when you grow up in a

dysfunctional home is that, inadvertently, you send mixed signals to people. You learn that other people, in the outside world, didn't live in the same context as you. I see this as President. I don't believe in psychobabble—you can overdo all that, but I think I have to be acutely aware that I grew up as a peacemaker, always trying to minimize the disruption.

When you are President, and go the extra mile, others will interpret it as weakness. In Haiti, I pretty much had to invade the country because people didn't believe me. When I finally had the planes in the air, they believed me and got out of there. That's happened all my life. . . . People underestimate your resolve because you go out of your way to accommodate them before you drop the hammer.[52]

The workaholism alluded to by Fick could also be interpreted as an attempt to actualize some of the social and economic gains promised in his election campaign; or simply as a desire to perform well in one of the most demanding jobs in the world. A "strong need for approval"[53] and an inability to stop working are practically job requirements for the presidency.

A Toxic Brain Disease

From the inside of an expanding social movement, it is often hard to judge one's own success. Does one popularity surge indicate bigger surges to come, or does each new wave of book buyers warn of a soon-to-be-saturated market for a given idea? Recovery stars at HCI conferences tended to adopt the first scenario.

The euphoria was palpable in 1988 when more than 700 people attended a regional HCI conference on codependency in Clearwater, Florida. Regionals seldom drew crowds of more than 300. Obviously, the company was doing something right.

Conference chairperson Sharon Wegscheider-Cruse kicked off the conference by praising those who gathered into a packed ballroom at the stately Belleview Biltmore for showing up. That so many people had recognized the usefulness of the conference material was evidence of just how far the recovery movement had come, she said. That the rest of the world had not also signed up was evidence of just how far the movement had to go, she added. The audience laughed.[54]

During the 1980s, quite a few therapists suddenly declared themselves experts on ACoAs and codependency. To them, recovery was a hot new concept, something to be tapped, trapped and exploited.

Wegscheider-Cruse, on the other hand, had studied with the legendary Virginia Satir (who had also written about "family roles" determined by birth order). Throughout her professional life, Wegscheider-Cruse treated, spoke and wrote about alcoholism and dysfunctional families.

The four family roles Wegscheider-Cruse wrote about in 1981—Hero, Scapegoat, Lost Child and Mascot—had long since been adopted by therapists of alcoholism and dysfunctional families. Seven years later in Florida, the topic was no longer the families themselves but their codependency—those denying, enabling and overcompensating behaviors that kept the family machinery oiled and lubricated at the expense of the individuals involved. Codependency therapy encouraged people to become self-determined, as opposed to playing the "little helper," the "little husband," the peacemaker or any number of other, equally time-consuming and ultimately unrewarding roles. In this respect, recovery from codependency was similar to the ideas of more mainstream self-help authors: Realize the ways in which you have been deceiving yourself and decide not to do that anymore.

In a *Changes* interview that stirred up much controversy, Wayne Dyer chose to emphasize self—"There is no substance outside of myself that I ever felt controlled me" and wellness—"I think people should see themselves as loving and whole and complete and at harmony."[55] In contrast, codependency emphasized being born into a sick family system and developing a personality that adapted to that system despite its excessive demands and lack of reciprocity to the individual, carrying the results of that learning into a new family, work situation and other adult relationships.

And come to think of it, there were a lot more sick family systems around than just alcoholic systems. Thus, in playing up the importance of codependency, the recovery field was announcing a drastic turf expansion. Nearly all of the public—96%—was in some way codependent according to the popular definition at the time. But without a clear understanding of codependency as something bad, there was little incentive for the public to get help for it. Offering this generalization was like starting a nail. In Florida, Wegscheider-Cruse drove that nail home, sinking the head with authority.

"We now know," she told the packed ballroom, "that codependency is a toxic brain disease."[56] Her husband, Psychiatrist Joseph Cruse, had laid the groundwork for some time in his talks regarding the role of neurotransmitter norepinephrine in stimulating the codependent "high." Left untreated, Wegscheider-Cruse warned, codependency progresses. As a brain disease, codependency starts out causing migraines, but can also eventually cause gastritis, colitis and heart disease. Wegscheider-Cruse did not offer a distinction between codependent stress-related illness and ordinary stress-related illness, which has been linked to the same illnesses named above. She said that codependency, if left untreated, could kill you.

Symptoms of codependency included drinking, smoking, gambling, overeating, working too much, unhealthy relationships, being too sarcastic and flirting. Treatment for codependency consisted of "emotional surgery," Wegscheider-Cruse said. The therapist surgeon "lances" the "emotional abscess," allowing people to function again. "It's not for sissies or cowards," she added.[57]

Concerns from Within the Field

William O'Hanlon, a student of famed psychiatrist Milton Erickson, expounds a new school of thought—brief therapy.

Brief therapy is just that—clients seldom return after more than ten sessions, and most stop after four or five, or even one. Clients, not therapists, determine the goals of the therapy. They also provide their own solutions with the therapist's help. Basically, the therapist's job, or part of it, is to find out how the client has already resolved similar problematic situations in the past.

O'Hanlon comes from an emerging breed of therapists who feel that their own beliefs influence the outcome of therapy more than any other single element. In one famous experiment, handlers of rats who had been brain-damaged (but which the experimenters thought had unmolested brains) performed better than rats with intact brains whose handlers had been told (falsely) that they were working with brain-damaged rats. All of the handlers were required to put their rats through mazes and record the data of how well they performed.[58]

In a book he co-authored with Michele Weiner-Davis, O'Hanlon compares this experiment, conducted in 1966 by J.R. Burnham, to therapists receiving a file from a new client's former therapist.

> Suppose you have just received a new referral along with background information such as, "Mary is incredibly resistant to therapy," or, "John is minimally brain-damaged," or, "This is a multiproblem, court-referred family." In what ways do you think that this information might influence your expectation of what is possible (or not possible) in therapy?[59]

Long-term therapy, with its penchant for labels and the "characteristics" that accompany them, may add to their client's woes, O'Hanlon says. He explains, quoting family therapist Jay Haley:

> To label a child as "delinquent" or as suffering from "minimal brain dysfunction," or to label an adult as an "alcoholic" or a "schizophrenic," means that one is participating in the creation of a problem in such a way that change is made more difficult . . . . The way in which one labels a human dilemma can crystallize a problem and make it chronic.[60]

O'Hanlon's message is that therapy constructs, however helpful or descriptive in understanding patterns of human behavior, may have very little to do with the kinds of thoughts and constructions needed to help people change their behaviors. The brief therapy he advocated never attained great popularity, perhaps in part because brief also meant inexpensive.

Worsening Relations with Managed Care

As for expenses, by 1990 the shift to HMOs, PPOs and the like had taken hold. Relations between insurers and chemical dependency providers became fragmented. For example, treatment approval would initially be granted, only to be reversed by a retrospective review committee. Physician Paul Teodo, director of chemical dependency treatment at Central DuPage Hospital in Winfield, Illinois, said this new breed of conflicts led to "an unfortunate situation."

> The provider contracts with managed care to charge them certain fees, agreed upon for certain services when deemed to be appropriate, at the discretion of the (third-party) payer. . . . A payer can at any time decide to review a client's medical record. And if a physician or psychologist determines that there was a pre-existing condition, or that the patient has not been fully forthcoming as to his history, a retrospective review can overturn the initial decision (to authorize treatment). Since the legal agreement is between the patient and the provider, the provider's only recourse is to go back to the patient for a bill the patient initially perceived to be covered at 80 percent. In the eyes of the patient, we tend to be the bad guy.[61]

While such incidents may not have been common, they reflected the changing waters of reimbursement. And the sudden failure of treatment providers to communicate with insurers was not only a matter of length of stay. It became increasingly more difficult to reach an understanding as to what constituted appropriate treatment in the first place.

Health-care consultant Leroy Kelly of Massachusetts was a member of then-Governor Michael Dukakis's commission to examine utilization reviews, particularly to find out how well insurers were complying with government-mandated benefits regarding chemical dependency. His comments made in a 1991 interview reflect the state of change occurring in the insurance industry.

"I think there were abuses on this side of the system such as overdiagnosis of chemical dependency in order to reap insurance benefits,"[62] Kelly said.

Rick Esterly summed it up, saying "the pendulum has swung too far in the other direction."[63] Occasionally treatment advocates would attempt to create state legislation mandating tighter controls concerning circumstances in which insurers could deny coverage, Kelly said. "But for every bill that made it to the Senate floor, there were in the hallways, without exaggeration, four or five hard-case insurance lobbyists."[64]

These lobbyists came armed with studies indicating that outpatient chemical dependency treatment in most cases was just as effective as inpatient; while the treatment side had studies showing that inpatient treatment, when appropriately administered, was more effective than outpatient treatment. The insurers were winning on the political front.

In their negotiations, providers observed painful contrasts with the good old days of the early- to mid-1980s, when they enjoyed the luxury of addressing problem areas in a patient's life—things considered to have caused the chemical dependency or aggravated the pattern. "We have had little problem sitting around with managed care establishing (treatment) criteria," Kelly said. "But we have had problems with interpretations of the criteria. The areas patients are stuck in and don't want to change are what they need our help with the most."[65]

Insurers were not without a ruthless profit mentality of

their own. They denied payments to some based on pre-existing conditions, (as chemical dependency must be, almost by definition) and took revenge on others later in their lives. In a 1991 interview, Harold Hughes, a former Iowa senator and a patients' rights advocate, said the following: "I've been on the road two weeks, and everywhere I go people come to me with sad cases of insurance denials. One man can't secure a license to work out of his home because he goes to a 12-step program. Another can't get admitted into a nursing home because he was admitted to treatment once."[66]

At the time, Hughes was organizing a patients' lobby called the Society of Americans in Recovery (SOAR). The grassroots organization would press for "responsible treatment, responsible coverage, and the right to have access to treatment,"[67] Hughes said. But a lack of funds kept SOAR grounded. People who didn't already have access to treatment were not well off. Some couldn't afford the society's five-dollar membership fee. For a couple of years, Hughes tried to obtain funds from other sources, then gave up. Sometimes, payers denied coverage because they found claims frivolous. "We have seen claims submitted for people who are codependent but not chemically dependent, or one-time Driving While Intoxicated (DWI) who are not out of control" sufficiently enough to merit six weeks of treatment, said Christie Kriha, a medical utilization review manager for Blue Cross of Minnesota.[68]

By the early 1990s, skyrocketing health care costs and the advent of managed care brought about a new era for chemical dependency. By the end of 1989, treatment centers in large cities were reporting 50% patient drop-offs. Large chains such as Mediplex, Parkside, Koala, Center System and Comprehensive Care underwent financial restructuring in the fall of 1989—selling their assets to larger corporations, merging with other treatment centers or closing their doors permanently.[69]

During the boom years between 1980 and 1988, membership in the National Association of Addiction Treatment Providers had more than tripled. By 1992, the number dropped to 530 facilities, and two-thirds of the nation's treatment centers had closed their doors.

The result was widespread nervousness. Virtually everyone in the professional recovery field was affected. After all, the therapists who specialized in chemical dependency had been the first to expand into treating adult children of alcoholics, codependents, bulimics and sexual abuse survivors. They had been the ones to determine linkages between these newly-discovered or newly-emphasized illnesses in terms of how codependency often "underlies" chemical dependency—and later, how "trauma" underlies codependency. If insurance companies were suddenly going to play hardball, they would either have to find ways around the review committees, or find people who could afford to pay cash for their services.

CHAPTER SEVEN

Codependency:
Heightening "Awareness"

D o you worry about what other people think of you?" asked a flyer for a small therapy center. "Are you afraid of criticism? Are you more than 10 pounds overweight?"

"If you answered yes to one or more of these questions, you may be suffering from co-dependency."[1] This was one piece among the reams of promotional literature available during the *U.S. Journal* Training's Second Annual National Conference on Co-Dependency held at the Scottsdale Princess in Scottsdale, Arizona in August 1990. Not all of the brochures advertising treatment centers and individual therapists were as blatant as the above, but target audiences were nearly as wide everywhere.

A year earlier, at the First Annual National Conference on Co-Dependency, a specially convened panel created a definition for codependency, which read as follows: "Codependency is a pattern of painful dependence on compulsive behaviors and on approval from others in an attempt to find safety, self-worth and identity."[2]

The "Scottsdale Definition," as it was enshrined in HCI literature, was hailed as an "historic" accomplishment. Prior to the 1990 conference opening, a meeting was held by essentially the same panel of 25 or so of the biggest names in codependency who were asked to address the challenges ahead. One of the largest challenges was that codependency still carried no medical weight, and thus was not useful for insurance billing.

Despite the Scottsdale Definition, experts seemed to harbor extremely diverse opinions on codependency. Some of the interpretations of codependency at the time included:

- "For me, co-dependency is another title for using relationships to avoid dealing with the trauma of our own emotions."[3]–Long Beach, California therapist Marsha Utain.
- "Co-dependency is so global it can't be put in a box. It is the absence of a relationship with self."[4]–Minneapolis, Minnesota therapist Terry Kellogg.
- "Codependency is delayed identity development syndrome."[5]–Edina, Minnesota therapist Robert Subby.
- "A culturally conditioned response. It makes more sense to define it as an over-functioning person in relationship with an under-functioning person."[6]–Atlanta, Georgia marriage and family therapist Gus Napier.
- "I define it as any suffering and/or dysfunction that is associated with or results from focusing on the needs and behavior of others."[7]–Baltimore, Maryland physician Charles Whitfield.
- "[It is] a spiritual illness—ultimately, a conflict in gods."[8]– Phoenix, Arizona therapist and Codependents Anonymous co-founder Ken Richardson.
- "It is an emotional abscess that causes pain. The person wants relief for that pain and it sets off a craving for

help."[9]–Rapid City, South Dakota physician Joseph Cruse.

Joseph Cruse's saying, "Scratch an alcoholic and a codependent will bleed,"[10] was obviously gaining favor. These professionals were strong supporters of the disease model of alcoholism–but apparently not the "naive" disease model, or the one that emphasized genetics. The theory that alcoholism could be explained as a response to stress, an improvement over the disease model, was still heresy. Yet disease model supporters at the Scottsdale meeting explained codependency not only as a "hole in the soul" or as a "disease of lost selfhood," but as "the -ism underlying all addictions"! Experts who knew that the disease model was under attack by another school of researchers were concerned by such descriptions.

The panel format went as follows: *U.S. Journal* president Gary Seidler asked for clarifications about the future of codependency–including thoughts on whether it was possible or desirable to help the concept's credibility within the medical community. Later, people broke up into small groups to address relatively concrete issues such as codependency treatment, reimbursement, interplay with chemical dependency, relapse and so on.

Some experts complained about the vagueness of the term and questioned whether codependency had already outlived its usefulness. Recovery star Terry Kellogg suggested that codependency is a global condition responsible for wars and other social ills.[11] Joseph Cruse, a participant in the alcoholism "intervention" of First Lady Betty Ford, continued his interminable explication of a "medical model" for codependency. Cruse argued from conference to conference about the codependent "high," which he compared to the euphoria of a cocaine addict.[12]

This ongoing disparity threatened to undermine the optimism in the air about "how far we've come."

I asked the assembly of self-help authors how they would address several criticisms of codependency that were well in circulation by 1990, including the following four:

- No clinical diagnosis for codependency;
- A tendency to diagnose women that some saw as "blaming the victim";
- An inherent cultural bias that leads to a disease label given to some of the sharing and care-taking practices of minorities and other cultures;
- The danger of codependency being used as a catch-all diagnosis making it easier for professionals to miss serious psychological problems.

Responses to these criticisms varied. Anne Wilson Schaef, who called attention to the concept in *Co-Dependence: Misunderstood, Mistreated*, published four years earlier in 1986, now wanted to drop the term "codependency" (or "codependence") altogether. Schaef's change of heart seemed to stem from her own globalization of addiction concepts.

"Co-dependency denies the reality that people who are co-dependent are addicts," Schaef said. "Until we look at that, there is no hope of recovery."[13] Her comment, it seems, is evidence that not everyone was optimistic about the potential for strengthening the concept of codependency.

Another panelist, alcoholism consultant Terence Gorski, outlined the potential usefulness of the concept. Codependency, he said, describes a range of behaviors such as "unmanageable feelings, self-defeating behaviors, irrational thinking and dysfunctional relationships."[14] In his lectures, Gorski divided codependency into two degrees—mild and severe— as well as onset—"early" and "late."[15]

Yet Gorski remained fundamentally critical of the generality his colleagues applied to the term "codependency". He called it a "garbage-can diagnosis" and said, "If you can't determine who is *not* codependent, you can't determine who is."[16]

More typical responses came immediately after the four criticisms of codependency were relayed to the panel. First, Keith Miller, author of *Sin: Overcoming the Ultimate Deadly Addiction*, rambled about the dangers of "intellectualizing." Although in Miller's estimation he could intellectualize "with the best of them," he would rather have convened this pre-conference gathering of experts with a 12-step meeting.[17]

Jean Rigaud, a registered nurse who was at the time clinical director of Cottonwood Centers in Tucson, Arizona, commented on her anxiety when the 12 Steps were not mentioned in conversations relating to codependency treatment and recovery.[18] Many of the dozen or more panelists who had spoken before Rigaud may not have mentioned the steps by name, but all of the experts did use language that was, at the very least, friendly toward 12-step concepts and vernacular.

George Nash, medical director for Sierra Tucson, one of the nation's largest and best-known treatment centers said, "AA called alcoholism a disease 28 years before the AMA followed suit. I think we're witnessing something similar to that now."[19]

Then, Ralph Earle, president of the American Association for Marriage and Family Therapy, said, "I would like it known that we have heard criticisms being brought forth, and that we are dealing with them."[20]

Rounding the corner, Joseph Cruse underscored the need for a clinical diagnosis. His wife, Sharon Wegscheider-Cruse, who had once used this medical model as the basis for calling codependency a "toxic brain disease," answered next, allowing now that "some of the criticisms (of codependency) are deserved,"[21] and added that the recovery field needed to beware of people looking for gurus.

After the round table, the panelists split into five groups, each tackling a separate set of challenges facing codependency. In one sub-group, I asked Joseph Cruse how "spirituality" factored into codependency and whether he worried that the inclusion of this concept might hinder codependency's acceptance as a diagnosis.

Cruse replied, "Well, obviously, if someone is going to commit suicide, that person has a spiritual problem."[22]

"Why isn't it just a psychiatric problem?" I asked.

Cruse was a few sentences into his reply when Gorski repeated my question: "Why isn't it just a psychiatric problem?" As a treatment advocate, Gorski was concerned that religious issues were interfering with treatment—hence the recoveries—of atheists and individuals of different belief systems. He related a lecture in which the speaker said, "chemical dependency and codependency are spiritual diseases, and the only way to recover is to turn your will and your life over to the care of a Higher Power. I choose to call that Higher Power God!" Gorski recalled:

I was sitting next to a representative from a Health Maintenence Organization. After the presentation, I asked him what he thought. "I can't believe you people want insurance reimbursement for providing spiritual programs," he said. "If we begin underwriting all spiritual programs, we would have to honor payment claims for people who attend church on Sunday."[23]

Though it gradually smoothed itself out, there was a sense of rift as a result of raising a set of obvious questions. This rift is similar to what happens in 12-step meetings:

- Arguments or reactions against something someone has phrased in the discontinuous language of "I-centered" sharing; the animus for "intellectualizing" while employing only the non-pathological definition of the word;
- Misapplications of the Tenth Tradition (which discourages the intrusion of outside controversies into 12-step meetings but has no bearing on individual thought or on situations totally outside the context of 12-step groups);
- A tendency to answer the question, "Why are we here?" with, "Because we must be!"

It was surprising that so few of the recovery experts seemed concerned or even interested in the theoretical underpinnings of the concepts they'd been using in their work for some time.

HCI author Charles Whitfield was one who did respond by diagnosing the opposition, saying critics just "don't understand"[24] the concepts. Whitfield explains:

> This is not surprising, since most of us come from a dysfunctional family and society that is run by actively codependent, dysfunctional politicians who interact with actively codependent, dysfunctional educational, vocational, religious, communication and industrial systems.[25]

Whitfield's caveat that "we can still learn"[26] from critics on occasion reads more like a hedge against being diagnosed himself rather than dispassionate consideration.

Perhaps the attitude of most recovery stars was best

summed up by another HCI author John Friel at this same meeting: "Spirited debate about codependency is extremely important, but you measure the value of a theory by its usefulness. There are thousands of people who use [codependency] and to whom it makes sense."[27]

In the Middle Ages, there were thousands of people who used witchcraft and to whom it made sense. One of these was the great Paracelsus, who in 1527 burned his official pharmacopoeia (the 16th century equivalent of the *Diagnostic and Statistical Manual*) because, explained one historian, "he had learned from the Sorceresses all he knew."[28] Between their magical rites, which would eventually disappear from medicine, and their pharmacology, which remained, how did the witches determine what was useful? Or did they just say, "It works if you work it, so don't intellectualize?"

On one point the experts agreed: an overbroad description of codependency makes diagnosis impossible. If the field wanted insurance companies to reimburse for treatment, everyone would need to clean up their acts.

The Post-traumatic Stress Disorder (PTSD) Model

In contrast to the indecisiveness of the expert panel, the rest of the conference went well. Presenters told the 1,000 conference participants they were on the verge of a monumental breakthrough. Some compared the public awareness of codependency to that of alcoholism in the 1930s.

Scottsdale also marked the emergence of a new and critical sub-section of codependency—childhood trauma. A small percentage of presentations emphasized early experiences, not family substance abuse or lifelong patterns, as penultimate to understanding the patient.

Where codependency was once presented as the "ism" beneath all psychological (and, possibly physical) illnesses, it was now seen by some as a "symptom" of childhood trauma. So, just as codependency, for some professionals, created addiction, now trauma created codependency.

The *Diagnostic and Statistical Manual III-R (DSMIII-R)*, the barometer of medical practice, described Post-traumatic Stress Disorder (PTSD) as an outgrowth of "shell shock," which was first attributed to World War I veterans.[29]

According to the *DSMIII-R*, the PTSD sufferer has undergone an event on the outer reaches of human experience, including:

A serious threat to one's life or physical integrity; a serious threat or harm to one's children, spouse, or other close relatives and friends; sudden destruction of one's home or community; or seeing another person who has recently been, or is being, seriously injured or killed as the result of an accident or physical violence.[30]

The list of symptoms depict someone who has structured his or her life in an attempt to avoid thinking about or coping with what happened. This person has little future expectations, has difficulty concentrating, is easily and exaggeratedly startled, has trouble sleeping and often dreams of the event when he does sleep. Young children who have been traumatized by an event may lose some of their abilities to speak or remain toilet trained.[31]

The *DSM* criteria refers to memory repression as "efforts to avoid thoughts or feelings about the traumatic event and about activities or situations that arouse recollections"[32] of the trauma. It does not state that the person has no recollection. The exception—psychogenic amnesia—refers to an inability to recall "an important aspect of the traumatic event."[33] This criteria falls in sharp contrast to the recovery movement's theories that repressed memories of childhood sexual abuse cause PTSD; and that chemical dependency and codependency are depicted as ways in which patients avoid trauma and the impact of the abuse on their lives.

Therapists used "regression therapy" to help clients uncover long-repressed incidents of abuse ranging from witnessing nudity to satanic torture. Regression therapy is an umbrella term. It nearly always involves placing the client under a hypnotic or quasi-hypnotic trance, then asking the client to "go back" to the time the trauma occurred or might have occurred. In more extreme forms, regression therapy can involve explicit parent-child relationships with the therapist assuming the role of parent.

Given that symptoms of past sexual abuse can appear in behaviors as mild as perfectionism or problem drinking, it is not difficult to understand how prodding techniques could become necessary. After all, these clients are not shell-shocked children whose homes were demolished in a propane gas explosion. They very often come from the ranks of the "worried well," troubled by vague dissatisfactions such as a loss of community, economic uncertainty or any number of other problems.

They may nonetheless be troubled and be able to benefit from the counsel of friends or therapists. The decision to seek help is, of course, an individual one, to be determined according to one's concerns with costs and benefits. It seemed that many people discovered great benefits from "integrating the trauma," despite the high emotional and financial costs involved.

Scratch an alcoholic and a codependent will bleed—that much was clear before Scottsdale. Now there was a new layer: Scratch a codependent and a trauma survivor will bleed. Scratch a trauma survivor—particularly a "ritual abuse" trauma survivor–and God knows how many people start bleeding. Between sacrificed infants, MPD survivors and their alters, it's a deluge all right.

Ode to Clifford

Perusing through an old *Focus* magazine not long ago, I found the entire "letters" department consumed by the concerns of one heretofore unknown Clifford Ostrover, regarding the burgeoning recovery industry:

> I can not begin to count–50, maybe 100 books on these specific issues–*Co-dependent No More, Addicted to Misery, Recovery from Rescuing, Understanding Co-Dependency, Surviving With Serenity, After the Tears, Addictive Relationships, Healing the Child Within, Struggle for Intimacy,* etc. . . It's not as if most of these contain any new insight to these problems, they are just re-stating the same information over and over again.[34]

Ostrover also raised concerns about people "being opened up to their issues by the thousands (perhaps millions, as in the case of T.V. programs)" during "Inner Child" workshops.[35] He questioned the motives of colleagues who seemed to view our entire species as an untapped mental health market.

"If we, as clinicians, put forth an image to the public that we feel almost everyone needs therapy, we will surely self-destruct and lose all validity,"[36] Ostrover wrote. Atop his long letter, someone had chosen the headline, "Promoting Therapy," which got it exactly backward. Ambitious authors were promoting therapy through their legions of books, codependency cruises and inner child workshops.

Clifford Ostrover, a recovering addict with seven years

clean time, a certified addictions counselor with a Ph.D. in psychology, was trying to save his discipline from profit mongering and unbridled diagnosis. His letter consumed three columns of dull black type. In a magazine on the verge of folding, with its treatment-center advertisers crippled by insurance cutbacks, Ostrover argued for the promotion of "a sense of wellness, rather than dependencies!"[37]

But he must have known that people who are well are not as likely to have much incentive to buy armfuls of self-help books, are not as likely to check themselves into a center for eight days of treatment and probably wouldn't jeopardize their health insurance or "sell their homes to finance their recoveries" so someone could "validate their pain."

Reconstructing and Deconstructing

The observations of academics, contained mostly in journals the general public rarely reads, do not appear to be widely read among recovery stars either, if lack of mention and response signify anything. This is a pity, because what these "outsiders" have to say is often instructive.

Janice Haaken, a psychologist at Portland State University, for example, raises more critical issues in her 22-page paper, "From Al-Anon to ACoA: Codependence and the Reconstruction of Caregiving," than most recovery authors manage to do in four or five books. Haaken suggests that the expansion of AA-based disease ideology to include codependents or survivors of dysfunctional families represents "a search for deeper causality than a repressive, law-and-order approach to addiction."[38]

At the same time, she cautions, recovery makes escape from these generalized conditions more difficult, since "rigid" or "dysfunctional rules" are everywhere. She devotes much space to the split messages regarding feminism in recovery—

the simultaneous beliefs that women can rise above oppression and that women are ill; leaving some confusion as to who is responsible for these conditions in the first place.

The conceptions of the family also changed as more people left Al-Anon meetings for ACoA and Codependents Anonymous just as Al-Anon introduced a larger conception of alcohol in the family than was possible through AA. Haaken argues that the results of these changes were mixed. Codependence is much more the fruit of the mental health field than was the early Al-Anon of the 1950s. Hence, support group members are more likely to be assertive and less conscious of the humanity of those representing an evil "system" or disease process:

> The notion of a family-transmitted disease for which neither parents nor children are personally responsible depersonalizes the destructive experiences of the past so that hostility toward parents can be expressed without guilt or doubt. Whereas Al-Anon argued that anger is useless against a disease, codependence writers are more apt to believe that anger is harmless when directed toward a disease.[39]

As for families, they had better be in recovery too. They cannot be openly dysfunctional—drinking, overeating, abusing, etc.—nor can they appear "perfect." It is interesting how recovery authors romanticize the family, then vilify them for not living up to these romantic ideals. Concepts such as "unconditional love," "honoring uniqueness" and a bill of "rights" far beyond those guaranteed by the Constitution place the therapeutically unsophisticated in an untenable position.

The very self-esteem of an individual or a family can be used against them. Never having been in recovery opens a person to some very serious diagnoses. What, for example, are we to do with the people who think that a certain amount of dysfunction comes with the territory of being alive?

In order to accept fully the pronouncements of code-pendency experts, one must totally reconsider civilization as it has been taught thus far. Most world religions revere their founders, which denotes hero worship that results from low self-esteem. The entire institution of science, with its fetish for "controlled experiments," could be accused of rigidity and secrecy. Politicians are codependent because they are people pleasers, always trying to portray a false image of themselves. Major cities are case studies in unmanageability, foreign countries are behind the times, and one can pretty much write off the mental health of anyone choosing to live on the South Pole.

Even the angry, aggressive polar bear of Alaska has bound-ary issues, consistently failing to respect the integrity of other living creatures. Butterflies, however, are serene. They never talk, and so are never inappropriate. Butterflies have also made themselves teachable through months spent in an ego-deflating cocoon. They have died in order to be reborn. Therefore, butterflies are good and polar bears are bad. Remember this truth—my Higher Power revealed it to me only moments ago. He wants you to have it.

Codependency as a Post-Graduate Course

In *The Idea of a University*, John Henry Cardinal Newman distinguishes philosophical knowledge from that which is merely mechanical; and although not wishing to diminish the latter says of the former:

When I speak of Knowledge, I mean something intel-lectual, something which grasps what it perceives through the senses; something which takes a view of things; which sees more than the senses convey; which reasons upon what it sees, and while it sees; which invests it with an idea.[40]

That, Newman says, is the goal of liberal education as opposed to mechanical instruction.[41] One would hope that education in counseling psychology would be at least as much philosophical by the above definition as technique-oriented and practical. It may be that recovery, "the field," cannot yet be called recovery, "the discipline," even though most of the root subject matter has been a part of respectable disciplines for decades. Alcoholism research, family dynamics, Post-traumatic Stress and various interpretations of memory and repression were a part of college curricula before self-help blossomed into its current, disease-model paradigm in the late 1970s. There is no doubt that the explosion of popular interest in recovery affected these curricula.

It is also safe to assume that course material before the recent recovery era was, for the most part, delivered in a third-person format—talking about "them" who are alcoholic or who constitute dysfunctional families. It is already known that AA is modeled on a first-person format. In theory, at least, AA is strictly a matter of "I" and "we," and does not claim to know anything about any outside party or what other people ought to do.

Recovery literature cannot be broken down into such categories. Often written by mental health professionals whose interest is intensely personal, this genre of writing encompasses all forms of address—I and we, you and you all, he, she and they. A course syllabus for "Co-Dependency" offered by Pennsylvania State University's graduate program in counseling listed 48 items in its bibliography, 18 of which were HCI products.[42]

That 13 HCI authors and one magazine made up 37% of a graduate-level counseling course would not in itself be disturbing if the other 63% contained some balancing perspectives. There are a number of published articles and books critical of the codependency construct, none of which were included. The suggested texts for students of the course included: *Codependent No More* by Melody Beattie; *Diagnosing and Treating Co-Dependence: A guide for professionals who work with chemical dependents, their spouses and children* by Timmen Cermak; *When Society Becomes an Addict* by Anne Wilson Schaef; *Choicemaking: For codependents, adult children and spirituality seekers* by Sharon Wegscheider-Cruse; and *Adult Children of Alcoholics* by Janet Woititz.

The last selection is ironic: Woititz, who died of cancer in 1994, had become disenchanted with the codependency concept by the early 1990s, and ceased any participation in conferences built around it.

Students were to participate in an experiential group, attend lectures, read course material, write papers and visit treatment centers. There was no indication in the syllabus that the concept of codependency was a controversial newcomer to psychology—one that has been accused of harboring intolerable vagueness and sweeping generalizations; a tendency to diagnose women for their own oppression and a cultural bias against minorities. Instead, the Penn State course assumed legitimacy and appeared to base this assumption on a raft of self-help books and a few one-sided clinical contributions such as those of the psychiatrist Timmen Cermak.

Planners presumably designed this course to turn out Masters-level counselors who would be well-versed in codependency. Yet nothing was offered that might round out the students' impressions of the concept and nourish their capacity to evaluate it or defend codependency against its critics. According to the syllabus, if the course was successful they would be able to accomplish the following:

1. Identify co-dependency as a dysfunctional interaction system.
2. Learn to recognize symptoms of co-dependency in potential clients.
3. Discuss the dynamics of co-dependency in systems and treatment facilities, and list the features of co-dependency in counselor-client relationships and group settings.
4. List and describe the available treatment modalities for co-dependency.
5. Demonstrate needed counseling techniques for those working with co-dependent persons.[43]

Department heads at Penn State eventually abolished this post-graduate course in codependency. But it is important to remember that hundreds of currently practicing counselors were trained with the self-help books prescribed in that course and thousands more counselors-in-training are probably digesting similar material in universities across the country.

The Addictions Left

No matter how completely the PTSD model seems to have blanketed the recovery field, pockets of resistance remain. An article coming from one such pocket called "Who Are the *Real* Co-Dependents?"[44] was published in a 1991 issue of *FOCUS* magazine. Substance abuse counselor

Marguerite Babcock argues that codependency lacks solid research and springs from a "disturbed personality"[45] hypothesis for which there has never been evidence.

"Disturbed personality" was once a popular diagnosis for women who stayed married to alcoholics "to serve their own 'sick' needs,"[46] says Babcock, a clinical supervisor at the Center for Substance Abuse Training in McKeesport, Pennsylvania. That both disturbed personality and codependency should pathologize women in similar ways says more about some "helping professionals" than those ostensibly being helped.

The problem is that in order for something to be called a disease or a pathological behavior pattern, there must be some consistency to the pattern. Yet, Babcock says:

> Research has shown that significant others present no consistent response pattern that could be called a pathology. Addictions workers have been taught about only a limited number of responses, such as enabling and control, and unconsciously edit out other types of responses.[47]

The largest inconsistency lies in the society that produces the label. After thousands of years of telling women to be loyal and subservient to their husbands, societal beliefs suddenly change and label them sick for doing so. This is not merely a matter of "taking personal responsibility." It may still be the duty of battered wives to remove themselves from their marriages—certainly no one else can file their divorce papers—but a more humane position would be to take some collective responsibility for social codes that have permitted the abuse. As Babcock writes, "Confused and sometimes maladaptive experiments in coping with an impaired person do not equate with a pathology."[48]

The addictions culture that gives rise to disease labels may also suffer from confusion. Babcock makes the following observations:

> I have repeatedly heard addictions workers label any focus on others . . . as "co-dependency." What they were actually talking about ranged from affective disorders to personality disorders to the feminine sex role to global politics. Such dangerous sloppiness borders on a lack of professional ethics.
>
> During the last few years, therefore, I became increasingly convinced that the beast called "co-dependency" doesn't exist.
>
> But then something hit me. In the '80s, there were a lot of people who fed into the continuation of chemical dependency (a part of the definition of co-dependency). A lot of them are still around now; I'm hoping that will change. But they aren't, as a group, women and/or significant others. They are the people who sold us ideas like "co-dependency." They are the people who played fast and loose with the facts when doing advertising for their facilities, or who claimed to the treatment community that the simple-minded, quick-fix ideas that they had just dreamed up were the answers in therapy for addicts and those close to addicts. They are the Real Co-Dependents, the people who have really been involved in the continuation of addictions, in that they were more concerned with their reputations than with responsible examination through research and critical thinking of what is needed to help addicts and their families. It is too simple to say that this is a critique of commercialism in the addictions

field. One has to be commercial, whether selling health food or cocaine. But there is truth in advertising, and then there is self-aggrandizement.[49]

Babcock's Masters degree matches the education of most of the big names in codependency. Yet because she had not published a self-help book promising a newly-evolved being, few people knew her name. Babcock spoke at the 1991 National Lesbian and Gay Health Foundation (NLGHF) Conference in Washington, D.C. The foundation offered a wide array of topics at its annual meetings, with special emphasis on addiction and AIDS. While mainstream, Minnesota-Model treatment philosophies prevailed, just as they did at other addiction conferences, alternative views did find their way into a very thick conference program.

A lecture critiquing codependency was held in a small room on the basement floor. Babcock told the dozen or so people in attendance that codependency experts were "dry dope dealers" who generalized from a bed of sloppy thinking.

"They have no sympathy for the people they treat," she said, "their only interest is in continuing the addiction."[50] Also included in Babcock's overview were "a number of well-meaning professionals who have trusted the validity of research when it doesn't exist."[51]

These were the very same people who were being referred to as brave "pioneers," perpetually involved in pushing back the frontiers of knowledge: Sharon Wegscheider-Cruse, Claudia Black, Robert Subby, John Bradshaw and Anne Wilson Schaef.

Babcock, an obscure, backroom lecturer at the time, portrayed these vaunted leaders quite differently. Codependency support groups, she contended, were "like 1-900-lines"—a

place for the needy to connect. The new therapies maxi-
mized the problems of the well-adjusted and minimized the
more serious disorders that would not rapidly improve.

Babcock's presentation moved me in ways I hadn't expected. Despite the inflammatory language, her concerns in
general, even some of her specific accusations, struck me as
basically sound. Despite its healing tones, much of commercial recovery, from alcoholism to codependency and trauma,
had been influenced–all but taken over at times–by the
twin motives of selling products and services, and attracting
converts to a new belief system. Central to the newly identified codependent's spiritual searching was a realization that
one is profoundly flawed, and a deepening hunger for
therapy. For the first time, I found myself questioning my
habit of accepting a paycheck from such self-serving acts
based on questionable information. The so-called "ethical
seatbelt" was beginning to fray. As for the movement's
many seekers, they looked for information too–about themselves, and what sort of events might have shaped them into
becoming the people they turned out to be. As we shall see,
many were already finding answers.

CHAPTER EIGHT

A Climate of Accusation

T he letters arrived by certified mail on July 9, 1990–
12 days after Nick's 80th birthday. For reasons that
will become clear, pseudonyms are used for Nick
and other family members.

On condition of anonymity, his family and others have told
their stories of being accused of horrendous crimes against
their children, committed decades ago and "remembered"
only in psychotherapy. These stories, more often than not,
begin with a letter.

Two such letters, one to Nick and one to his wife Holly,
also 80, came from their daughter, Hannah, who lives in Salt
Lake City, Utah. During the months prior to the letters,
relations between both parents and Hannah, then 45, had
entered a neutral zone. Hannah had moved into a new home
with her husband and two children and had been "adjusting" by maintaining a certain distance.

Since Nick and Holly were planning a trip to California in
August 1990, they proposed stopping over in Salt Lake City.
Hannah said it wasn't good timing, workers were still in the

house and things were too hectic. She followed up with a Father's Day card, reiterating these reasons and urging her parents not to worry about her.

The certified letters, which arrived a month later, conveyed a very different message:

Dear Dad,

Know you were bewildered by my demand that you not come visit us in August. I know my reasons have been vague and confusing. First off, there is nothing wrong with my immediate family. Thank goodness they are happy and healthy, productive, functioning people. What is wrong is (our) family is a dysfunctional family, and I no longer want to expose myself to my family or their illness.

A few months ago I realized, through flashbacks, that you sexually assaulted me from four-and-a-half years through thirteen-and-a-half years old. These assaults started with fondling to forcing me to give you oral sex, to violently raping me at seven-and-a-half, and continuing the rapes until I was thirteen-and-a-half.

The incestuous, sexual assaults were painful, frightening and so horrendous that I had to block them out most of my life. I no longer have to do that because I know I am not crazy, insane or out of control. I know that I no longer have to be afraid or silent. You kept me silent by threatening to institutionalize me because I was crazy just like your mother. (Mom did spend some inpatient psych time after her husband died.) You kept me silent by making me believe no one would believe me, that people would believe I was insane because you said I was. You kept me silent because no one knowing you would believe you would commit such a horrendous, inhuman act. I have discovered I am not crazy—that no one doubts that you are incapable of the assaults you committed, and that I am not responsible for your behavior.

I have also taken a careful look at how your behavior affected me. You robbed me of my innocence, betrayed my daughterly trust, and made me feel incapable of functioning mentally, emotionally and creatively. I lived in terror and pain. You made me feel unlovable, sick and so despicable that no one wanted to stay close to me. I spent years degrading myself and feeling I would never be a functional human being. I spent years believing that whatever you said was true, and that I had no control over my body, my mind or my life. I spent years hoping you would love me like a father should, and I'd have a father who loved me unconditionally. One I could trust, one who would allow me to be free to be myself. I can no longer believe in that fantasy and continue the myth. I have come to realize that you were the perpetrator and responsible for all that has happened. I do not expect you to admit to what you did, or even to take responsibility for it. People with your type of illness usually never do.

I will no longer try to avoid you by making excuses or emotionally withdrawing. What I do expect—demand—is that you do not have contact with me or my family ever again. I do not want my family or myself to be subjected to your destructive, hateful, violent behavior. I will not allow you to cause me any further pain, fear or destruction of my self-worth. I loved you as a child and you used it against me. I still love

*you. I love myself and my family and I will not pay
the price you ask for love.*

*Unless you seek self-help from a therapist, or a
group like Parents United, I never want to see you,
hear from you or have letters from you. If you decide
to change, you can let me know through your therapist or counselor. Otherwise stay totally away from
me and my family. If you don't respect my demand, I
will take any action I need to keep you away.*

—Hannah[1]

The letter to her mother, Holly, was identical in places,
similar in tone, but slightly gentler. Nick had not seen Hannah
in four years. It had been longer for Holly. Both were bewildered and deeply hurt by their daughter's accusations.

Before he received the letter, Nick had always respected
therapists, although he didn't know much about what they
did. "Now I find out she's using all the words of these therapists. 'Dysfunctional, perpetrator.' I have never heard of this
before in my life!"

"I'm smiling because if it wasn't so tragic I'd think it was
funny," Holly said.

By all accounts, Hannah was the creative one in the
family. While living in Miami, Florida, she wrote a one-act
play, which was produced and aired by a local television
channel. She went on to get her Masters degree in drama. In
Germany, Hannah received a medal from the German government for another play she wrote for children.

Faced with their own incredulity and their sister's flair for
invention, siblings Nancy and Tom have concluded that
Hannah's memories of abuse are fictitious, though neither
doubts her sincerity. In October 1990, they heard the charges
firsthand in Hannah's therapist's office. At the therapist's

request, Nick flew to Salt Lake City from California, Nancy from New York and Tom drove from across town for the meeting.

When the therapist arrived to open her office, Nick introduced himself cavalierly. "I'm the monster," he said.

"My daughter read off the list of offenses," Nick recalls. "She had it all prepared and she just read it off. I looked at her face to face, eyeball to eyeball, and said, 'Look, Hannah, I'm telling you this never, never happened. And all your dreams and flashbacks are nothing but nightmares.'

"The therapist says, 'Oh, no, we have confirmed this by hypnosis.' I didn't know then that there was something suspect about hypnosis. To me, that was like saying, 'Your fingerprints are on the gun!' And I was taken aback."

After Nick's second denial, Hannah's husband said, "Then you'll never see your grandchildren again."

Nick said to his daughter, "Give me one instance where this happened and how it happened. Then the therapist broke in: 'You don't have to answer that, time is up for the meeting.' "

During her trip home, Nancy wrote her sister Hannah a letter. She wondered how in their tight living quarters, nine years of molestation and violent rape could have gone undetected. The family had lived in a small two-story house in Long Island, New York. Nick was working long hours in the city, starting a new business manufacturing women's clothes. Nancy had her own bedroom, while Hannah and Tom shared a room down the hall. Nick and Holly slept in the room adjacent to the two younger children.

In 1953, the family moved to Miami. Nick rented a two-bedroom apartment. The first year, Hannah shared a room with Nancy, then 21, who had returned home while her husband was in the Army. During the two years Nancy was home, she hardly recalled a time when her father and Hannah were alone together.

After returning home from that disastrous meeting, Nancy wrote Hannah a second letter. Yes, Nancy agreed, Dad was controlling and he had made mistakes as a parent. But he was no rapist. Nancy reminded her sister that they had shared a bedroom in a small apartment. "Logistically, I know that these acts were impossible," she wrote. "I resent (the therapist's) implied idea that we were aware, but chose to ignore any signs because we didn't wish to know. There are no recollections by Tom, Mom, Dad or me, and there is no unspoken or spoken conspiracy to conceal a 'family secret.'

"I love Mom and Dad and I love you," Nancy's letter concluded. "I mourn for the loss each of you will experience because of the solution you have elected to apply. I grieve for the pain such a decision must evoke in all those involved."

Subsequent letters to Hannah came back unopened, return-to-sender. The entire tragic saga reminded Nick of a Russian fable:

A woodcutter in declining health lived with his children and grandchildren deep in the forest. Times were tough and food scarce.

"You ought to take that old man out into the woods and let him die," the wife told her husband. "He is taking food from our children's mouths. Besides, he won't live long, anyway."

This the husband could not do. The old man was, after all, his father. But after hearing the same complaint day after day, the son finally gave in. He bundled up the woodcutter and laid him on a sled, hitched the horses and drove away, taking his own children along for the ride.

Several miles away he stopped, now deep in the heart of the forest. He unhitched the horses, leaving his father tied to the sled. As he began to ride away his children stopped him.

"Daddy, daddy, the sled," they cried. "We'll need it for you someday."

Amidst the open photo albums and old letters scattered across the card table in this comfortable home, Nick and Holly's avowed disownment of their daughter is difficult to believe. There's a picture of Hannah with her firstborn and another one of Hannah, smiling and waving from a mountain overlook.

These days there is little left to do but speculate. In 1989, when Nancy visited her sister in Germany, Hannah confided that she was having some bad dreams. She was also having problems with her husband, whom Nancy described as "not a talker." The two of them went into therapy with an Army psychiatrist. Had the seed been planted then, or later?

Only Tom, the middle child, has been able to maintain contact with Hannah. He too recalls the two-bedroom apartment in Miami during the early days of Nick's business. "I don't think it could have gone on for a year, much less 10 years," Tom says. The allegations have strained their relationship, as well.

"I haven't spoken to her except recently. She said she felt that we had taken an enemy position, that we didn't trust her perceptions or her memory, and therefore we were her enemies."

Nick and Holly differ on whether to go public and use their real names. He wants to, she doesn't. "We don't have that much time left," says Holly. "I don't want to live the few years I have left this way. As far as I'm concerned," she adds, "I don't have a daughter."

When I reached Hannah, she asked how I had gotten her number (through Salt Lake City Directory Assistance). As to the story on the repressed memory controversy, she said she would have to think about it. When I called back a couple of days later, she declined to be interviewed. People in her position seldom talk if they know you have talked to their parents. Below is the conversation:

Hannah: I have very meticulously tried to create a life for myself. I would rather not be involved in this, and I do not know why my parents wish to be involved in this. I could understand if they were being sued, but they are not being sued. And I would rather be left out of it. I just want to get on with my life.

AM: Do you believe your parents when they say that in their hearts, they are certain that they did not do these things?

Hannah: I would rather not comment on that.

AM: Better for me to get all sides. Better for you, too, since you are the only one who can express your truth.

Hannah: I understand that and I appreciate that. I would just rather not be involved.[2]

On October 24, 1990, shortly after the confrontation in the therapist's office, Nick wrote to Hannah for the last time:

Hannah,

    You always urged me to express my anger and feelings. You were right, it's time to let them out. I was a loving, caring father who tried his best to love, protect and shelter you, to inspire you to be loving and caring, to enjoy and appreciate music, art and the finer things in life, to give you luxury comforts

*and to achieve the best possible education. I sup-
ported you emotionally and financially.*

*Even after you were married I gave you ten thou-
sand dollars for the down payment of your home,
plus an interest-free loan (partially repaid) of six
thousand dollars to buy a car. (Loan has never been
fully repaid.) You are an ungrateful child. You are
intrigued and bedeviled in your subconscious mind
by false-based, evil, obscene, vitriolic thoughts so strong
that you consciously believe them, and are able to
spew them out in total disregard of the consequences
to me and your mother. Some day you will awake to
the truth and realize the havoc you have done to the
entire family.*

*I am angry and deeply hurt. Because I have failed,
I will deal with my anger and hurt and they will go
away. But I have been grievously offended by your
disgraceful, despicable, abhorrent behavior and I
don't think I shall ever forgive you. No one likes to
look at or be reminded of their failures. So Hannah,
goodbye and good luck, for you will need it. Remember the sled may await you, too.*[3]

Nick swears the relationship with his daughter is over, no
matter what. Still, he doesn't object when Holly says, "If she
came back tomorrow, he'd melt." Early in 1993, Nick legally
disinherited Hannah from his estate.

Can This Profession Be Saved?

Until the early 1970s, sexual abuse was almost as quiet on
the national scene as in the families in which it occurred.
Father-daughter incest was thought to be rare. Research
since then has refuted this idea. A pair of well-known stud-

ies have placed the frequency of sexual abuse of girls as high as one in three by their 18th birthdays.[4]

Prevalence rates differ according to the criteria under which they are based. What is abuse? Does it mean penetration by an adult in the same family? What about a grab on the buttocks by another student? Variables such as these help explain why the field is wide open, with estimates from 15 studies since 1976 ranging from 6% of the population to 62%.

In a 1994 issue of *Society*, Berkeley sociologist Neil Gilbert criticizes methodologies prevalent in the more liberal estimates, characterized by inclusive screening questions. One such question was posed by Diana Russell, who reported a 54% sexual-abuse victimization rate among girls by their 18th birthday: "Did anyone ever feel you, grab you or kiss you in a way you felt was threatening?"[5] Gilbert counters such overgeneralizations, saying:

> When one thinks of child sexual abuse, an incident of attempted petting, a touch on the leg, and an unwanted pat on the buttock hardly come to mind. By lumping together relatively harmless behavior such as attempted petting with the terribly damaging ordeal of child rape, advocates have inflated the estimates of child sexual abuse to critical proportions.[6]

Even so, in recent years the one-in-three figure has gotten a lot of promotional play. It is rapidly gaining the popular acceptance of other tragedies that are easier to measure: that drunk drivers account for nearly half of all traffic fatalities, or that smoking kills 300,000 people each year. Moreover, high estimates lend credibility to the likelihood that it has happened to any given person, particularly if the epidemic is "hidden" from society and even victims themselves. Gilbert observes:

> Of course, there is a relation between the size of a problem and the extent to which its cause is attributed either to social forces or to personal factors. If 4 percent of the labor force is unemployed, these workers are unskilled, unmotivated, or temporarily down on their luck; if the unemployment rate goes to 24 percent, they are victims of a depression. If 5 percent of females are sexually abused as children, the offenders are sick deviants; if 50 percent of females are sexually abused as children, the problem is "normal" male socialization to take advantage of females.[7]

Lurking beneath prevalence rates is a more complicated question: Of those who have been sexually abused in childhood, how many "repress" the memory of the events? The idea of repression dates back to before Sigmund Freud, and was a key element in his description of the unconscious mind. Dreams, for example, did not simply recap the events of the day—they expressed powerful emotions or wishes through a filter of what the conscious mind could accept.

At an 1896 meeting in Vienna, Freud went public with a controversial theory: Incest is responsible for many, if not most, psychological problems. This "seduction theory," as it was called, proved unpopular among his colleagues.[8] Freud himself discarded it after a few years. He substituted the idea of infant sexuality and unconscious fantasies in its place.

The political implications of this move were enormous. Moreover, it is not at all clear that repression, which Freud called "the cornerstone on which the whole structure of psychoanalysis rests,"[9] even happens. David Holmes, a psychologist at the University of Kansas, says the field has yet to respond adequately to his 1974 paper undermining repression. In his 60 years of research, no one had ever produced evidence that people repress painful desires or events.[10]

Experts failed to reach an agreement on repression at a 1990 conference sponsored by the McArthur Foundation. "We spent three or four days hashing it out," Holmes said. "We reviewed all the research evidence. Everyone agreed you can't prove it in the lab—but, boy, you can sure see it when it happens."[11]

Yet when the experts reviewed videotapes of psychiatric interviews, no one could agree on when or if a subject was repressing. "And if you can't get two people to agree, you have no validity,"[12] said Holmes.

Berkeley sociologist Richard Ofshe agrees: "There has been no evidence for it in one hundred years. The whole idea of repression is a coke dream. It was Freud's idea of how to save his failing career."[13]

A string of recent books have also attacked psychoanalytic theory, causing *Time* magazine to wonder "Is Freud Dead?" on the cover of its Nov. 29, 1993 issue.[14] Among other critics quoted in the lead article was Frank Sulloway, a visiting scholar of science history at Michigan Institute of Technology, who said: "Psychoanalysis is built on quicksand. It's like a 10-story hotel sinking into an unsound foundation. And the analysts are in this building. You tell them it's sinking, and they say, 'It's O.K.; we're on the 10th floor.' "[15]

The issue has special relevance today, given the current uproar concerning "repressed memories." In recent years, critics from a variety of disciplines have attacked the recovery movement's preoccupation with self, causing many naive observers to rethink the idea that "if it's helping people, why tear it down?" Arguments over the nature and accuracy of repressed memories have generated sharp criticisms, showing that many of the ideas previously sanctioned as "help" have in fact been one-sided presentations of highly controversial issues.

Accusations of ideological over investment surfaced as a school of therapists (who had already cornered the incest market by touting themselves as "specialists") linked a host of individual problems—ranging from job loss to failed marriages—to sexual abuse concealed from memory. Thus recovery-oriented therapists were accused not only of participating in controversy, but of importing a reductionist polemic to areas previously considered a part of life and not controversial.

The divergence of opinions on recovered memory is not, as some have claimed, comparable to the "controversy" over whether the Holocaust really occurred. Holocaust denial is the crucible of a handful of extremists. As an issue, it has no academic standing. Doubts as to the reliability of repressed memories, on the other hand, have come from leaders at some of the nation's most highly recognized universities including Berkeley, Stanford, UCLA, Harvard, Yale, Carnegie Mellon and Johns Hopkins. The AMA has also issued a statement warning that the methodology of uncovering repressed memories is "fraught with problems of potential misapplication."[16] The American Psychiatric Association and the American Psychological Association have followed suit with warnings of their own.

A string of recent court cases with favorable judgments for the accused parents underscores the legitimacy of repressed memory as a controversy. In a 1995 judgment, Presiding Justice William Groff of the New Hampshire Superior Court wrote: "The phenomenon of memory repression, and the process of therapy used in these cases to recover the memories, have not gained general acceptance in the field of psychology; and are not scientifically reliable."[17] While advocates for the concept can also buttress their claims to legitimacy with court decisions and the backing of some prominent scholars, the controversy as a whole is a long way from Holocaust denial.

In the beginning, repressed memory lawsuits ran almost exclusively one way. Aided by the "delayed discovery" statutes adopted in 23 states to accommodate them, accusers sued their parents. Repressed memory also played a key role in many criminal cases; notably in the murder conviction of George Franklin, discussed later in this chapter. It is important to stress that the stakes riding on the validity of these memories are very high. To the extent that flaws may exist in widely-held (but controversial) theories supporting the delayed recall of traumatic memories or in the methods therapists have used to elicit and confirm them, this issue has led to the needless destruction of thousands of families and placed many innocent individuals behind bars. The tumultuous differences over repressed memory run much deeper than the political retaliation of a supposedly well-organized body of perpetrators in denial, as some have suggested.

Buying into Recovery

In 1988, B. Dalton's bookstore chain agreed to establish a recovery section, which was a tremendous breakthrough for the industry. This created legitimacy for recovery as a separate genre on par with psychology, history or science. Now publishers could showcase their interrelated products in one place.

Previously, books on eating disorders might have been found in "Diet and Nutrition." Books on alcoholic families were found in "Psychology" or "Marriage and the Family" sections. Within months, other booksellers followed suit. "Addiction and Recovery" remains a separate category in virtually all national bookstore chains today.

By 1993, sales of adult children and codependency books peaked. The foothold of recovery publishers on the book market gradually weakened as larger publishers lured the smaller companies' most successful authors with six-figure advances and promises of greater exposure. That is exactly what happened to HCI in the early 1990s. First Wayne Kritsberg, author of *The Adult Children of Alcoholics Syndrome*, went to Harper & Row. Then, John Bradshaw and relationships author John Lee of *The Flying Boy*, went to Bantam, and Janet Woititz and Robert Ackerman to Simon & Schuster.

Despite the undeniable interest by major publishers in exploiting the recovery genre, few made more than a cautious investment in the form of 10 to 15 new titles a year. Today, even this level of commitment has been scaled back. By early 1993, "backlist" recovery titles had overtaken the new releases in sales. Despite having been on the shelves for at least five years, old standbys such as *Codependent No More*, *Adult Children of Alcoholics* or *Bradshaw On: The Family* were now outperforming the new releases.

Books by parents accused of sexual abuse, skeptical experts and "retractors" (individuals who first thought they had recovered memories of abuse but changed their minds), also landed, appropriately, in the addiction-and-recovery sections of bookstores. After all, recovery books had played an indispensable role in the dissemination of incest survivor literature. And if there was a controversy, it was not limited to therapists' offices by any means. Talk shows, 12-step groups such as Incest Survivors Anonymous and survivor literature helped to saturate the culture with the same assumptions summed up most famously by Ellen Bass and Laura Davis in *The Courage to Heal*: "If you think you were abused and your life shows the symptoms, then you were."[18]

Paul McHugh, head of psychiatry at Johns Hopkins Medical School, called *The Courage to Heal* "the *Malleus Malificarum* of the incest movement,"[19] referring to the infamous 16th century witch-hunter's manual. Sales of the book testify to its influence. There are many similar books, an entire genre, promoting the idea that because abuse is so painful it is common for children to repress its memory. The authors received a substantial amount of air time on *Oprah* and *Sally Jesse Rafael*, which reached millions who may have never picked up a recovery book or gone to therapy.

Sales in one sub-genre, sexual abuse recovery, continued to climb. Borrowing from recovery literature, popular sexual abuse authors used generalized checklists and tendentious mass-diagnosis to advance explanations far more serious than those used for coping with alcoholism.

Psychologist Renee Fredrickson provided one such "symptom checklist" in her book, *Repressed Memories—A Journey to Recovery from Sexual Abuse*.[20] Fredrickson's list of symptoms are very similar to previously published ACoA or codependency "traits," only with a darker cast. For example, whereas Melody Beattie said some codependents "become withdrawn and isolated;"[21] Fredrickson wrote that victims of sexual abuse might agree with, "I am scared to be alone or to leave my house."[22] Whereas codependents on Beattie's list might "expect themselves to do everything perfectly;"[23] sexual abuse survivors on Fredrickson's might agree with, "I do some things to excess and I just don't know when to quit."[24]

On the other hand, there is a whole class of symptoms on Fredrickson's list that do not appear on ACoA or codependency lists, such as "I sometimes wake up feeling as if I am choking, gagging, or being suffocated" and "I have a strong sense that something terrible has happened to me."[25]

So it is disingenuous for therapists to rebut the entire case for false memories, as some have tried to do, on the grounds that many of these memories happen "spontaneously" and outside of therapy. Nor is anyone claiming that therapists, incest-recovery authors or fellow survivors are trying to brainwash people or deliberately implant memories. As a number of recent books by University of Washington psychologist Elizabeth Loftus, Richard Ofshe and others demonstrates, the process of acquiring a false memory happens naturally enough.[26] It does not require the participation of anyone with sinister motives—which is precisely what makes the situation so frightening.

The entire issue of repressed memory remains hopelessly controversial. Predictably, survivor advocates have diagnosed the False Memory Syndrome (FMS) Foundation and books criticizing memory retrieval as part of an anti-recovery "backlash." Some, such as co-authors Laura Davis and Ellen Bass of *The Courage to Heal* and Charles Whitfield, have responded with anti-backlash manifestos.

Anti-backlash responses resemble the traditional alcoholism field's responses to critics of the disease model. The most prominent habit both fields share is the upward skewing of odds, coupled with the reframing of odds as certainties. Some people say that a few of the memories may be false. Some people say that a few alcoholics may be able to drink safely again. Both are token concessions, which hold no meaning.

Testimonials

In a blazing silk dress matching her blue eyes, Marilyn Van Derber Atler looked positively radiant. A 1958 Miss America, Atler has had a lot of practice looking good "on the outside," apparently masking a pain she did not begin to comprehend until she was 24 years old. Atler told her story to 100 or so people in the auditorium of North Miami Community College, the crowning event of a two-day seminar on sexual abuse in February 1993.[27] The event was sponsored by the Joan E. Childs Institute of neighboring Hallandale, Florida, at that time one of approximately two dozen therapy institutes affiliated with the John Bradshaw Center in Rosemead, California.

A year or two earlier, the comedian Roseanne Barr turned heads by announcing that she recently remembered being abused by her mother at six months of age.[28] Like Roseanne, Atler was another celebrity quick to claim commonality with legions of abused children. Atler claimed her father, a prominent businessman, admitted the abuse to her privately, but threatened to kill himself if she told anyone.

The story would not be so remarkable had it ended there. Atler claimed the abuse took place from ages five to 13 years—yet she did not remember any of it until she was 24 years old. The warmly appreciative audience apparently needed no convincing.

Atler said she shut down the dark realities of her growing-up years by creating a separate entity who she called "the day child," who would cope and excel and handle whatever came her way. The tragedy was that the job of handling the worst that came her way was left entirely to her disembodied twin, "the night child." It wasn't until a pastoral counselor asked the question—had she been a victim of sexual molestation?—that "the floodgates opened" and the memories returned.[29]

Atler's lecture was well-rehearsed (identical almost word for word with a tape of a previous speech) and hard-hitting. In content and delivery, the words conveyed a strength of political activism one rarely heard at recovery conferences. "We must do our work," she reminded audiences, "not only for ourselves but for the children."[30]

She gave short shrift to the FMS Foundation—"My father would have been president of that organization and given them a million dollars"—and all but dismissed a question as to whether her perpetrator had been abused in his child-hood. "I don't know," she replied, "—and, 'frankly, Scarlett, I don't give a damn.' "[31]

It seems odd that Atler's memories returned the first time someone asked her if she had been sexually abused. Had the pastoral counselor's question been asked when she was 12, or 16 or even 20, what would Atler have answered then?

"No one did ask me,"[32] she replied when asked.

Vicki Lawrence, founder of a group called Incest/Sexual Abuse Survivors and Friends of Florida is a firm believer in repressed memories. Lawrence strained when trying to sum up the scope of abuse: "The judges don't understand, the lawyers don't understand, the doctors don't understand, even the psychologists don't understand totally, what we're dealing with in incest victims. It's all starting to come out now."[33]

One senses a fear among these people—that perhaps even the most ardent advocates of reform around child sexual abuse issues have underestimated the problem. The purpose of Lawrence's group is to remedy that problem with tougher child-abuse laws. Incest activists have found a sympathetic ear among legislators. In 1992, Florida joined 22 other states by extending the statutes of limitation in civil cases involving sexual assault to four years "from the time of discovery" or after the abuse is remembered.[34] In other words, a 40-year-old who has suddenly remembered being molested by her father at age five has four years to sue—even though the alleged incident took place 35 years ago.

Boiling Points

During the course of an investigation on repressed memories, I contacted Eleanor Goldstein, publisher at SIRS Mandarin. Goldstein, together with SIRS Mandarin researcher Kevin Farmer, published a book called *Confabulations: Creating False Memories, Destroying Families*. I joined them in 1992 in attending a meeting of roughly 600 mental health professionals and accused parents, sponsored by the FMS Foundation.

There were a number of interesting presentations. Paul McHugh of Johns Hopkins focused much of his lecture on the work of 19th century neurologist and psychiatrist Jean-Martin Charcot, who is regarded as one of the greatest figures in French medicine. He was the first to distinguish between the ordinary wasting away of the muscles and lateral sclerosis, as well as between multiple sclerosis and paralysis. His systemic neurology paved the way for the discovery of Lou Gehrig's Disease.

Charcot is also known for exploring the relationship between hypnosis and hysteria, and passed the interest onto his most famous pupil, Sigmund Freud. Charcot learned belatedly that some of the symptoms his "hysterical" patients exhibited, notably seizures, resulted from being housed in the same wing of the hospital as the epileptics. Once Charcot followed the suggestion of an assistant and housed the two groups separately, the hysteric patients' epileptic seizures stopped.[35]

McHugh argued that flashbacks have never represented

events reproduced so much as worst fears imagined. "Abandon flashbacks as confirming abuse," McHugh warned, "they are, rather, much more likely worst fears generated in the context of therapy; and may represent not post-traumatic states from the abuse, but post-traumatic states induced by therapy."[36]

Women who had "retracted" or taken back their memories also spoke at the meeting. Some of them had lawsuits pending against their former therapists. Like detonated TNT caps on opposite sides of an implosion bomb, ultimate accusations had met with ultimate denials at the epicenter of a "critical mass,"[37] a metaphor borrowed from Renee Fredrickson.

Divining the Past

Gary Stout of Michigan provides the following account of his sister-in-law's experience with repressed memory therapy:

> The schools told her her son was hyperactive. The counselor referred her to a therapist, who expanded on it. It's hard to get much detail on what's going on in her life now, since she has decided that her dad abused her and that I am guilty, too. My presence causes her great emotional turmoil.
>
> Supposedly there were five individuals that her father had murdered. There may have been an unsolved murder or multiple killing, but how much of that is legend I don't know. She said, "I remember my father doing that, and I remember him burying them in the front yard, in the car." He just put the whole car in the ground.
>
> The therapist gave her a stainless steel divining rod with a forked end, like I've seen guys using twigs trying to find water. She was holding it a special way—you have

to hold it the right way. Almost like the Ouija board thing. She's following that around saying, "Here! It's down there!" She and her husband just tore up the yard. Her husband was an auto mechanic. Twelve- and 16-hour days were not unusual for this guy. She was stretching them to 20 and 22. But he was trying to support her emotionally, trying to keep everything intact.

Finally her mom and stepdad moved to Texas. The mom's reputation was ruined. How do you bring someone back to reality when they have moved into a nether land? It doesn't make sense to me.[38]

In 1994, John Bence was conducting a class at the Seminole Vocational Educational Center in Largo, Florida, when a detective appeared, read him his rights, handcuffed him and took him to the Pinellas County Jail. For the next four days and three nights, Bence sat in his cell thinking, "This can't be happening. It isn't real. This kind of thing doesn't happen to innocent people."[39]

Tori Bence, then 24, had told detectives that her father began raping her at age seven, and it had continued until she was 17. Among the crimes cited in the 16-count indictment, John Bence had allegedly jumped out of a closet and sodomized his daughter on one occasion. On another, he placed a knife inside her vagina and at the same time had oral sex with her.[40]

She didn't remember any of this until Christmas 1992. While talking to a friend, suddenly, Tori testified, she remembered her father leaping out of the closet. She began seeing an unlicensed therapist who had uncovered memories of sexual abuse in her own life. The therapist encouraged Tori to file criminal charges against her father, which she did. If convicted of capital sexual battery, John Bence faced life in prison with no possibility of parole for 25 years.

Clearwater attorney Denis De Vlaming, who represented John Bence, began checking into the allegations. Medical records from Tori's childhood had long since been destroyed. Her pediatrician said he could recall nothing about a knife wound to the vagina, and said he would have recognized such a wound had one been inflicted.

It is possible for a knife to be placed inside someone's vagina without causing a wound. But when De Vlaming found a similar incident described in *The Courage to Heal*, the prominent incest survivor self-help book, the case against John Bence began to unravel. Tori had read *The Courage to Heal* as part of her therapy. The book also contains an account of a father jumping out of a closet and sodomizing his daughter. A third incident, in which Tori recalled her father tying her hands with clothesline rope, was also in the book.[41]

Once confronted with the similarities between Tori's memories and the book, prosecutors declined to press forward with the case. A judge dismissed all 16 counts of sexual battery against John Bence and the Pinellas County school system allowed him to return to work. Still, De Vlaming remembers the Bence case as one that could have gone either way for his client.

"The prosecutors felt, 'If she's giving us all these details, she must be telling us the truth,'" De Vlaming said in an interview. "But that's very fallacious. We discovered that a self-help book had basically told her how she had been molested."[42]

In the end, De Vlaming said, "It was too coincidental to have these multiple incidences of abuse and say, 'These things happened to me;' and 'They also happened in the book.'"[43]

A Stalled Discussion

Since the FMS Foundation's inception in 1992, a flurry of arguments and counter arguments have been tossed back and forth. Every position has been articulated and re-articulated, to the point at which both sides—incest therapists on one side, the FMS Foundation on the other—can anticipate the other's arguments and responses several moves in advance.

Repressed memory is a polarized topic reflecting not only different perceptions of presumably shared experiences, but different values and belief systems among its combatants.

The motive of economic interests must also be considered. When John Bradshaw's reputation was unfairly tarnished by a rumor that he'd returned to drinking, he sought out—and received—a full and unconditional pardon through *Changes* magazine.[44] But when the subject turned to the careers and reputations of others wrongly accused, his outlook changed. Bradshaw's skill at wordplay ranks higher than that of any other recovery star. In his most recent book, *Family Secrets*, he defines the word "repression" by saying that "these memories [of abuse] can be forgotten as a result of psychological processes whose nature is not fully understood"[45]—or documented; or verified to the satisfaction of reputable psychologists and psychiatrists in the field.

Research support for the concept of repressed memories is almost totally lacking. Stories about incest and stories about someone falling off the wagon are not exactly analogous. But some of these abuse incidents would be unbelievable even in *The Twilight Zone*. It is much easier to imagine an alcoholic relapsing than a CEO of a major retail chain having the time and energy to moonlight as a satanic priest, decapitating his pets and holding rituals in the woods. These are just a few of the charges recently leveled at one South Florida executive in a lawsuit brought by his two daughters, both of whom claim to have recovered their memories in therapy.

This man had no public venue through which he could be quickly exonerated. He could not even contest the suit without alienating his own board of directors, who maintained it would be better to pay the requested $150,000 settlement than weather the adverse publicity of a trial. His case is exceptional.

Richard Ofshe has called repressed memory "the major psychological quackery of the 20th century."[46] Ofshe investigated Synanon—which was a cult, plain and simple. Its mission was to cure drug addicts.

The cult of recovered memory is much more difficult to describe or define. It exists in no one place, nor is it subject to the dictates of a single leader. Instead of stopping drug addiction, recovered memory therapists tend to see addiction and a whole range of other behaviors as symptoms of underlying Post-traumatic Stress. Instead of "emotional haircuts," recovered memory therapists often give unfounded reassurances similar to the following passage from *The Courage to Heal*: "It is natural that you have periodic doubts of your experience. But that's because accepting memories is painful, not because you weren't abused."[47]

During a telephone conversation with Ofshe, I asked what his observations were concerning the similarities between the widespread acceptance in the early 1970s of Synanon and current theories of memory retrieval: "They both illustrate the fragility, a lack of a kind of critical mass in the mental health field," Ofshe answered, adding that the absence of a single dominant body of coherent thought has made psychology vulnerable. "The practical skills of mental health professionals—their depth of knowledge and confidence are so slim—they are influenced by the mass media, the same as we all are."[48]

When Synanon launched its public relations campaign, therapists eagerly bought into it. Experts endorsed the methods that were slowly turning Synanon into a destructive cult and lent them credibility. Failure to do so would have meant dishonoring the metaphorical common man, whose street smarts had formed the basis of Synanon and to whom mental health professionals felt somehow indebted.

Couldn't the same be happening with so many professionals embracing the mind's wholesale ability to repress a decade or more of sexual abuse, torture and even murder, despite the hugely controversial techniques used for retrieving those memories? Failure to do so would mean dishonoring the survivors—a political crime in this day and age—or even "re-victimizing" them by failing to believe their truths.

Elizabeth Loftus successfully implanted false memories of being lost at a shopping mall at a younger age in five out of five subjects. In each case, Loftus employed a sibling to assist with the experiment, who "helped" in the recollection process.[49]

When the space shuttle Challenger exploded in 1986, Emory psychologist Ulric Neisser saw an opportunity to test ordinary human memory. The day after the accident, Neisser asked his freshmen students to write down where they were and what they were doing when they first heard the news. He put their responses in a drawer.

Three years later, Neisser reassembled many of those same students, now seniors, and repeated the question:

Where were you when you heard that the Challenger had exploded? He also asked them to rate their degree of confidence in their memories.

Many of the students answered incorrectly, some said they were in a bar with their friends when in fact they were in their dormitories studying or vice versa. Some said they heard the news from another student when in fact they had seen the broadcast on television. The most striking of Neisser's findings were the almost inverse correlations between certainty of belief and accuracy (assuming that the recollections the day after the event were the accurate ones). Many of the students who were "positive" they remembered where they were had it wrong, while those whose recollections were accurate tended to be less sure.[50]

Members of the survivor community are familiar with these studies, and they are not impressed. As Vicki Lawrence says, "Being lost in a shopping mall is one thing. Being fucked by your father is another."[51]

Responses from incest specialists are less graphic but qualitatively similar. "Trauma sets up new rules for memory,"[52] writes psychologist Lenore Terr, whose interviews with 20 children whose abuse was documented revealed some amnesia. In fact, Terr says, repeated assaults correlated with more forgetting than with children who had been abused or traumatized only once.[53]

According to Harvard psychiatrist Bessel Van Der Kolk, repeated molestation causes children to "disconnect" emotionally in ways that affect memory as well. "The emotional sensations related to trauma are remembered through a different memory, either as bodily sensations or visual images,"[54] Van Der Kolk writes.

John Bradshaw cites Van Der Kolk's work as evidence for

the existence of repressed memories.[55] But he does not address those critics who note that Van Der Kolk seems to have arrived at this knowledge through speculation, without supporting evidence. Even if such a thing as repressed memories can happen, they ask, how do you tell a true repressed memory from a false one?

Given the enormous influences of peer groups, recovery literature and the testimony of experts such as Lenore Terr and Harvard's Judith Herman—not to mention overtly suggestive techniques of therapists who pressure patients to come up with images of abuse—how does someone guard against "confabulation" (defined as the recall of images which may contain seeds of literal or metaphorical truth, but which have then been greatly enhanced by imagination or suggestion)? This, no one seems to know for sure. Columbia University psychiatrist Richard Gardner said:

> There is no question that people repress memories, but how is it that people who have been subjected to any other trauma known to humanity somehow remember it? People who were in concentration camps in World War II do not have to go to therapy to remember their experience. I say wait until we in the mental health profession have developed criteria to distinguish true from false.[56]

Ofshe stopped short of even this, "The fact that you can be reminded of something doesn't mean you repressed it," he said. "We don't wake up to the alarm every day with the conscious knowledge of everything that has happened in our lives."[57] People forget things, Ofshe said. With a little help, memories from childhood can be retrieved. Some of these retrieved memories will be innocuous, others irrelevant, still others painful. When a patient is given time to ponder whether exploitative sexual acts occurred—and the suggestion that perhaps something did happen—it is easy enough to produce dozens, perhaps hundreds of images of whatever the therapist or others have suggested.[58]

Reviewing the Evidence

Despite the thousands of pages on contemporary bookshelves about how the mind represses traumatic events, a sobering counter argument can be gleaned from only five pages. Most of the ink in support of repressed memories is anecdotal. The studies most often cited are examined by Harvard psychiatrists Harrison Pope and James Hudson in a 1995 issue of *Psychological Medicine*, published by Cambridge University Press.

Pope and Hudson note that since sexual abuse is widespread, afflicting a conservative 10% of women and 5% of men, there are at least 14 million survivors in the United States. "If repression occurred in only 10% of these cases, at least 1,400,000 [sic] Americans, and millions more worldwide, now harbour such repressed memories. Given this huge pool of predicted cases, one might expect to find in the literature various published studies of patients exhibiting well-documented cases of repression."[59]

Credible accounts of *psychogenic* amnesia, the authors stipulate, must exclude "cases in which victims simply tried not to think about the events" or pretended they did not occur; cases of ordinary forgetting. "Some experiences, though clearly meeting published research criteria for sexual abuse, may not be particularly memorable to a child."[60] For repressed memory to be proven, it must be documented, and it must be "too striking to be normally forgettable."[61]

Pope and Hudson then review four of the most widely-cited studies purporting to demonstrate repressed sexual abuse. While it is always best to read both sides of any issue, the following summations are presented for the benefit of the mildly curious who may have assumed that more evidence existed, amidst less genuine controversy, than is the case.

The Herman & Schatzow Study (1987):

Claims: 14 of 53 women in a therapy group for incest survivors displayed severe amnesia of the abuse.

Problems: Whether it is fair or not, Pope and Hudson chose to discount amnesia of abuse occurring at age five or earlier, citing previous studies indicating that children have "nearly complete amnesia for events before the age of three, and substantial amnesia for events before the age of six." This requirement reduces Herman and Schatzow's pool of subjects. Although 40% of the 53 subjects obtained corroborating evidence of the incest, it is not clear how many of those had amnesia. And some of this corroboration consisted of discovery that this same perpetrator had also abused someone else.[62] Pope and Hudson write:

> In short, it is not certain that any of the 3 subjects met both the criteria of clear amnesia and clear confirmation of trauma. Indeed, of the four case examples given, three do not meet the criteria (1 and 2 did not have amnesia, and 4 had virtually no confirmation.) Case 3 apparently had at least partial amnesia, and good confirmatory evidence. But even this case, it appears, is not actually a real person, since the authors explain that "all examples cited are composites of several cases."[63]

The Briere & Conte Study (1993):

Claims: 59% of 450 patients who had been sexually abused

had, for at least some period of time, been unable to remember the abusive incidents. (This appears to have been the source for John Bradshaw's opening statement in a *Lear's* Magazine article, that 60% of abuse victims repress the memory.)[64]

Problems: Evidence for the above claim consists of the fact that 59% of the study subjects answered "yes" to the question: "During the period of time between when the first forced sexual experience happened and your 18th birthday was there ever a time when you could not remember the forced sexual experience?" The study seems to assume that a "yes" answer to the above question means a traumatic memory had been repressed. But no evidence is mentioned that might confirm that this abuse occurred. "Neither is it clear what portion of the subjects had experienced abuse sufficiently traumatic that they would reasonably be expected to remember it always,"[65] Pope and Hudson write.

Moreover, the fact that the study subjects were, according to Briere and Conte, "recruited by their therapists," who are elsewhere described as belonging to "an informal abuse treatment referral network," leaves open the possibility of suggestion.[66] Given that there has been no experimental evidence for the repression of memory, it is up to investigators to prove that this repression does occur if it is to be established as scientific fact.

The Loftus, Polonsky & Fullilove Study (1994):

Claims: 19% of 52 women with abuse histories reported having forgotten the abuse "for a period of time and only later had the memory return."[67]

Problems: No independent confirmation that abuse occurred. No exploration of whether the incidents in question were repressed because they were traumatic, minimized or denied because they were embarrassing or forgotten because they were insignificant.[68]

The Williams Study (1994):

Claims: 38% of 129 women selected from hospital admissions between 1973 and 1975 (when the oldest woman in the sample was 12 years old and the youngest was ten months) did not report this abuse to an interviewer until 17 years later when the subjects were now between the ages of 18 and 31:

- Even though these same women had previously been asked detailed questions about sexual abuse in their pasts (including incidents they had not themselves perceived as abusive but which others might have).
- Even though many of them had volunteered detailed descriptions of other painful or embarrassing childhood incidents.
- And even though their sexual abuse was already confirmed in hospital records.

Williams concluded that most of these women had repressed the memories of their assaults.[69]

Problems: That conclusion rests on the inference that non-reporting equates with amnesia—a leap in logic, Pope and Hudson contend. Half of the non-reporters had been under age six at the time of the abuse, leaving the door of normal childhood amnesia conspicuously open. Williams noted that these hospital visits occurred over the course of criminal investigations stemming from reported abuse. The abuse itself was not always violent; about a third involved touching and fondling only (which, while admittedly repugnant, could have been forgotten). More significantly, a number of studies performed since the early 1960s have documented that somewhere between 25% and 50% of people underreport life events such as doctor visits, hospital admissions and car accidents for indeterminate reasons.[70] As for the memory of abuse, Pope and Hudson cite a 1990 study by D.D. Femina which, like the Williams study, also found a 38% non-reporting rate among 69 young adults whose childhood victimization from mostly physical assaults had been documented. Femina and colleagues then conducted "clarification interviews" with eight of the 18 "deniers." When confronted in the second interview, all eight turned out to have remembered the incidents. For varied psychological reasons, they had simply withheld the information from investigators.[71] Pope and Hudson continue:

> For example, one woman, "whose mother had attempted to drown her in childhood and whose stepfather had sexually abused her, minimized any abuse at all on follow-up." But in the clarification interview, when presented with this history, she admitted, "I didn't say it cuz I wanted to forget. I wanted it to be private. I only cry when I think about it." Similarly, one man, who as a boy was frequently beaten by his father, also minimized any history of abuse on the first interview. When presented with the history in the clarification interview, he acknowledged the beatings but said, "my father is doing well now. If I told now, I think he would kill himself."[72]

Thus, Williams' 38% rate of non-reporting might be readily explained as a combination of cases of early childhood amnesia, cases of ordinary forgetfulness and perhaps many cases of failure to report information actually remembered.[73]

Pope and Hudson claim that "we found only four applicable studies in the literature" on the repression of memories of child sexual abuse.[74] They are not examples from the academic literature in support of the mind's ability to repress years of painful abuse–they are the literature. The repressed memory and Multiple Personality Disorder (MPD) experts tend to buttress their arguments with the above studies, particularly those of Judith Herman, John Briere and Linda Meyer-Williams.

Finally, if the standards to which Pope and Hudson would have us adhere to in order to be convinced seem a bit stingy (what with the exclusion of all alleged victims under six and the number of cases they lump into "ordinary forgetting"); consider this: If abuse is so widespread, and repression so common, as the Renee Fredericksons and John Bradshaws of the world have claimed, why has this repression been so difficult to prove?

If the theories that an entire body of psychotherapists seems to have embraced were true, there should be ample research evidence of sexual acts perpetrated upon children, the traumatic character of which requires no interpretation–acts proven to have occurred, their memory in victims demonstrably repressed. If the evidence could show that some people have experienced this phenomenon, it would be easier to accept the explanation for others who cannot supply evidence and in such a favorable climate should not be asked to do so. Where is this evidence?

The High Costs of Memory

Therapists who want to help America rediscover its abuse memories stress the long-term benefits of healing. What they often neglect to discuss are the costs. At a lecture for the 1993 FMS meeting, Psychologist Jack Leggett, vice president for clinical services at Integrated Behavioral Health, outlined abuses of an unforgettable sort, on behalf of clients supposedly suffering from Post-traumatic Stress Disorder (PTSD) and Multiple Personality Disorder.

> One plan [that] my company manages the services for has seen 88% increases in three successive years. That is, an 88% average increase each year, one year more than doubling the costs for mental health coverage. These costs have been driven largely by inpatient treatment offered for adolescence and chemical dependency. But as we get on top of those and start managing those cases, the game changes.[75]

It changes in the direction of treatment for sexual abuse which the client has not yet fully appreciated or recalled. Although Leggett found that "specialists" in multiple personality and repressed memories charged more than twice as much as did "generalists" over nine months ($1,522.80 a case for specialists, compared to $608.22 for generalists), the words "MPD" and "PTSD" seldom appeared on claim forms. Specialists preferred non-controversial diagnoses such as major depression and anxiety disorders.

"The problem," Leggett said, "is that providers who style themselves 'expert' in these areas tend to be the ones who view symptoms of almost any type as indicative of memories of underlying sexual abuse."[76]

Those who wind up in this kind of treatment can drive up health costs for everyone. In "a case that is, unfortunately, not unlike others," reviewers at Integrated Behavioral Health noticed that 17% of one company's employees had used the mental health benefit on their policies. This stood out. Other companies were averaging utilization rates of 8% to 10%. Of that 17%, two-tenths of 1% was using up 30% of the total mental health dollars spent on the company.[77]

Looking further, insurance investigators found repeated hospitalizations, some of which lasted for months at a time. Patients and every member of their families were seen two to four times a week for hypnotic regression—"hundreds and hundreds of sessions, frequently with substantial deterioration over time."[78]

"I got treatment plans, they demanded that I authorize six months inpatient care on an 'abreaction' unit where people would be tied to a bed in five-point restraints, hypnotically regressed to recover their memories and abreact the trauma,"[79] said Leggett.

Nor are the costs necessarily congregated to inpatients. This same treatment provider billed between $2 million and $4 million for outpatient therapy in a single year; with one patient racking up $250,000 with eight to 10 sessions a week over four years, and a dozen others with outpatient bills hitting six figures inside of a year.[80]

The chemical dependency notion of "treating the whole family" slides neatly into sexual abuse therapy. "I've got a therapist seeing everybody in the family up to three times a week, sixteen sessions a week," Leggett said. "Do the numbers. Instead of averaging 10 to 20 sessions, you average between 50 and 200 sessions a week at $90 an hour."[81]

Once the abuses are discovered and funds to the providers cut off, some of these same patients need genuine treatment to recover from those abuses caused "iatrogenically" by treatment. Meanwhile, whether the treatment is good or bad; families, employers and individuals must make up the 20% to 50% not covered by insurance. Leggett said he has frequently seen individual co-payments of $100 a week. One therapist billed 21 hours with the same patient in a single day.[82]

Until insurers learn to contain the huge costs inflicted by a tiny percentage of mental health policy holders and their "specialist" helpers, the following trends are likely to continue:

- Higher deductibles. More businesses will have to drop out of the coverage marathon.
- Reduced benefits. All childhood behavior disorders will be eliminated in many plans. So will chronic illnesses. Many plans will choose to stop covering behavioral health altogether.
- Less state money for victim's assistance or aid to the poor.
- Higher taxes. Patients pay only 5% of their total health costs now. Public and private reimbursement systems split the balance. Government funds are getting hit just as hard as private insurers by questionable hospitalizations and unnecessary or harmful treatments.[83]

"If a mental health benefit gets into national health care, we'll all be paying for this stuff,"[84] Leggett said.

The Therapists

How, exactly, do therapists specializing in sexual abuse traverse these delicate issues when they surface? What role do they, themselves play? Regarding these questions, Gayle Brooks, a psychologist at the Renfrew Center in Pompano Beach, Florida commented:

> We get caught up in truth sometimes. It's not so important that we get at the truth. I'm sure that there have been some families that have been injured in some way. But because we have not been dealing with sexual abuse openly as a society, perhaps for awhile we need

to really err on [the side of] believing people, because for far too long there has been such a push to suppress it. And I think we need to be encouraging people to be able to speak about what has happened. And if there are going to be a few people in there who are speaking out of other reasons, that may occur. But I think for the larger majority of people, that may be their truth that they are speaking about.[85]

Joan Leshner, a Masters-level counselor in Miami, Florida responded:

I don't know if I would go along with the belief that it happened to someone if they were just speaking from their head and said, "Well, my father abused me when I was five," and I didn't see a *body* validating it. And when I say that, I mean people that had penises in their mouths all of a sudden start choking. They're lying on my mat and they go, "I don't know what's happening," and they gag and make these horrible noises.

And I also believe they don't want to believe this is true. This happens all the time. The first time it comes out on the mat, like, for example, "Oh, my god, I think he—oh, god, please don't let it be true! It's not true, right, Joan? It's not true!"

And I say, *"Well, of course it's not true if it's not your truth . . ."* Only if it gets repeated over and over and over, over a long period of time, then maybe we'll think it is truth.[86]

Unlike the traditional office Brooks keeps at the Renfrew Center, Leshner's office is host to a mattress on the floor and at least a dozen stuffed animals. Leshner is casually dressed.

She sits on the floor. She thinks ABC's *PrimeTime Live* took hypnotherapist D. Corydon Hammond's comments out of context in its profile of him. Hammond is a leading exponent of the theory that the United States houses an array of underground satanic networks. *PrimeTime* had taken a hidden camera into one of his lectures.

Most misleading, said Leshner, "the interviewer interviewed the (accused) parents. My people's families look *so good* on the outside. They are deacons in the church."[87] Her view of the television piece was shared by angry survivors on computer bulletin boards across the country, who were now referring to the magazine show as *SlimeTime*.

The following passage is taken from Hammond's *Handbook of Hypnotic Suggestions and Metaphors*. "Screening Procedure to Assist in Early Identification of Ritualistic Abuse Victims" is taken from the sub-section on "Metaphors with Multiple Personality and Trauma Patients." Italicized items on the list "are believed to be more likely to elicit a fear reaction in ritualistic abuse victims," Hammond says. Thus, "as a tentative clinical tool for which there is currently no data on reliability or validity, I have begun asking hypnotized MPD patients about their fears:"[88]

"Is anyone inside afraid of . . . ?" [Patients not diagnosed as MPD may be asked, "Is any part of you afraid of . . . ?"]

1. Heights	2. Doctors
3. Dentists	4. *Stars*
5. Speaking in Public	6. *Fire*
7. Being teased	8. *Knives*
9. Crowds	10. *Blood*
11. Sudden Noises	12. Being Criticized
13. *Being photographed*	14. *Dying*

15. Large open spaces   16. *Candles*
17. Sick people   18. *Feces*
19. Dogs   20. Cats
21. *Animals being hurt*   22. *Robes* [89]

"It's real scary to see who's doing some of this work," commented Joan Childs, another Masters-level therapist, curled up on a sofa in her plush suite overlooking the Florida Intracoastal Waterway. "This is such a delicate thing. This can destroy families."[90] As mentioned earlier, the Joan E. Childs Center was one of 20 or so counseling centers to whom John Bradshaw lent his name nationwide. However, at the time of this interview in 1993, Bradshaw was in the process of withdrawing his affiliation from most of them. Now she would like to clarify how easy it is to wrongly perceive recovered memory work.

One of her clients began recalling traumatic memories from infancy, of being invaded somehow, a diaper being rudely tugged off. The culprit turned out to be a rambunctious puppy. A therapist can never be too careful, she says.

At the same time, the problem of sexual abuse is immense. Childs quotes an article from *Lear's* magazine—one in three girls is abused by their 18th birthday, and one in five boys.[91] "Multiple Personality Disorder has always been much more common than was once thought, Bradshaw and Alice Miller are bringing it out of the woodwork, but it was always there," she said.[92]

Childs arranged for two of her clients, a South Floridian and his sister-in-law in New England, to meet with me and discuss the memories of childhood sexual abuse they recovered while attending Childs's workshops. Tom, who was 51, told how a year earlier he was thumbing through his own self-help book looking for a way out of his suicidal thoughts. Tom made his first million by his 40th birthday as a real-estate broker who also fixed up homes. But he was not happy.

"I was truly a human doing, not a human being," he says. "I was a workaholic."[93] For as long as he could remember, Tom had always felt as if he were two people. Half of him was loving, caring and sensitive, the other half was "cold, aggressive and manipulative," he said. "Which side was the real me?"[94]

After retiring at the age of 45 with a net worth of several million dollars, the edifice he had worked so hard to maintain began to fall apart.

"It got worse then. I had no way to keep the stuff buried."[95] The "stuff" had been going on since Tom was 16, the year he put a loaded shotgun into his mouth and pulled the trigger. For some reason it didn't fire. Now with opportunities most people only dream about, Tom wished he could give his money away and live on the streets. The thought of crashing his car into a tree seemed like "the perfect answer, because life insurance would pay."[96] He even got together 200 Valium pills so that if the time came when he simply did not want to live anymore, he would be ready.

Tom checked himself into the Institute for Living, in Hartford, Connecticut. While there, he was interviewed by a hypnotherapist.

"The guy was doing a work-up, when out of the blue he said, 'Were you ever abused as a child?' With that came a vision of a child huddled up protecting himself against a wall."[97] Tom guessed the child's age at about six but wasn't sure. There were many blank spaces in his past. Elementary school was pretty much a blur and he had few photos to use as references.

Not long after his release from the Institute for Living,

Tom saw the movie *Prince of Tides*. Based on the Pat Conroy novel, the movie tells the story of a man haunted by sexual violence from his childhood and his eventual psychiatric breakthrough. Walking out of the movie Tom found himself thinking, "You know, there must be help for me, too." Then he asked himself, "Why the hell did I say that?" [98]

With the help of another therapist, he started getting more pictures of his past. The flashbacks still seemed distant, but they were coming. Then Tom attended a John Bradshaw/Joan Childs-sponsored weekend retreat, and had the opportunity to do some work with Childs. He's glad he did.

"Joan opened the doors to sexual abuse," Tom said. "She just gives you permission to let it out. When the floodgates were opened, I was hooked."[99]

Tom's mother died three years before he started treatment. While she was alive he called her everyday. They were close, much more so than he and his father, whom Tom remembers as "physically there but preoccupied with things of his own."[100] Yet at the time of the interview Tom remembered his mother as an "extremely domineering, violent person"[101] who on a weekly basis dragged him upstairs by the hair for "punishment enemas, huge ones." This picture is darker and more detailed than his previous image of the enemas.

"I kind of knew but I wasn't putting it all together," Tom said of his fuller memory. "I remember all of the pain of it, getting smacked around if any of it leaked out, if I didn't hold in the whole bag."[102] At the retreat with Childs, Tom also remembered his mother lying down with him when he was eight or nine and fondling him sexually. This was new.

Though he did not own a gun, Tom began to fantasize about having one and wiping out his whole family. "I must have killed them all a million times," he said. "Just shooting them, stabbing them, cutting their arms and legs and fingers and feet."[103] Going into a McDonald's and blowing people away was not such a strange idea, he thought. In fact, he felt he was near the level of rage it must take to do that.

In August 1992, Tom called Adult Survivors of Childhood Abuse (ASCA) Treatment Center in Bellflower, California, and reserved a two-week slot. The clinic, run by psychiatrist and HCI author Mohan Nair, specialized in memory retrieval. Its full-page ad in *Changes* magazine drew the eye to its pinkish-red backdrop over which is laid a close-up photograph of a knot of petrified wood and the following message in bold yellow type: "REMEMBERING INCEST & CHILDHOOD ABUSE IS THE FIRST STEP TO HEALING." In the background is a list of 29 problems including "irritable bowel, low self-esteem, obesity, A.C.O.A., depression, hopelessness, rage, religious addiction, substance abuse, relapse, parenting problems, sexual fear, sexual compulsion, mood swings, self mutilation and multiple personality." The ad promises to "help bring up forgotten memories through our powerful combination of massage, body work, hypnosis, psychodrama and sodium brevital interviewing."[104]

"I got the truth serum and that opened some doors,"[105] Tom said, referring to the sodium brevital interviewing. Sodium brevital is a trance-inducing drug that ASCA and other clinics have used as the centerpiece for a technique called "narcoanalysis." Many people mistakenly refer to the drug (or its chemical cousins, sodium amytal and sodium pentothal) as "truth serum," perhaps believing that people who are hypnotized are more likely to tell the truth. In fact, people under hypnosis are more likely to believe that what they are saying is true, but their heightened suggestibility undermines the accuracy of these perceptions.

In 1987, the Arkansas Supreme Court disallowed all "hypnotically refreshed" testimony after receiving evidence that hypnotic subjects often fill in memory gaps with invention, which they unconsciously convert to the realm of fact with astonishing emotional certainty.[106]

ASCA staff videotaped Tom's sodium brevital interview then had him watch the video every day for two weeks.

"A therapist is available" to help interpret the interview, Tom said. "You are kept under close scrutiny."[107]

Following his release from ASCA, Tom's memories became clearer over the next several weeks. Now back in individual therapy with Childs, he remembered that his brother had raped and sodomized him several times by a rock pile while a friend held him down. The brother had already admitted to bullying him. After Tom confronted him through a letter several months before going to ASCA about physical and emotional abuse, the brother recalled an incident Tom had forgotten.

"He said that one day, I had him pinned and I wanted to bash his head in with a rock."[108]

However, the brother had denied any sexual molestation and Tom had not confronted him about that. The only reason he maintained any contact with his older brother was for his father's sake. But as long as he did have contact, Tom thought he might as well get whatever verification he could.

"I try to verify pieces of the memory without bringing up the total issue," he said. "I'd ask my brother, 'Did you remember behind the barn, behind a rock pile and the pond?' And he said yes. It fills up a lot of my picture. I'm filling it in and I'm verifying it. I know inside me it's all happened."[109]

Tom said he's a lot happier these days. He doesn't feel the conflict of being two people anymore—one who wanted to live and let live, the other who wanted to die and take others down with him. A lifelong fear of snakes has abated. He's thinking about writing a book about his recovery. In 1993, he was still going to therapy every now and then, but not in the same intensive way as before.

Seeing Tom get better helped his sister-in-law Cheryl's decision to see Childs, too. Cheryl is the wife of Tom's younger brother Steve, who still lives in the New England area and whom Tom calls "a daredevil kind of guy."[110] Cheryl attended three weekend retreats in a row. Childs considers Cheryl a good test case because "she fits all of the symptoms"[111] of a sexual abuse survivor, yet prior to therapy had no inkling that she was one. Tom's resolution triggered Cheryl's decision to find out if there was something in her past that she too might have been blocking out. At the first retreat in South Florida, Cheryl jokingly asked Childs why she couldn't hug people.

"So we went into a trance," Cheryl recalled, "and my body reactions just went into a little ball. After that I just wanted to know more."[112] At a second three-day retreat in North Carolina, more emotions came but still no memories. It wasn't until the third and final day of a third retreat with Childs that something happened.

"There was another girl going through something," Cheryl said. "She was abused by her father, and seeing her go through it opened something in my mind."

Cheryl's first abuse image came during an exercise in which participants were writing with their opposite hands. "Everything falls into place once you get a little piece," she said. "My mind must have been ready to receive it."[113]

Cheryl saw an image of someone standing naked before her in the basement of the house in which she grew up. The face was not clear at first and initially she had thought it might belong to her uncle. After further work with Childs, however, she came to remember that it was actually her grandfather's face, and that it was her now-deceased grandfather who had molested her. Like Tom, Cheryl feels much better since this discovery.

"It is possible to get the person wrong," Childs said. "It's like anything else."[114]

During our discussion, Childs said that seeing other people find their memories can help a person find his or her own.

> People are connecting on a feeling level, and they're looking at someone's work. That gives them permission to allow themselves to feel their own feelings and connect with their own experiences. All of a sudden they're in process work. It's like a domino principle. It's like a nudist colony, people just strip right down and all that toxic shame just comes out. It's a cleansing and a healing. Another person sees that happening, and somewhere inside their own psyches, they say, "It's okay for me to feel this way, too." It's more powerful [in a group] than one-on-one because you're getting validated.[115]

According to ASCA social worker Rebecca Davis, it is rare for a patient to go through the program and not recover a memory of sexual abuse. Therapists make recall easier by pointing out subtle reactions to questions that a patient may have missed.

"Sometimes they won't say anything," Davis said, "but we'll see that they have a lot of rapid eye movement and their breath is coming fast. Then you can say, 'When you were asked this question, you became extremely agitated.' "[116]

"We never tell people that what you remembered is real," said Mohan Nair. When asked by memory experts for a response to growing concerns that therapy patients could be led into inaccurate beliefs, Nair tittered "You mean 'False Memory Syndrome'?"[117]

When asked about the FMS Foundation, Childs said:

> I don't know much about what they're saying. I am not an authority in that particular context. Doing this for 15 years, I've seen people who have been blocked, and through regressive hypnosis have had corrective experiences. And I don't need any more evidence than that. It's just like past-life experiences which have also been corrective. There's a 50% chance they're right, and a 50% chance I'm right. I'm very careful, very cautious. And if it's [not] really authentic, if it's not true, it will get booted out eventually."[118]

Tom brushed off the possibility that many of the sexual-abuse memories being discovered these days are not real in a literal, historical sense. "So what if a therapy is based on false information," he asked, "if it could yield positive results for the patient?"[119]

Afterthoughts

In science, the burden of proof is on the people making the claim, and the people making these claims have failed to supply the proof. This obligation is doubly relevant since abuse memories require abusers, and if false memories have been created, nourished and championed as true, then an appalling cruelty has taken place.

How many falsely accused parents will die of old age before their adult children have second thoughts about the accuracy of their memories? To the extent that young children have been pressured through suggestive questioning to "reveal" abuse at the hands of grandparents or day care workers, what will happen to these children when they grow older, expose themselves to the ambiguities surrounding this issue, and begin to reconsider their own roles in their family's estrangement, in people having been bankrupted and imprisoned because of things they told authorities? These people who advertise how much they care about the rights of children—how much do they really care?

Yet the seven-year, $13-million McMartin Preschool prosecution in Manhattan Beach, California[120] and the unsuccessful Bobby Finje prosecution in Miami, Florida led by then-State Attorney General Janet Reno, showed ample evidence of child abuse by investigators. Abuse, here refers to the suggestive questioning by experts who fed answers, withheld play time until they answered correctly or urged children to "be brave" for the other children and tell the experts the information they needed.

Does it concern these champions of the child that their own hyper-vigilance has led to an increase in unnecessary and traumatic rectal and vaginal examinations by pediatricians? Given the oceans of reasonable, legitimate doubts that have been raised in recent years about the possibility of suggestion and the headlong rush to combat abuse, real or imaginary, it is difficult to understand how this trumpeted compassion for children can be actual. Instead, it is hubris, self-righteousness, anti-intellectualism, bigotry and the zeal of people who want to reform society. And if some children have to get swept along in this tide of reform, so be it. Much of the blame for this wave of cruelty and this climate of accusation can be placed squarely at the feet of the recovery movement.

Alas, adults are also vulnerable to suggestive techniques and skewed investigations. The ASCA Treatment Center and those like it are commercial memory mills, whose upsurge in hospital units at a time of declining revenues for alcoholism and chemical dependency is too closely linked to have been a coincidence.

With child abuse and repressed memory accusations running rampant, the boundary between what is public and what is private has broken down completely. In both child abuse and memory repression, the conscious and semiconscious motives of accusers have become so suspect that they end up clouding the entire issue. Between custody disputes and revenge toward a former spouse, sincerely-held beliefs as a result of faulty questioning and ideologically overinvested therapists, and the tabloid triumph of emotional conviction over cerebral doubt, it becomes almost impossible to sort out the true from the false.

The following are assumptions we should consider for a course of action, or non-action, when it comes to the treatment of alleged abuse:

- **We err on the side of doubt because there are other people involved.** Abuse necessarily implies an abuser. The evidence from experiments with ordinary memory, hypnosis and successful implantation of false memories does not lend credence to the belief that bad ideas are eventually discarded on their own weight. If anything, the evidence shows that people can cling to false beliefs at least as tenaciously as to accurate ones, if not more so. It is unfair to disrupt the lives and liberties of individuals with accusations when other more plausible explanations exist for what is thought to have occurred.

- **We err on the side of doubt because to do so is in accordance with scientific principles.** Doubt is generally the province of science; faith is generally the province of religion. There is nothing wrong with having religious beliefs; however, a great deal is wrong with leaping to conclusions based on guesswork and then claiming that one science has somehow been represented in having made this leap of faith.

Hypotheses and speculations may lead to knowledge; however, they themselves are not knowledge. To the extent psychology would like to retain its status as a social science, mental-health practitioners would do well to curb their habit of "erring on the side of the survivor" when establishing that an event has unambiguously occurred not only in some metaphorical way or in the survivor's mind, but in the actual world.

- **We err on the side of doubt because it is the right thing to do.** Art and fiction have their place: The place of art is art, the place of fiction is fiction. Both mediums represent and reinterpret reality in useful ways, as do dreams. It is ironic that so many people have championed the mind's ability to repress by demeaning the imagination ("Why would people say these things if they weren't true?"). Much of what becomes knowledge begins as imagination. The capacity to wonder leads to systematic reflection, which leads to theorizing. But when someone, such as a carpenter, is building something, he must distinguish between proven and unproven theories. A good carpenter does not slap his work together or seek to cover up his mistakes, even if he knows he can get away with it. If his helper is doing inferior work, he will order it torn down and begun again "right," by which he means more than "as specified." There is a moral force behind this use of "right."

The authors of an article on claims of Satanic Ritual Abuse (SRA), which appeared in a 1993 *Christianity Today* issue, understand the relationship between what is right in a building sense and in an ethical sense. In the article, sociologist Robin Perrin and psychologist Les Parrott III note some of the discrepancies between some of SRA's widely publicized claims and the evidence, beginning with those of Lauren Stratford in *Satan's Underground*. Stratford claims to have been raped by satanists and to have given birth three times during her high school and college years. After being unable to locate a single witness to any of these pregnancies, *Cornerstone* magazine investigators called her entire story a "gruesome fantasy."[121] The investigators "did find people who knew Stratford during the years she was allegedly pregnant, but all claimed emphatically that she was never pregnant during that time."[122] Nor could Stratford herself produce any evidence or witnesses that she had ever been involved in a satanic cult.

Stratford's sensational story of being used as a baby "breeder"[123] and witnessing human sacrifice attracted the talk show circuit, including *Geraldo* and *The 700 Club*. Yet not one person from these shows verified her story. Faced with escalating doubts and criticisms, her original publisher finally recalled *Satan's Underground* from store shelves (it was later released by Pelican).[124]

"What I have written in my books, I have written in the spirit of truth," said Stratford in an interview with the *Bookstore Journal*. "If there are any errors, they are errors of memory and not lies."[125]

Addressing the question of why witnesses were so hard to find, Perrin and Parrott write:

As we watched the recent confrontation between federal agents and the Branch Davidians in Waco, Texas, we could not help noticing that the press seemingly had little trouble locating defectors willing to provide details of the practices of David Koresh and his followers—this despite the fact that speaking out against Koresh could be dangerous. . . . Yet, when it comes to Satanism, a "megacult" supposedly so pervasive and sinister that the Branch Davidians pale in comparison, no one has stepped forward to lead us to an ongoing cult or to the remains of bodies used in human sacrifice, or to any other physical evidence that supports the stories of SRA.[126]

A study by researchers Bob and Gretchen Passantino is based on the same question in statistical terms. Their article, published in the *Christian Research Journal* (and cited by Perrin and Parrott), reads in part:

Let's suppose there are 100,000 adult survivors [of SRA] who represent only a small subgroup of the conspiracy. They are the ones who were not killed; eventually escaped the cult's control; got into therapy; "remembered" their abuse; and were then willing to tell others about it. . . . If we conservatively peg the average number of abusive events per survivor at fifty, that would give us 5,000,000 criminal events over the last fifty years in America alone. And not a shred of corroborative evidence?[127]

They go on to say:

Physical and sexual abuse, involving cultic activity or not, is plainly evil and influenced by Satan—whether or not it is done in his name. An individual's satanic abuse, real or imagined, should be taken seriously. . . .

Still, we must avoid the danger Paul warns about in 2 Corinthians: "I am afraid that as the serpent deceived Eve by his cunning, your thoughts will be led astray from a sincere and pure devotion to Christ" (11:3). We have an obligation to listen to our Christian brothers and sisters, but we also have a scriptural obligation to evaluate what they say. We cannot fall victim to sloppy thinking or judgment based on a mixture of fallacies, nonevidence, and subjectivism. "He who chases fantasies lacks judgment" (Prov. 12:11). We must rely on careful Bible study, prayer, worship and the fellowship and wisdom of other believers while we retain our commitment to compassion for the victims.[128]

Even if one decided to discard SRA's claims while retaining the legitimacy of other recovered memories—say, of more common sexually abusive acts such as fondling—the same assumptions have given rise to both claims. It is only slightly more cautious to only suspend beliefs about bizarre claims of human sacrifice and cannibalism while retaining belief in the rest, than to believe it all. These stories differ in content, not form.

The ethical dimension of caution in fact finding extends beyond the possibility of injuring someone through faulty inference. Inaccurate claims of abuse injure the accuser and the accused, regardless of side benefits such as the emotional support of others or a favorable judgment in a lawsuit (though the benefits to accusers are certainly more noticeable). But these injuries are inevitable consequences of participating in something that is harmful in itself—the building of a faulty structure.

The line or standard separating reliable structures from

faulty, truths from fallacies, is indeterminate and value-laden. In any endeavor, it is better to proceed on the basis of what has been shown to be true, rather than what might be true. This superiority is not only structural, it is ethical.

It seems rather antithetical to say, as Joan Childs has, "I'm very careful, very cautious. There's a 50% chance they're right, and a 50% chance I'm right."[129] That a method capable of producing false memories may also happen to produce some true ones is no defense. One person who can elaborate on this point is psychologist Gary Schoener, who since the mid-1970s directed the Minneapolis Walk-In Center, which has become a lightning rod nationwide for abusive psychotherapy complaints.

"One of the key things in research," Schoener said in an interview, "is to ask, 'Who should *not* have this therapy?' We have interviewed several hundred people who have claimed serious upset or injury where regressive therapy played a significant role. And we don't advertise our services, we're not out there trying to find them."[130] Schoener estimates that 3% to 5% of ex-clients injured in some kind of therapy actually follow through with a complaint. "It becomes real to us when people say, 'There are five others or 12 other people who have had similar experiences, and I'm the only one willing to take action.' "[131]

Schoener is also an expert on "reparenting" therapy. The element of regression—of "going back" to a younger age, and in so doing often becoming dependent on the therapist—overlaps with memory retrieval therapies. Both therapies also rely on a similar justification, that they help people.

Psychologist Harry Boyd of Norman, Oklahoma, chaired ethics committee hearings which in 1978 expelled reparenting founder Jacqui Schiff from the International Transactional Analysis Association (ITAA). Regarding claims of beneficial outcomes from controversial therapies, Boyd said:

> It's the argument that justifies snake oil or any other hype you can impress upon the public through your own charisma. Yeah, people who take snake oil probably feel better doing it. But the person who sells it, and uses credentials to sell it has some things to answer for, it seems to me. You can't just talk about things making people better. What made who better? Compared to what? Do the results justify the risks? How are the claims evaluated? People aren't asking these questions. I've worked hard most of my professional life doing my trade, and I don't like people ripping it off.[132]

This point of view has been that of the majority in Western culture. In this sense, the proponents of disease theories for alcoholism, codependency and family dynamics are correct in portraying themselves as embattled underdogs, even though their views have dominated a large corner of the mental health marketplace since the mid-1980s. It is that Western culture that many of these therapists seek to overthrow. Proponents of questionable therapies have seized upon the fashionable assault on science and enlightenment standards for knowledge now taking place in universities. In so doing they have discarded the viewpoints that are most desperately needed today, such as this one from the "*Meditations* of Descartes:

> I lay down the rule also, that we must wholly refrain from ever mixing up conjectures with our pronouncements on the truth of things. This warning is of no little importance. There is . . . nothing in the current Philosophy which is so evident . . . that the learned, not

content with the recognition of what is clear and certain, in the first instance hazard the assertion of obscure and ill-comprehended theories, at which they have arrived merely by probable conjecture. Then afterwards they gradually attach complete credence to them, and mingling them promiscuously with what is true and evident, they finish by being unable to deduce any conclusion which does not appear to depend upon some proposition of the doubtful sort.[133]

Descartes describes his entire philosophy as a countermeasure to the above, "lest we in turn should slip into the same error."[134] This philosophy is the foundation of our law and our culture. The implications for tossing it aside are enormous. For, once we proceed in the direction of embracing theories "of the doubtful sort" and begin to act on those theories, we begin building structures of valid inferences on foundations of sand. Nowhere is the tragedy of converting wishful theories into fact more evident than in the casualties of fringe psychotherapies of the last 20 years, both in patients themselves and those who have suffered as a result of their insights.

"You have to look at this the way you look at drugs," Schoener said. "If you had a drug that helped a third of the people a lot, helped another third some, hurt a third of the people and then a handful died, do you think that drug would get on the market?"[135]

If such a drug were recalled, a certain percentage of people who would have been helped—perhaps a large percentage—would no longer be helped in this way. Therapies cannot be "recalled;" they can only weather shifts in public opinion and either survive or not. Toward this end of influencing public opinion; former accusers, psychologists, psychiatrists, experts in the memory field and the more than 17,000 accused parents have challenged the current body of information about buried "memories" of sexual assault as theoretically ill-founded and unacceptably prone to misapplication and error.

In a speech before the 1993 meeting of the FMS Foundation, University of Pennsylvania psychologist Henry Gleitman, underscored the ethical dimension of logical, architectural "rightness." Gleitman listed half-a-dozen widely-held "assumptions" which have been misrepresented as truths, despite the fact that none of them have been proven and many of them may be wrong. The beliefs are:

- The all-importance of early childhood as more critical or more defining than any other stage of life.
- The idea that memory is permanent,
- that memories can be repressed and then extracted later in essentially unchanged form,
- that there are sure-fire techniques for getting to these memories, such as hypnosis or "truth serum,"
- that if you think you remember something, then it actually happened,
- and that the more confident a person is in a memory, the more likely that memory is to be true.[136]

Gleitman stated:

These are assumptions that have crept into our everyday notions as Americans, as citizens and indeed as psychologists, and that, I am sad to say, as a teacher and writer about general psychology, may well have helped to perpetuate—if for no other reason than by not emphatically and vehemently saying that these are assumptions.

We're swallowing so much of psychological truth on faith—no different from the faith placed in Ann Landers. Whatever effect childhood experiences have on a person is unknown. . . . Then there are those who have a line of argument which amounts to saying, "Yes, it's true, memory can be confabulated, but not repressed memory." Next it will be, "Yes, it's true that repressed memories can be confabulated, but not these repressed memories."

I would like to combat what I believe has come to pass. . . . What I can only call the suspension of common sense.[137]

The Death of Conversation

Wendy Kaminer's essay, "Chances Are You're Codependent, Too," appeared in a 1990 *New York Times Review of Books* issue, elevating criticism of the recovery movement to a new level. In the essay, she named HCI as one of the leading recovery publishers with 102 titles, citing sales figures from HCI co-president Peter Vegso at: 1.1. million *Adult Children of Alcoholics* copies sold; 500,000 copies sold of *Healing the Child Within* by Charles Whitfield; and 350,000 copies sold of *Bradshaw On: The Family*. She also sketched the contributions of four larger publishers including some of their sales figures.[138]

Most impressive, however, was what Kaminer said about the books themselves and the recovery movement as a whole. In astonishingly little space, she accurately conveyed the central messages of recovery self-help; contrasted these with the messages of self-help books of earlier decades; discussed how recovery borrowed from both feminism and religion while distorting the aims of each; analyzed several of the messages individually; tossed in literary allusions from

Dickens to Kafka; and placed her entire critique within a broader social framework of victimization and survivorship as cultural metaphors.

"Codependency offers a diagnosis, and a support group, to virtually anyone with a problem who can read."[139] Beginning where a lot of critics left off, Kaminer argued a few key points.

- On the spiritual dimension in recovery literature: This is not moral relativism; distinctions are made between healthy and unhealthy behavior. It reflects instead the need to believe that no one is unforgivable and everyone can be saved. Because within every addict there's a holy child yearning to be free, recovery holds the promise of redemption.[140]

- On the way in which this spiritual dimension expresses itself in dialogue: The suffering associated with addiction is purposeful and purifying, and it prepares you to serve: "Without my suffering, I would not be able to bear witness," Mr. Bradshaw says. Sin can be the low road to redemption, as Jimmy Swaggart made clear. Codependents take a familiar confessional pride in their disorders, as if every addiction were a crucible.[141]

- On the dominance of the recovery star over the consumer: Experts are always unique (their tritest pronouncements are packaged as news), but readers are fungible, suffering the same syndromes and needful of the same cures.[142]

- On recovery doctrine as a fear of life:

Merely buying a self-help book is an act of dependence, a refusal to confront the complexities of a solitary creative effort, as well as its failures . . . Self-help books market authority in a culture that idealizes individualism but not thinking and fears the isolation of being free.[143]

The truth about recovery could lie somewhere between descriptions offered by its strongest supporters and by its strongest critics. Recovery from addiction is characterized by difficulty and stumbling along the way, from the slips of the relapsing addict to the soul-shearing breakaway of the codependent from a tyrannical husband, parent or family. Part of the lesson is that the road is paved with failures and setbacks.

Many recovery stars urged their audiences to "move on," to have normal lives apart from all this self-seeking. At the 1990 Codependency Conference in Scottsdale, Arizona, which was discussed in the previous chapter, Sharon Wegscheider-Cruse told several hundred people that most of her everyday friends are not particularly involved with recovery, and warned against the dangers of guru worship and of the mythical fellowship "On and On Anonymous."[144]

This rather recent emphasis on moving on came just as talk shows and mainstream media were withdrawing from a pattern of unqualified endorsement for any set of ideas bearing a 12-step label. But the very fact that recovery stars tend to answer their critics by co-opting what they can— claiming that autonomy and at least a capacity for dissent had always been their aim—muddies the water and complicates the job of the critic.

For example, in 1993, when an interviewer writing for *Changes* asked John Bradshaw what he thought of "recovery bashing," Bradshaw replied, "I see a lot of critical parent in it, a lot of blaming . . . Critics have no sense of what's right about recovery."[145]

A moment later, he co-opts what he can: "It's helped me enormously to see a much broader sense of the recovery movement. Wendy Kaminer is missing it by calling recovery a fashion. It's part of a larger movement of consciousness, and I'm grateful to her critique for helping me to see that."[146]

So recovery is part of a larger movement of consciousness characterized by television talk shows; The Forum; the pursuit of capital as a path to spirituality; and a tidal wave of self-help stars from Norman Vincent Peale to M. Scott Peck, Dr. James Dobson and Dr. Joyce Brothers. It is my feeling that Kaminer did not write *I'm Dysfunctional, You're Dysfunctional—The Recovery Movement and Other Self-Help Fashions* simply to draw up an ideological family tree for self-help movements. It seemed more of a genogram, the kind of tree upon which Bradshaw bases his 1995 book *Family Secrets.* Genograms attempt to dig beneath the surface of intergenerational family relations. They illustrate how strengths and weaknesses can be passed from one person to the next. In co-opting a part of Kaminer's critique, Bradshaw had not responded to the genogram at all. He had dismissed that, but thanked her for producing such an interesting family tree.

How or if critics choose to respond to the movements of a criticized agency is their prerogative. Kaminer's approach was refreshing, she brought an opening salvo to the recovery field that could not simply be erased or dismissed as ignorant (though that is just what most recovery stars attempted to do).

Before Kaminer, only Stanton Peele's critique stood out, and it is not easy taking on a multi-billion-dollar industry single-handedly. Though academia was top-heavy with individuals who could have provided authentic, critical analyses of the recovery movement, few bothered. With Peele first, and then Kaminer and others, challenges were now on the record extending well beyond chemical dependency treatment and the disease concept of alcoholism.

Simply having someone ask the questions about political versus personal life in recovery and freedom versus dependence made the beginnings of a dialogue possible. A chapter called "The Recovery Boutique: Workshopping," from Kaminer's book, *I'm Dysfunctional, You're Dysfunctional,* was culled entirely from attending an HCI conference in Philadelphia, Pennsylvania on self-esteem and recovery targeted toward women.

Kaminer reported the audience demographics–"mostly white, female, and middle class"–[147] drawn from the presentations of four recovery stars. She gave half-a-dozen examples of recovery truisms which are actually assumptions:

- that feelings are "always okay;"
- that men are cerebral, women emotive;
- that the main goal of feminism is a draining climb up the corporate ladder;
- that emotional healing will change the world more than political activism ever could;
- that emotional, physical and sexual abuse are essentially the same experience;
- and that the unwillingness to bond quickly with strangers is a mark of low self-esteem.

She also noted the absence of a political dimension in any of these discussions and emphasized once again the exalted status of recovery experts compared to their audiences.

"Maybe there's nothing unethical about HCI conducting business in any manner the market will bear," she writes. "It's just that the women here seem so needy and the conference organizers are so slick."[148] What separates this chapter from her *New York Times* article is its immediacy and the fact that the writer not only read books and made phone calls but had seen the movement in action. She attempted to participate and convert monolithic lectures into dialogues.

"In nearly three days of lectures and workshops, I am the only person I hear question or challenge an expert," she reported. "I always take them by surprise, and the audience is always irritated with me."[149]

This is the problem, of course. It only takes a lengthy enough exposure to recovery subculture before one begins to suspect that even the seemingly open-minded forums, debates, points/counterpoints and round tables presented at conferences amount to little more than exercises in reinforcing the beliefs of the majority.

Why Would Anyone Make This Up?

In the years since the FMS Foundation organized in Philadelphia, a definite shift has occurred in public perception. It used to be that the only people who knew about repressed memories were accusers, their parents and therapists. Now a number of high-profile court cases, books and national television programs have alerted the public to what is being alleged, and the evidence to support it. At a February 1998 conference sponsored jointly by the Eleanor and Elliot Goldstein Foundation and Florida Atlantic University (FAU), changing times were never more apparent. Whereas researchers of the early 1990s had only a few experiments to go on in answering the common rejoinder

"Why would anyone make this up," a number of studies are showing that it is in fact quite easy to convince psychologically normal, untroubled adults of events that never happened to them.

Elizabeth Loftus asked, "What is going on in psychotherapy?" Specifically, what effects in the areas of memory could researchers gain using human subjects and practicing techniques such as hypnosis, guided imagery and dream interpretation (techniques that have commonly been associated with recall of traumatic memories)? To help answer that question, Loftus enacted the "lost in a shopping mall" experiment alluded to earlier in the chapter. She managed to convince subjects that they had been lost, had cried and been rescued by an old man or woman, simply by having an older sibling participate in the experiment who claimed to also remember the incident.[150]

Ira Hymen, of Western Washington University, then took a step closer to traumatic memory by convincing a quarter of his subjects that as children they had each attended a wedding where they spilled punch all over the bride's parents and suffered embarrassment. Hymen also managed to get his subjects to remember that they had once suffered an earache so painful that it required a trip to the hospital.[151]

The keys to implanting memories are repetition and suggestive techniques. In other experiments, Loftus has successfully induced memories that, as children, subjects had:

- Slipped and cut themselves on a window.
- Caught their fingers in a mouse trap.
- And saw a colorful mobile hanging over their cribs the day after they were born.

Subjects were told only that they were participating in an experiment on memory. Part of the experimental procedure involved corroboration from a close relative that these events had not actually occurred, so far as they knew. When subjects balked at the suggested events, the experimenter would say, "Let's try some guided visualization to see if we can find out how and where this might have happened." It wasn't necessary to remember (how could someone be asked to remember something that did not happen?), only to imagine for a moment how such an event might unfold.

Loftus and her colleagues found that people undergoing guided imagery had increased confidence that a fictitious event occurred. Loftus refers to this phenomenon as "imagination inflation."[152] Sometimes the results are dramatic. For example, in a joint experiment with a prominent Italian psychologist, Dr. Lombardo, subjects shared dreams which were then interpreted by Dr. Lombardo to mean that they had been lost in a large public place. The subjects would share a dream they'd had. Lombardo would remind the subjects that he was a renowned expert on dream interpretation, perhaps mentioning that a few weeks earlier, he had seen another patient who had a similar dream, and that person had been lost in a large public space at a young age. Before a dream interpretation session, 40% of the subjects' confidence increased that before the age of 10 they had been lost in a public place. After the dream interpretation session, the rate of false confidence in the getting-lost experience rose to 89%.[153]

In the volatile field of questioning children, Stephen Ceci, a distinguished professor at Cornell University, and colleagues asked 4-, 5- and 6-year-olds a series of questions: Had they ever dropped a cantaloupe on the sidewalk from a hot-air balloon; gone ice fishing; caught their hand in a mouse trap? The experimenters asked the same questions repeatedly over an eight to 14 week period. With repeated exposure to the same question, Ceci found that up to 60% of the children could be induced to have memories of dropping the cantaloupe. Moreover, even after being told that the memories had been implanted by experimenters, it proved all but impossible to get the children to erase a memory they had once believed. Ceci said "If a kid started at a 20% error rate and over 12 weeks, that error rate goes up to 50%, we might get them back down to 30%, but we can never get them all the way back down to the original point."[154]

Daniel Schacter, Dean of Psychology at Harvard University, spoke of his work using Positron Emission Tomography (PET) to study the neuroscience of false memory. While his results are not conclusive, his studies can shed new light on how we remember and how we forget. Like many memory experts, Schacter does not discount the possibility of repressed memories of traumatic episodes, but feels that caution is called for, given the mind's felicity in conjuring up false events and the widespread availability of suggestible influences.[155]

While the discussions presented new information, some things have not changed since the early 1990s. I saw some of the same faces in the audience that I had seen five years earlier when I first began investigating the memory issue. These were the parents who used to meet every week at the SIRS building in Boca Raton, Florida. For most of them, their adult children remained estranged with no contact whatsoever. One couple's daughters had returned, but the subject of the lost years is never mentioned. Two of the fathers I interviewed have since died.

These parents speak of donating to charities in their grandchildren's names, so they can feel they have given something and the gifts will not be returned. They talk of moving on with their lives. Their testimony is proof that although the tide may at last have turned in favor of those accused, the memory wars are far from over.

CHAPTER NINE

The Metastasizing of Metaphor

Everyone hates his parents,
It's in the Torah,
It's what history shows,
In fact, God said to Moses,
'Moses, everyone hates his parents!
That's how it is,'
And God should know
Because God hated his
      —From "Falsettoland," music and lyrics by William Finn

I n recent years, recovery stars have often argued that critics do not understand their work. This is probably true. Emergent recovery ideas have assumed an acceptance of earlier ones. The incestuous society presupposes the dysfunctional family, which presupposes the alcoholic family, which presupposes a disease of alcoholism. Those with perspectives informed primarily by psychology, sociology, philosophy or medicine have a difficult time understanding John Bradshaw's theology of recovered memories, or Charles Whitfield's new paradigm for healing the culture from its own institutionalized codependency.

Bradshaw, Whitfield and Anne Wilson Schaef are probably the three recovery stars who have most successfully exploited addiction as a metaphor for a broad range of social ills. All have responded aggressively to reactions in the mainstream media. In the second edition of *Co-Dependence: Misunderstood, Mistreated*, Schaef discusses the controversies surrounding recovery, naming only one book, Stanton Peele's *Diseasing of America*:

> Why, might I ask, are these sophisticated critical thinkers not being open to the exploration of the *truths* that exist in the new awareness about addiction and codependence? In recovering circles, the kind of thinking that we see in many of these articles would be nailed as "stinkin' thinkin' " (confused reasoning characteristic of the addictive process), and people would be encouraged to do their own work and get clear before they dumped their own issues onto others.[1]

Schaef alludes to articles appearing in *Family Circle*, *Playboy* and the *New York Times Review of Books*, mystified by the media's anti-recovery "bias." "I do know," she concludes, "that as I have tried to read some of this material, I have felt covered over with a slimy goo, and that in trying to respond, I am forced to enter into a system that I perceive as unhealthy and that I do not like."[2]

For present purposes, the word "before" in Schaef's critique should be addressed: As in, "people would be encouraged to do their own work and get clear before they dumped their own issues onto others."[3] The idea of doing one's own work is not in itself threatening. In this book I have, on occasion, noted the places in which my interactions with one recovery star or another "touched off issues," and how my own unresolved emotions in turn affected the interactions. For this added dimension I owe my thanks to the recovery stars themselves and their contributions. The issue here is that the same people who for years have been saying that "recovery is a journey, not a destination," now want critics of the recovery movement to be perfectly serene and in touch with their issues before publishing their negative critiques. Yet, if recovery is a journey, not a destination—a process, not a result—we can never be all-the-way clear; our work is never all-the-way done.

Nor is this mandate of getting clear first one that Schaef has cared to follow in her own life. In 1992, she settled a multimillion dollar lawsuit brought by Vonna Moody, a client of Schaef's from 1975 to 1985. During that time, Moody alleges that Schaef initiated sexual relations with her on numerous occasions and borrowed $6,000 for a Puget Sound, Washington, real estate investment. According to records in Boulder County District Court in Colorado, Schaef diagnosed Moody as a "sex addict." In a deposition, Schaef said that standards of care in the 1970s and early 1980s "allowed sexual intimacy with patients."[4]

Schaef has never denied the sexual relationship although she claims that Vonna Moody was never her client. She explains more than 500 checks totalling $9,700—all of which Moody had recorded and described in check registers, and still possesses as cancelled checks—as payments on a cabin they owned together and for a women's support group Schaef led but which was "not therapy."

Moody remembers it differently. She says each of those checks were payments for individual appointments which she had scheduled with Schaef as her therapist.

"I don't know what I gave her $10,000 for, if it wasn't for therapy,"[5] Moody said in an interview. As for the women's "intensives," Moody recalls, Schaef guided them, set the tone in each one and confronted group members regularly.

"She was the main one,"[6] Moody says. In a deposition, Schaef insisted that intensives were not therapy and that "treatment" based on 12-step concepts was not psychotherapy.

Had Schaef repaid the $6,000, she might have saved the suit. She had borrowed money from several clients and former clients ($36,000 from one), but she insisted Moody's was a gift, not a loan. Letters were exchanged, including the following handwritten one from Schaef to Moody about why the idea of repaying the $6,000 did not "feel sober." The letter dated February 20, 1989, reads in part:

> *I had done so many things for you for which no monetary value could be placed and I could see why you would want to give to me out of what you had.*
>
> *As I thought over these interactions, I remembered when Pocus, your old barn cat, was near death and you seemingly had no other choice than to take him back to the barn and ask neighbors to feed him and I took him into my house and nursed him until he was well again.... Or the time that your horse had hurt her foot and you were nervous about what the vet said to do and I told you (which was exactly what the vet had said) and I gave you support to follow through with the treatment when you were shaky and in tears ... Or the time that we invited you to live in our house when you had no home and were moving from one motel to another ... Or the way I shared my children with you because you had none ... I think my kids are a great gift for anyone to get to know and they still consider you a part of our family ... Or the many*

Christmases, Thanksgivings and other holidays that you were part of our family and spent with us . . . Or the time that I loaded up the kids and drove all night to Nebraska because you thought you were "losing it" . . . Or the times that I invited you along on my trips because I knew that you liked to travel, had no one to travel with and I enjoyed your company . . . Or the many times all of us considered you part of our family, reached out with love and took you in because we cared about you . . . As I thought about all this, I realized that it is always important for me to feel like I am giving back to people who are so generous with me and I felt that it would be rude and uncaring not to accept your insistent offer so I accepted it graciously, took you at your word and considered the matter closed.[7]

Moody emphatically denies that she ever insisted the money was a gift. "It was always a loan," she says.[8]

Diane Fassel, Schaef's business partner and co-author of *The Addictive Organization*, was also named in the suit. Moody alleged that Fassel knew Schaef was exploiting the therapeutic relationship and allowed it to continue. Schaef and Fassel settled for a $250,000 payment to Moody. A spokeswoman for the American Psychological Association's public affairs department was unsure about what standards, if any, governed "dual relationships" in the late 1970s. It is entirely possible that Schaef's assessment is correct. Both sexual relations and investment transactions between client and therapist, however, would be considered unethical today. Furthermore, both would seem to fall well within the range of unhealthy power imbalances described by Schaef and Fassel in *The Addictive Organization*.

In the updated preface to *Co-Dependence: Misunder-stood, Mistreated*, Schaef recounts a turning point that occurred some time after she had been "in recovery": "I had to admit I was an addict . . . a relationship *addict* . . . just like any other addict. And then my recovery took off."[9]

What is a relationship addict? Schaef has written a book about that, too. *Escape from Intimacy—Untangling the 'Love' Addictions: Sex, Romance, Relationships*, lists two pages of "characteristics of relationship addiction," two of which are: "Relationship addicts are very controlling;" and "Relationship addicts are consummate 'cons.' "[10]

It seems highly unlikely that Schaef, who began publishing books in the late 1970s, could have completed her own work regarding relationship addiction before publishing several book-length sermons on societal dysfunction.

Perhaps when recovery stars talk about doing your own work before you criticize them, they are not talking about any obvious psychopathologies in the persona of the critic: the criticisms themselves are evidence of the pathology. The evidence of "doing your own work" is that you come around to their point of view—or those points of view which tend to legitimate their status as experts and enrich them financially.

Juanita Benetin, who represented Moody, describes questioning Schaef as a frustrating experience. "You ask a question and you don't get an answer," she recalls. "And then she tries to convince you that the reason you don't 'get' her answer is because you haven't done your own work. It's like having a conversation with someone in which you think you're being rational—and the other person is having a whole different conversation. And yet they're answering you."[11]

"Columboing" for Secrets

The work of John Bradshaw has attracted a large audience and has come to define what recovery is all about. By extending and synthesizing popular concepts of alcoholism theory and incorporating elements of family systems, 12-step folk wisdom, transactional analysis and New Age metaphysics, Bradshaw has created a cosmology of the spiritual seeker's path to wholeness.

Family Secrets: What You Don't Know Can *Hurt You* is an archaeological manual for unearthing the treasures of childhood and family, as well as the demons that continue to wreak havoc. The treasures don't get very much ink, but then they are not the problem.

Bradshaw seems to confound his critics. Wendy Kaminer singles out this Bradshaw quote: "We cannot have an identity all alone; our reality is shaped from the beginning by *relationship*."[12]

She replies: "Our reality is also shaped by the larger cultural environment—our race, religion and socioeconomic status—as well as by the weather. Somewhere along the line we still become accountable for ourselves; the factors that shaped us are moot."[13]

In *The Mismeasure of Woman*, Carol Tavris comments on Bradshaw's employment of the ubiquitous "96 percent" estimate as to family dysfunctionality which originated with Sharon Wegscheider-Cruse:

> Oddly enough, no one considers this pessimistic computation as a sign of a Grandiose Self-inflating Personality Disorder, whose symptoms are the belief that "I'm cured and you're not" and the claim "Give me ten minutes, and I'll tell you what's wrong with you."[14]

As any recovery writer would acknowledge, ideas do have consequences. The belief that one has been fundamentally bent by childhood leads to a range of plausible solutions on how to be made straight–in therapy, in support groups, attending recovery conferences or reading recovery literature. Critics such as Kaminer and Tavris do not so much dispute the truth or falsehood of Bradshaw's views on identity or the family, as some of their practical implications and the authoritative vestments in which they come clothed.

Entering into a debate on almost any of a thousand "truths" Bradshaw sprinkles throughout his work is a perilous enterprise. How, for example, might one go about assessing the notion that "The wounded inner child is the major cause of addictions and addictive behavior";[15] or weighing the position that children from dysfunctional families suffer from "the loss of I AMness"?[16] Sympathetic readers–those already allied with, or inclined toward acceptance of the advanced metaphors, the promoted explanations–can fit themselves into these metaphorical constructions with ease.

Even a more empirically minded reading of those two statements–which are by no means unique, and whose like can be found on almost any page of Bradshaw's work–could yield favorable interpretations of what is being said. Most addiction theorists acknowledge some psychological causation these days. It is therefore plausible that childhood "wounding" could at least contribute to addiction later in life. Similarly, any family deserving the name "dysfunctional" probably inhibits the individuality (or the "I AMness") of its members almost by definition. If one is even a little generous, these statements sound reasonable enough.

The fact remains that "wounded inner children" cannot really be the cause of anything, because there is no such entity as an "inner child". This may seem obvious enough but after encountering Whitfield's assertion that the inner child is "far more than a metaphor. It is reality,"[17] (a claim he reiterated to me in person), I can afford to take nothing for granted.

HCI author Pamela Levin, a registered nurse with a long track record in reparenting therapy (and an inspiration to Bradshaw, who cites her work favorably in *Healing the Shame That Binds You*) also refused to give ground on the term's metaphorical status. During an interview, Levin once said that she had "seen" the inner child in a part of the brain.[18]

Like so many others on the recovery circuit, Bradshaw has exploited every imaginable avenue of addiction possible, wringing every drop of water from that conceptual towel, all the while insisting that he is not engaging in metaphor. Perhaps he makes this point because he would like readers to try on the expanded view of addictions he has advanced and summarized in borrowed one-liners such as "a pathological relationship to any mood-altering experience that has life-damaging consequences";[19] or, elsewhere, "any process used to avoid or take away intolerable reality."[20]

The "damage," again pulling from just one list, would certainly include whatever you might have imagined plus being subjected to "contempt, criticism and blame, judg-mentalism and moralizing, perfectionism, the striving for power and control, or people pleasing and being nice."[21] If you were so shame-based to think of niceness as an at-tribute in people that is, well, nice, then you have not read *Healing the Shame That Binds You*. There we learn that "People-pleasing nice guys and sweethearts also act shame-less and pass their shame along to others . . . Being nice is primarily a way of manipulating people and situations."[22]

There is something flattening and ultimately impersonal

about this widening of definitions. With the removal of meaningful distinctions between the post-traumatic stress of Holocaust survivors and ACoAs (a comparison in his book on the family that Bradshaw adopted from another recovery author), or between "joy addicts" and heroin addicts, Bradshaw comes close to trivializing the very sufferings he has set out to recognize. The damage that causes an inner child to be wounded, as well as the resulting addictions, could be almost anything. Thus it is hard to imagine anyone not wounded or anyone not addicted. How helpful is it, then, to be told that one such abstraction causes another?

But then the matter of causes, or sources, has enchanted philosophers from Heraclitus (who believed that the sun's fire was nourished by the exhaled breath of oceans) to Hume (who asked his contemporaries to prove causes were anything other than their own exhalations, knowing full well that, strictly speaking, they could not do so).

The art of divining causes for things has also tempted mystics to the stage. Bradshaw counts himself an admirer of Rupert Sheldrake, the maverick biologist whose speculations on the nature of reality make Heraclitus look conservative even by today's standards. Sheldrake is referred to here as a mystic not to demean him, but to separate his methods from those of careful, systematic thinkers deserving the name "philosopher." Here is one of his fairly typical rumination on the linkage between evolutionary theory and memory:

It is possible that we do, after all, live in an amnesic world that is governed by eternal laws. But it is also possible that memory is inherent in nature; and if we find that we are indeed living in such a world, we shall have to change our way of thinking entirely. Through morphonic resonance, formative causal influences pass through or across both space and time.[23]

Sheldrake is careful not to represent such musings as fact. But without advancing an argument as to why these things "must be so," the reader is only left with impressions about what "might be so," no different from the counsel of a Tarot card reader or someone who casts bones on the ground and interprets their patterns. Here is Bradshaw on Sheldrake:

Sheldrake calls the fields that transmit behavior *morphogenetic fields*: literally "fields of energy that give form." If we applied his theory to the family as a social system, we could say that a family with its special personality operates like a species, and that when a threshold of new behavior or habit is reached in a family, everyone in the succeeding generations will know them. They may be good behaviors or virtues or bad habits or vices. Once the threshold of new behavior is reached, the behavior is passed into the group mind or family energy field. Each descendant knows the new behavior, although not everyone will necessarily act it out. It may even skip generations.[24]

To follow the impulse to discovery, to search for new and more vital explanations and somehow improve humanity and Earth in the process, is to partake in one of life's greatest joys. No doubt our most venerated disciplines have originated and evolved by pursuit of whimsical impulses. But the act of reframing, reducing and analyzing-in-terms-of is not itself knowledge.

While not wishing to dampen anyone's creative spirit, other people do not always make the best canvasses for one's bursts of inspiration. Despite containing elements that are probably very helpful, Bradshaw's work nourishes the imagination in ways that could easily lead one into inaccurate and possibly harmful interpretations of one's past. He now seems aware of this—an appendix in *Family Secrets* is devoted exclusively to the dangers inherent in the work and the possibility of incurring false memories.[25] Other recovery stars who specialize in incest and buried trauma are not nearly as careful. Whether these words of caution will prove sufficient is another question.

"Man, I sure get tired of doing mop-up work for that guy,"[26] grumbled Michael Yapko, a psychologist who has written several books on the role of hypnosis in therapy; and, most recently, on the possibility of encountering false beliefs of childhood sexual abuse.

I interviewed Yapko during the 1992 annual meeting of the American Association of Marriage and Family Therapists in Miami, Florida. The interview focused mostly on the growing interest Yapko was observing in the subject of sexual abuse and in other traumatic experiences submerged in the unconscious. Since Yapko is an acknowledged hypnotherapist, other therapists occasionally call on him to request his expertise in determining whether or not a patient had been sexually abused.

"By the late 1980s, I was getting that call, no exaggeration, at least once a day." Though Yapko was reluctant to engage in therapy oriented toward the past, that did not stop him from listening to the results of these hypnotic forays, once these same clients had taken their business elsewhere.

Now the calls come from accused parents. "The parents I see are like Mr. and Mrs. Elmer Fudd. They're accused of killing neighborhood kids in human sacrifices, setting them on fire, pouring gasoline down their throats and burning them with cigarettes. The fact that there aren't any medical records or scars only points to how brilliant their coverup has been."[27]

I spoke to Yapko more recently to discuss the 1992 interview, it's relation to Bradshaw, and what Yapko had meant by "mop-up work." He began with a qualification:

> In a general sense, you have to appreciate that any model from which any body of work operates is generic and neutral in nature, whether that is Bradshaw or cognitive therapy or psychopharmacology.
>
> A critical evolutionary step in my profession is the recognition that anything that has the power to heal has the power to hurt.[28]

In that case, I asked if he regarded Bradshaw's pain explorations, such as cognitive therapy, simply as "a model" with no inherent dangers?

> I wouldn't go that far. Some people have been greatly helped by Bradshaw. But because he's working in an arena more emotionally charged, the risks go correspondingly up. He reframes things in terms of family abuse and dysfunction, giving people a considerably more pathological approach.[29]

To Yapko, "original pain" and much of the entire recovery school of thought exemplifies "the robo-approach to life—to move forward by looking backward."[30]

He stated, "It would never occur to me to have someone look at themselves or call themselves a survivor. If there is one thing I have said to my clients, it is that you are more than your history."[31]

Suffering and Secrets

Transactional psychotherapist Alan Jacobs agrees. After WTTW, Chicago's PBS affiliate, aired several hours of a Bradshaw seminar during a fund-raising drive, three of Jacobs' clients brought their newly-magnified pain into his office. Two of these clients, Jacobs said "were hurting in ways I had seen them hurt before. But at least in the office I could get them back together before they went out."[32] The third client's distress was more acute.

> He was terribly upset with all of this so-called pain from childhood that Bradshaw had induced—and I mean induced—him to experience. Specifically, he started feeling pain about the way his parents had treated him. I had been studiously peeling that onion with great care because I felt that this patient was self-destructive.[33]

Jacobs said that he and the client had constructed a "suicide contract" (a standing agreement stating that the client agrees to take certain countermeasures in the event he begins to entertain suicidal thoughts) and that no disasters occurred. But there had been reasons for concern.

This raises several questions. First, is it Bradshaw's fault that someone who watched his video had a negative reaction? Some people are neurotic, they react negatively to different stimuli: a plane flying overhead, a cockroach darting across the floor, a newscaster who seems to be talking directly to them.

Second, if there was something uniquely disturbing about what Jacobs's third client saw on WTTW, was that disturbance necessarily bad? Maybe this pain could be regarded as accelerated awareness of how the patient's parents really had treated him. Maybe peeling the onion with great care wasn't the only way to go, and perhaps the shock and suddenness of the patient's feelings about his parents would benefit him in the long run.

Even if there was a direct cause-and-effect relationship between the patient seeing Bradshaw on television and his reaction; which was an unequivocal setback to his progress, it still isn't necessarily Bradshaw's fault.

Most people who climb aboard Bradshaw's interpretive structures not only survive, but are glad they made the trip. And as his audiences increase, he has added safety ropes in the form of wandering therapists designated by a ribbon. Does this not reflect concern for a potential hazard, as well as a concrete effort to minimize that hazard?

How easy would it be to become emotionally overwhelmed by a glut of negative interpretations of one's family past, in which sacrifice is reframed as codependency, duty as rigidity and rules and religious observance as religious addiction?

And if over the course of a two-day seminar one was surrounded by people who had been or were becoming similarly disillusioned with their lives—and who together did the exercises, cried, heard secrets too shaming to disclose elsewhere, yet were affirmed all the more for the disclosure—it is possible that after two days of this, one might be ready to hear whatever the person in charge offers toward emotional reconstruction and spiritual release.

Carl Jung's comment to the effect that "neurosis is always a substitute for legitimate suffering"[34] has been quoted by many. (John Bradshaw, for one, seems fond of the statement.) The statement somehow sounds right, but what does it mean, and what are its implications?

Different therapies tend to put forth different explanations for the existence of distress, acute anxiety and despair. Freudian psychoanalysts might search for causes hidden in the unconscious. Followers of Albert Ellis might isolate and examine the "irrational beliefs" that have made this despair seem unavoidable. Brief therapists might prefer to zero in on ways in which a client has solved similar problems in the past.

Recovery-oriented therapists, whether under the rubric of addiction or codependency, "original pain" or Post-traumatic Stress, tend to treat distress, anxiety and despair as necessary stages for growth. There is a saying in 12-step groups: "The only way around (the suffering) is through!" This has a commonsense wisdom about it suggestive of a farmer: The only way to pull your tractor out of the mud is to pull your tractor out of the mud. The only way to fix your problems is to reexperience them and work through them. The ability to face up to the actual size of a problem in order to solve it is considered a hallmark of adulthood.

Yet when the problem being discussed concerns not tractors but semiconscious "issues" and vague "processes," it is easy for the saying, "the only way around is through," to become the exclusive property of advocates of a particular way of thinking. Gradually, this group of advocates comes to regard "legitimate suffering" as an esoteric technique to which they own the patent. Reliance upon antidepressants, or on talk therapies that do not emphasize therapeutic constructs such as "deep process, original pain or the underlying trauma" can be seen as ways of avoiding necessary and legitimate suffering.

Like a straight line on a map, the road to recovery leads through the suffering. There will be dangers along the way, and many toll booths. The toll booth keepers can give some directions for free. For detailed directions and tips on how to avoid various predatory beasts, you will need to pay them extra. It is worth it, because some of these dangers can be extreme.

Heart of Darkness

Renee Fredrickson's *Repressed Memories: A Journey to Recovery from Sexual Abuse*, is a classic of the genre. An intriguing aspect of *Repressed Memories* is its inclusion of organized, highly sophisticated satanists in the pool of sexual abusers.[35]

Like Bradshaw's *Family Secrets*, *Repressed Memories* is a self-help book, a guide. There are no academic standards to which self-help book authors are responsible. Instead, the author's credentials or perceptions in academic training, journalistic acumen or personal experience supply the credibility. That he or she may hold a Ph.D. or an M.D. does not oblige the author to prove a given thesis, as might be expected in the settings that conferred the degree. In the realm of self-help, proof is in the telling. *The Courage to Heal*, probably the most influential self-help book for incest survivors, does not claim to be anything other than a collection of anecdotes woven together by the insights of two non-experts.[36] The measure of a self-help book's "validity" is its sales.

When a psychologist writes a self-help book such as *Repressed Memories*, she is essentially saying, "These are my impressions based on my training and my professional experiences." It is a reader's prerogative to buy or not to buy, believe or not believe, essentially no different from the experience of enjoying or disliking a movie.

This said, it is clear that Fredrickson's perception on the prevalence of sexual abuse is fueled by her views on the male sex role. She does not say how prevalent it is, only that

"Millions of people have blocked out frightening episodes of abuse, years of their life, or their entire childhood."[37] But one can get some idea of the scope Fredrickson intends to convey through the following speculations:

> More males fill the offender role than females. We know that the hormone testosterone increases sex drive, so there may well be a physiological component to sexual compulsivity. Another factor is intricately bound up in the sexism that exists in our culture. The expectations of the societally defined roles for males grooms them more so than females for the controlling, dominating, sexually focused offender role.[38]

So in the absence of statistics on prevalence of sexual abuse, we nonetheless have been told that millions of victims exist whose trauma was so horrible they had to block it out; and that being a male sets one up to be an offender. Fredrickson notes the fact that some families have more than one sexually abusive member, and adds, "Chances are slim in a sexually abusive family system that a child will get past the age of five without being abused."[39]

For a while, Fredrickson, a Minnesota native, thought sexual abuse might be "some strange anomaly of the Southern patriarchal system."[40] She then discovered the problem was widespread, extending even to enlightened Minnesota, the no-smoking state, home of the Hazelden Foundation and the Multiphasic Personality Inventory.

Encouraged yet alarmed by the rapid rise in attendance at her memory repression lecture (and by orders for the tape of that lecture made to accommodate the demand), she reached the turning point of her 18-year career as a psychologist.

"I began to listen to my clients with focused attention to

the possibility of buried memories. Strange dreams, half-finished sentences, strong reactions to abuse issues, and imagery that persistently bothered my clients began to take on new meaning."[41]

The clients responded with fuller disclosures. One woman "described unbelievable acts of human sacrifice committed by a large group of neighborhood families in a small Midwestern city."[42] With Fredrickson's help, the client "bravely accepted that cults are real, even though treatment and intervention were still in their infancy."[43]

In her investigations, Fredrickson learned that these cults possess encyclopedic knowledge of mind-control techniques such as hypnosis, magic tricks, hallucinatory drugs and behavioral psychology. The very outrageousness of their manipulation (which extends to torture and cannibalism) is doubly cruel, for "What better way to keep a secret than to make sure that what is told is so crazy and awful that anyone who tells will never be heard?"[44]

The more likely explanation—that Fredrickson co-created these atrocities with her clients, then matched each new dream or feeling to fit the beliefs—seemed out of the question to her. Fredrickson, on the possibility of widespread ritual abuse, stated:

> The torments of the Holocaust are not confined to that time in history or that country. If people could get away with mass slaughter then, they can get away with it now. Humans and the nature of evil have not changed significantly in forty years. It is plausible that sadists with a similar bent are alive and well and acting out their disease today in America.[45]

John Bradshaw said of Fredrickson: "I consider Dr.

Fredrickson to be one of the leading authorities in the area of sexual trauma."[46] Through such endorsements, Bradshaw acquainted readers with positions he would rather not take himself. There must be areas of disagreement between Fredrickson's views (say, on the prevalence of "mass slaughter" in the United States today [47]) and his own. Perhaps he does not consider these differences important enough to state, or simply prefers to let readers sort these things out for themselves.

In any case, the goals of *Family Secrets* and *Repressed Memories* appear to be far more similar than different. Both books provide tools for the reinterpretation of long-held attitudes and beliefs about one's family. If the numerous examples and case studies are any indication of what lies in store, these reinterpretations will almost always be sinister. Both promise a light at the end of a dark tunnel, placing stock in the adage, "You have to get worse before you get better."

There is, however, a significant difference in the style of the two books. Fredrickson takes the reader straight to hell from the first page, stressing the enormity of the problem of sexual abuse and the lack of resources available for treatment. Bradshaw, on the other hand, goes to Oz. "The Secret History of Dorothy" alluded to in Chapter Four of this book ends happily. Her trauma integrated, Dorothy even visits Uncle Henry on occasion and lets her children come along. Of course, none of her good fortune could have come about without the help of good witch Glinda, who is both therapist and spiritual guide.[48]

In gothic tones, Bradshaw warns of a difficult yet "soulful" journey ahead, taking pains to stress that one may uncover good things as well as bad. One senses a frantic energy behind this discussion of finding the "rich depth and mysterious power of your family,"[49] as if the sorcerer were trying to undo an evil spell. Fredrickson makes no such overtures, and her book is more thematically consistent as a result. But sympathies for survivors were at their most unqualified pitch in 1992, when Fredrickson published *Repressed Memories*. By 1995, the tide had begun to turn.

During a two-day workshop in Coconut Creek, Florida, on "Finishing Business With Mother," Bradshaw announced his plans for the book *Family Secrets*. That was in 1992, a year in which the FMS Foundation was an unorganized group of 50 accused parents. By the time his book appeared in 1995, FMS Foundation membership had swelled above 17,000, and attracted the attention of newspaper and television journalists, including CBS's *60 Minutes*, ABC's *PrimeTime Live*, and Ofra Bickel's *Frontline* documentary for PBS.

Recently courts, who in the past were the survivor movement's strongest ally, have been reconsidering some of their earlier judgments and the arguments that brought these judgments about.

In a precedent-setting case, a California court dismissed a repressed-memory lawsuit on the grounds that the plaintiff's contentions rested on "junk science" and hence did not meet the Frye standard governing expert testimony. The plaintiff, 27-year-old Nancy Zeltzer, claimed to have remembered being molested and tortured by her father 20 years earlier. Zeltzer came to these recollections following therapy with a certified marriage and family counselor.[50]

In August 1995, the Michigan Supreme Court, also citing the Frye standard, ruled that experts would no longer be allowed to testify that certain behaviors in victims are "consistent with other child sexual abuse victims"[51] in child sexual abuse cases because "its foundation is too unreliable as a detector of sexual abuse."[52] Ordinary abuse cases (those not involving repressed memory) have been caught up in the same zealous protectionism that has affected the phenomenon of repressed memory.

Kelly Michaels, a former New Jersey child care worker who served five years of a 47-year sentence before being released, plans to file a $10 million lawsuit against the county who she says maliciously prosecuted her for fictional crimes. The New Jersey Supreme Court, in overturning Michaels' conviction, found that all 20 children in the case had been led, bribed or threatened by investigating social workers.[53]

And George Franklin, who in 1990 began serving a life sentence for the 1969 murder of Susan Nason, is now a free man after serving five years in prison. A federal judge in Oakland, California, overturned Franklin's conviction after determining that his daughter, Eileen Franklin-Lipsker, could have learned details of her best friend Nason's murder from newspaper accounts. Contributing to the prosecutors decision to not retry Franklin was Eileen's later memories of her father committing still other murders. For at least one of these murders, Franklin has an iron-clad alibi and has been exonerated by DNA evidence.

Franklin is suing his daughter's therapist and her prosecutors. From his daughter, Eileen, he asks only one dollar.[54] The case attracted national attention (including a television movie) as the first time testimony based on repressed memory that had sent someone to prison.

In the *Family Secrets* appendix, Bradshaw leads his discussion on the memory controversy with the Franklin case. In describing the controversy as "not only a pressing legal problem but a clinical one,"[55] Bradshaw himself cites the $500,000 judgment awarded Gary Ramona by a California court, which found that a therapist had improperly led his daughter to believe he molested her as a child.[56]

As shown by the cautionary words on pages 86 and 87 of *Family Secrets*, as well as in the appendix, Bradshaw wants his readers to know he is closely following the recovered-memory controversy.

The warnings are clear. Memory can be contaminated by suggestibility, Bradshaw writes, so "not every memory should be taken at face value."[57] Memory can become distorted by current desires, including a desire to please the author of a self-help book, such as himself. He would like to assure the reader unequivocally that he has no need for anyone to remember dark family secrets: "I would much prefer that you uncover long-forgotten memories of a pleasant kind: a joyous family outing, a special birthday party, the day your dad read you a story or your mom rocked you to sleep."[58]

Though the inclusion is commendable, and certainly more than most other incest authors have been willing to do thus far, Bradshaw offers an unremarkable summary of the false memory debate. His discussion contains no new insights and offers no solutions apart from the following:

> The bottom line for this book is that I want to warn you to be very careful and thorough in probing your family's secrets. Recovering traumatic memories is a very delicate matter. If you feel like you are uncovering such memories, you should seek out a reputable person who has experience in these matters. Leave no stone unturned in finding another family member who might be able to verify the abuse, and use all other objective means available to verify your memories.[59]

In light of the fact that these cautions appear, and the fact that readers will connect Bradshaw's statements: "You should seek out a reputable person who has experience in these matters,"[60] with "I consider Dr. Fredrickson to be one of the leading authorities in the area of sexual trauma,"[61] this reads more like a legal disclaimer than any sort of bottom line.

Having hallowed the journey and cautioned against the possibility of error, Bradshaw then sets out with the reader in an earnest search for memories. *Family Secrets* includes a three generation model of various family systems and exercises to assist the reader in his or her own search for secrets. Death is no barrier; the door to diagnosis is always open. A "Four-Generational Family Map of James Jeder, 1994," for example, traces the family tree of a 54-year-old English professor who is also an alcoholic and a womanizer with a clandestine attachment to pornography. His wife Karen has "trouble with intimacy." The dysfunctions are placed beside each name in a chart resembling electrical circuits.[62]

It is no wonder Jeder has problems. His father, Shane Jeder, was an alcoholic and a sex addict; and his mother, Heather Jamison Jeder, suffered from depression, psychosomatic ailments and "unresolved incest." She was pregnant when they married.

But they are not being blamed for Jeder's troubles: Shane's mother was an alcoholic who was also pregnant when she married; Heather's mother was an agoraphobic with an eating disorder. Her millionaire father did some "strange sexual acting out."

But they are not at fault: Three of their eight parents were alcoholics, two more were depressed and another "incested" his daughters. The sexual offender was Boyd Jamison, born in 1865, a self-made millionaire who left behind a secret pornography stash when he died in 1941.[63]

The book offers plenty of guidance for people who are interested in retrieving buried memories. Readers are advised to go on archaeological digs, obtaining as much information as possible about one's parents, grandparents, and great-grandparents. Bradshaw calls this exercise "Columboing," after the Peter Falk television character.[64] They are to play "What If?" using the following types of questions as guidelines:

> What if the man you call Uncle Joe was actually your father? What if your moralistic mother was having an affair with your best friend's father next door?
>
> Any family photos you have access to can be a mine of information and memory triggers. . . . What do the people's expressions and body language tell you about their relationships? . . . If most of the pictures show a carefully posed, "perfect" family, can you recall how you were feeling behind your smile?[65]

In *Homecoming: Reclaiming and Championing Your Inner Child*, Bradshaw explains:

> If your family of origin is not in recovery, it is almost impossible to get support from them while you're in your own recovery process. Often they think that what you're doing is stupid and they shame you for it. Often they are threatened by your doing this work, because as you give up your old family roles, you disrupt the frozen equilibrium of the family system. You were never allowed to be yourself before. Why would they suddenly start allowing that now? If your family of origin was dysfunctional, it is the least likely place to get your nurturing needs met. So, I advise you to keep a safe distance and work on finding a new, nonshaming, supportive family. This could be a support group of

friends, it could be the group you joined to work on your inner child, or it could be any one of the myriad 12-Step groups now available all over the country.[66]

The use of other "safe" adults as support systems, or even as parents for the inner child, is a common theme in recovery literature. The supportive, nurturing group of friends returns in *Family Secrets*. In the following passage, Bradshaw describes how these groups might "validate" any feelings associated with childhood incidents recalled in the work:

> After you've shared a memory, a member might say: "I saw your lips trembling. I heard your voice rising. You hunched your shoulders, lowered your head, and clenched your hands. You sort of looked like a child. It was clear to me how afraid and sad you were and how painful that experience was for you." By validating the experience, group members help the person own it.[67]

These seemingly neutral "observations," offered up as an example of what supportive feedback in a group might look like, appear to be aimed at helping the person who has shared a memory feel acknowledged, or "validated." If the event shared was something the person had always remembered, a response of the sort Bradshaw envisions might be helpful, even kind. But if "sharing a memory" means speculating on events that might have happened, or interpreting dreams, or in other ways engaging in an active search for childhood abuses, then even this seemingly straightforward feedback about lips and hands and shoulders could contribute to an individual's evolving belief that abuses did occur. Such a finding would be consistent with the group's (and Bradshaw's) beliefs that traumatic memories can be repressed and that Columboing for secrets is a good way to unearth them.

One could just as easily imagine a different kind of feedback which acknowledges the individual but entails no sweeping assumptions about the nature of memory or the events of a hidden past. In the counter scenario I propose, after you've shared a memory, a member might say:

> Last week you said it was two strange men who abused you. Now you are saying you believe it was your father and your brother. I know your friends in the 12-step group say you need to "face up" to the truth about your past, but do they know more about your history than you? For months you've been trying to 'put a face' on your attackers. With all due respect, how do you know that there were any such individuals? Have you thought about the role played by your therapist, who told you that getting fired from your job and losing custody of your kids was not the cause of your depression? If you are going to play "what if?" and "try on" the possibility that these things happened to you, don't you owe it to yourself to try on the possibility that they did not; that you have been subjected to enormous pressures brought on by peer groups, literature, television movies and even your own therapist, whose cumulative impact has led you to doubt your most fundamental perceptions and certainly your potential to function without their help? Isn't it possible that they have used your intellect and your capacity for introspection against you, not because they are evil but because they have been similarly deceived and blinded to the ways in which they do, in fact, benefit; that in your search for subtle meanings you have barked at a reflection and

lost the bone that was in your mouth, which was your very identity, your strength, those things you are searching for but possess nonetheless? And is it possible that it is this side of the equation which now demands the feeling, the owning, the facing-up-to, the recovery?

As someone who attended some group therapy in the early '90s, I have seen perceptions being skewed in the direction of finding abuse. The core of this issue wasn't that some people were harboring images of horrible events that didn't happen. It was the methods employed by therapists to heal the past, which almost had to produce false memories in a certain percentage of clients. These therapists would lead workshops citing inflated statistics on the prevalence of abuse; use guided imagery for regression and suggestibility; directly or indirectly equating and reinforcing the discovery of abuse with "growth" and failure to make such discoveries with "denial."

Using these combined influences over months or years, how could one not produce images—or, more often than not, a lengthy series of images—that were metaphorically significant, emotionally powerful and factually erroneous? This method was doomed to inaccuracy, it was destined to misrepresent the past—and, contrary to what some of the therapists were beginning to say, whether these pictures were literal or metaphorical representations of a person's experience does matter!

It is the method, and not the individual therapist that packs the most significant influence. People could easily produce questionable memories in the supportive environment of their own peer groups or even alone. The principals in memory controversies, large and small, were incidental to their methods. The particular peer group, the particular book and the particular therapist or even recovery star all were incidental to the climate of suspicion their methods created, out of which emerged these intractable tales of horror.

Recovery Stars and the Memory Controversy

Charles Whitfield continues to defend buried trauma, another metaphor that has become a reality. Similar to his inner-child workbook, his recovered-memory therapy involves writing things down and "telling secrets to safe people."[68] But unlike the inner child, who is instantly real if her outer host says she's real, victimization secrets require a victimizer, who may be sent to prison if certain things are written down and certain not-so-safe people are told. Instead of pausing before this rather solemn circumstance, Whitfield forged ahead unhesitatingly. He even required members of a workshop audience in Seattle, Washington to sign a "Statement of Safety"—the equivalent of a loyalty oath—which reads in part: "This is to certify that I am not a False Memory Syndrome Foundation member. I also do not side with them or seriously advocate their point of view that most delayed memories of trauma are false."[69]

Whitfield estimates that only 2% of people claiming to have been falsely accused of sexual abuse based on recovered memory are telling the truth. He does not indicate how he arrived at this number.[70]

There is another number worth mentioning: zero. It represents the total number of bodies connected with organized satanic cult activity despite a seven year search by the Federal Bureau of Investigation (FBI). Supervisory Special FBI Agent Kenneth V. Lanning published a summary of that study.[71]

The following scenario is my conjecture as to how *Family Secrets* reached its finished form: Bradshaw knew of the potential for false memories to be created before FMS became an issue. In the past, he had seen other recovery stars pulling up memories through their own suggestive methods and it had horrified him. He devised a system of archaeological digging that seemed safer, but would still access the original pain—which could just as easily be an emotional injury, he wasn't partial to finding sexual abuse in particular.

His earlier books outlined the dysfunctional family, the nature of toxic shame, the inner child, and how to love and find love despite one's past. *Family Secrets* seemed to mark the therapeutic summit, his Summa Theologae, the symphonic climax in which deepest darkness is reconciled with the light of understanding and forgiveness.

But something went wrong. While writing the book, he watched the development of the memory controversy with interest, half-hoping it would all go away. When it didn't and it seemed that Columboing and playing "What If?" might actually be dangerous, Bradshaw gave his image a makeover by tacking on the appendix and writing "The Secret History of Dorothy," making sure to emphasize resolution with family members and even a type of forgiveness.

While *Homecoming* also includes a section on forgiveness, it does not contain this emphasis on "staying connected with your family."[72] It must be a rather difficult and dismaying position to be in, learning that so many people have used his books and workshops to discover their memories, when he himself is not sure about the validity of these memories.

Such stories are plentiful among parents who meet through the FMS Foundation. An estranged sibling shares this typical account in *True Stories of False Memories* by Eleanor Goldstein and Kevin Farmer:

Pat quotes John Bradshaw often and talks about "doing the work" to "heal the child within," which has included hypnosis and role playing. . . . How much more time, energy and money will she spend trying to get healed?[73]

I interviewed a woman who will be referred to as Gerry. She recounted the time period leading up to her sister's confession that she had been raped as a child and that her father had killed the family cat to terrify her into silence: "John Bradshaw was a significant influence on her. At the end of October 1990, when we were still living in the condo, she made us watch Bradshaw shows on PBS."[74]

By July 1991, and with the assistance of other supporting influences, the sister found her memories and thought it would be a good idea for Gerry to dig into her own past as well.

"She didn't say I had been sexually abused," Gerry recalls, "but the message was implied strongly that this happened to us all. I would say, 'You're telling me that your reality is reality and my reality is not reality? This is insane!' And she kept saying, 'That's your problem. You're repressing it.' It was so frustrating!"[75]

A 70-year-old woman active in the FMS Foundation tells about a planned visit scheduled by her daughter on Mother's Day. The daughter brought her therapist, and the two of them laid out the years of molestation and rape committed by the woman's husband with her knowledge and consent. The mother emphatically denies that the abuse, only recently discovered in therapy, took place. On the only subsequent visit, when the daughter left, she picked up an expensive vase, threw it on the floor and shouted, "I give you back your shame!"

"There are people who go into these groups to learn how to hate," the mother says. "They come on Mother's Day, holidays, Christmas. If their message is sincere, why do these hateful things?"[76]

Through letters, many accusers have severed all ties with their families. There is a remarkable similarity among them. The following letter was written to an elderly couple by their adult daughter, from whom they have been estranged for several years:

> *THINK HARD–YOU'LL REMEMBER*
> *I will not give you specifics. I don't owe you an explanation, nor is it my responsibility to prove I was abused. Everyone has the right to tell the truth about her life and so I have and shall continue to do so. I am the strongest and the healthiest I have been in years. You can tell the world I'm crazy, but this won't go away. Understand, however, that if you malign me and if I find out about it, I will shout from the rooftops the things you did to me. I do not want to and will not see you or talk to you.*[77]

During an interview, therapist David Calof, who attempts to counterbalance FMS concerns, said that patients have shown him scars inflicted during satanic rituals. One dimension of his argument in support of the reality of repressed memories is that "somebody has to explain why the patients get better when they are treated as abuse victims."[78]

It seems that people have been explaining this for quite some time now. The patients get better because someone recognizes them, talks to them as human beings, validates some kind of suffering in their lives and shows them a way out of that suffering. The improvement is real, not manufactured. But the lessening of psychiatric symptoms among survivor patients does not imply that what they have survived actually occurred in a literal way; any more than the lessening of symptoms among members of the Unification Church implies the truth of the teachings of the Reverand Sun Myung Moon; or the improvement of AA members implies the truth of Bill Wilson's speculations on an "allergy" to alcohol.

In a 1993 issue of *Changes*, John Bradshaw tells an interviewer:

> I offer people $100,000 to find a place in my books or lectures where I've blamed anybody. . . . They're missing the point, which is that the intention of your parents isn't even relevant. It's the internalized father that the little child made a fantasy god of; it's the fantasy we're working on in the workshops. If you call your dad after a workshop and read him off, you're missing the whole point.[79]

Having a Funeral for Your Mother

Though I did not conduct that interview, Bradshaw had said the same thing to me in a previous conversation. I had asked him about a prolonged guided-imagery portion of a "Finishing Business With Mother" workshop he had given in 1992, in which he commands his audience to visualize lowering their mothers into the ground.[80] Later, I discussed his answer with psychiatrist David Halpern of the Mt. Sinai Medical Clinic in New York, who had stopped by a meeting of accused parents. First, I described the taped meditation:

> *See yourself on a country road. There are green fields all around you. See the trees and the flowers. It*

comes up to a little hill and at the top of the hill you look down, you see an old cemetery there. . . . See the gravestones. . . . (Music starts. Musician Steven Halpern—no relation—does some nice things with a Moog synthesizer.) *See that one of those gravestones has [your mother's] name on it. Look at the dates!* (From somewhere, a slow drumbeat begins.)

Now let your mind flash back. You're at home and the telephone rings. . . . It's the hospital. Your mother is dying! . . . Now you're driving there. . . . This is it! A nurse is there. Your brother's there, your sister's there. You can hear [your mother] breathing heavily. (Halpern starts with a funereal accompaniment on the piano.). . . *Hear her say, "I'm so sorry for the way I hurt you." See that wounded little girl's eyes.* (Someone in the audience breaks out into deep, wailing sobs.) *Touch her hand, touch her hair. . . . It's so sad!*

It's just so sad that we never had what we both wanted! (Now others in the audience are weeping audibly.) . . . *See a smile, a little smile on her face. And then let her die. . . .*

Now you're in the hearse and you're going to the graveyard. To the headstone. . . . Just very slowly, casket's being lowered into the ground now.

It's over. Walk away now. You're all alone now. There is no magical mother to come and make it all okay. Just let yourself feel the emptiness. It's okay to cry. (People cough and hack and cry.) *You wish it could have been different. It's okay to grieve the dream—the kind of mama you wanted. . . .*

Now we're coming out of the meditation. This is an ending. We have the fall when the earth dies and then the winter. Then comes the spring. (Hopeful little groundhog trill on the piano.)[81]

As the meditation breaks up, Bradshaw tells the audience it's okay to hug someone or ask for a hug. Some of them are still sobbing.

After describing the meditation to Halpern, I then offered the explanation given to me, which roughly went as follows: that infants are narcissistic, they literally see themselves as a part of everything around them; that part of the grandiose worldview of the infant is to see the parent as all-good or all-evil, or both at different times; and that what we are saying goodbye to is the mythical, all-good or all-evil mother of our infantile, narcissistic imagination, so that we can have a real relationship with the real mother who remains.[82]

"That's what the words say," Halpern repilied when I finished. "What does the music say?"[83]

In *Healing the Shame that Binds You*, Bradshaw writes, "The *est* Training (The Forum now) confronts people's act: their melodramatic story. The act or story is the mythologized self: the phony performing self."[84]

Sometimes this may be true. Then again, various other groups could probably do the same thing. In the 1970s, these types of groups were large and easy to recognize: The Unification Church, the People's Temple, the Divine Light Mission and the Krishna Consciousness Movement are primary examples. In his paper, *Reparenting and Mind Control*, which appeared in the January 1994 issue of the *Transactional Analysis Journal*, Alan Jacobs writes about these and the cultural shift toward smaller and more numerous therapy cults:

Religious beliefs notwithstanding, they have been

criticized for controlling and restrictive techniques, seductive recruitment practices, manipulative indoctrination procedures, stroke bombing, consciously isolating people from family and friends, etc. They sell personal transformation through symbolic community attachment, semi-worship of a master, total emotional realignment and radical personality change. And, they often produce psychiatric casualties.

Concurrent developments in psychology have produced groups promising secular salvation through adoption of pseudo-humanistic values and claims of innovative ontological uniqueness and exclusivity which are similarly produced by a master.[85]

Representatives of the two primary cult watchdog organizations in this country, the Cult Awareness Network and the American Family Foundations, have expressed serious concerns about these groups. Forum graduates have often sought relief through FOCUS, a support group for former cult victims, according to director Carol Giambalvo, who claims her own involvement with the Forum nearly destroyed her family:

You feel like you're more in control of your life than ever before, if someone says "mind control," you laugh and say, "Who are you kidding? No one's in control of my mind." You don't see the emotional manipulation until you study the mind-control techniques.[86]

A low point for Giambalvo came when a Forum workshop leader confronted her act—her phony performing self—in front of 250 people, telling Giambalvo she had "created" her diabetes in order to manipulate her father. She burst into tears. Although the incident was painfully humiliating for her, Giambalvo quit her job as a legal secretary to do volunteer work for the Forum.[87]

Bold Beginnings

Jacqui Schiff was a psychiatric social worker who, in the late 1960s, lived in Fredericksburg, Virginia. Her most famous case literally appeared on her doorstep in 1966 in the form of an uncommunicative, severely unbalanced young man. After months of unsuccessful efforts to open his heart and mind, Schiff managed to get the young man to nurse at her breast, and that event was the turning point in a remarkable psychiatric breakthrough.

The patient was given a new name: Aaron Schiff. He later graduated from college and completed a two-year training program to become a clinical member of the International Transactional Analysis Association (ITAA). Aaron Schiff became the test case for a new therapy whose pioneers claimed to be able to treat schizophrenia without drugs.

As Alan Jacobs has observed, Schiff's writings reflect the loneliness of a legendary inventor. In a 1977 paper she writes, "My professional advisors offered no help; I was already beyond the range of their imaginations."[88] Alan Jacobs pulls this quote, and adds: "With this kind of thinking almost any level of confrontation can be ultimately justified by claiming that one is merely escalating over the pathological behavior and that 'coercive techniques are confrontive and not punitive.' "[89]

Alan Jacobs, incidentally, received part of his training from Jacqui Schiff. He has since become a major force behind getting the ITAA to take a second look not only at Schiffian reparenting, but the implications of "regressive therapies" in general. The tide has turned in the direction of taking that second look.

The only literature analyzing Schiffian reparenting from a psychological perspective seems to be Jacobs's *Reparenting and Mind Control*. This is difficult to understand, considering the number of people damaged by reparenting and the extent of the damages. The following is a quote from Schiff's 1977 paper that Jacobs discusses, beginning with his introduction to the quote:

> Schiff also wrote that *"what had been environmentally acquired could be extinguished"* and claimed success in decathecting a patient's violent "werewolf parent":
> "(The patient) perceived the werewolf as a threat to his survival, that its bizarre and violent behavior on some occasion might result in the police or someone else killing him, or that he might kill someone else. He believed that he could eject it totally, or kill it internally. . . . And he succeeded."[90]

The patient to which Schiff referred was her adopted son Aaron, the first of more than 1000 schizophrenics she claims to have reparented. The people who lived under Schiff's roof in Virginia and later at the Cathexis School in Alamo, California, were not her biological children. They were adults who had signed over their legal rights, or had a parent or legal guardian sign for them. As she explained in a 1969 issue of the *Transactional Analysis Bulletin*:

> Patients were asked to give up relationships with their previous families and to invest in forming new primary relationships. [Parents] . . . are asked to ex-

plain to the patient that they are giving him up permanently and to indicate clearly that the Schiffs are now his parents.[91]

In *Reparenting and Mind Control*, Alan Jacobs explains that: "Requiring this of patients creates fear and panic and quite naturally they seek some protective parent substitute who will give them a feeling of safety. What is required is that they trade their physical freedom for it."[92]

In 1970, Jacqui Schiff published *All My Children* with Pyramid Books. This account of reparenting by its founder contains numerous references to spanking adult patients, standing them in the corner and restraining them physically. The following passage describes a session with Aaron Schiff:

Naked, Aaron was strapped securely in a restraining chair. As I approached him with a large hunting knife, I was sure that he believed I would, indeed castrate him. To my dismay, he did not appear in the least frightened.

Maybe he really did want to be castrated! I thought fleetingly of those men who have submitted to surgery in order to become as much like females as they could be made. I remember how desperately Aaron had wanted the love he saw his mother lavish on her daughters. Perhaps mutilation was worth it, in his thinking, to get that love.

Then, as I laid the edge of the knife against his naked genitals, Aaron's face drained of color.

"What am I going to do?" I asked him. "Shall I start cutting you so you can never be a man?"

"No, no, please!" he whispered. "I want to be a man. Mom, I do want to be a man!"

"I don't believe you," I said. I pressed slightly with the knife, and his controls broke. He began to struggle and scream.[93]

Schiff describes this moment as another therapeutic breakthrough, the day Aaron decided to "take responsibility" for his sexuality.

In 1972, Margaret-Rose (Gans) Rubin testified before a city commissioner in Alexandria, Virginia, about Schiff's treatment of a 16-year-old male patient at the Schiff Rehabilitation Project:

Jacqui Schiff gave orders—finally after standing him in the corner and beating him with assistance from her son Aaron. Every time he mentioned his natural parents, a gallon of Octagon—that's a dishwashing liquid—was to be poured down his throat. . . . He was beaten for so many things. He was beaten with a paddle—a very heavy paddle—he was also switched. . . . She told him she wouldn't kill him unless it was absolutely necessary. . . . Danny was beaten repeatedly and if he breathed wrong he was beaten.

Jacqui gave orders to have him put in a restraining chair. It had a white seat and a belt at the waist and there were strings underneath—not really strings, they were ties that looked like pieces of a sheet that had been torn. They had gags which they made out of dishcloths. He was bound and gagged and left like that. He didn't get anything to eat ever when he was restrained. He was left like that for almost two days . . . Mrs. Schiff decided that the best thing to do with him was to punish him. He was taken around like a calf on a rope, his shoes were taken away so he couldn't run away. . . . They made a rope and knotted it and tied it around his waist and other people would pull on it when they wanted him to go somewhere. . . . They fed him only starches—no fruit, no vegetables. And if he didn't eat everything on his plate, he had a choice of either being beaten or restrained or going in the corner.

I heard Aaron yelling at him. He was saying that you are disgusting to wet your bed and I'm going to kill you if you ever do it again and he kept screaming at him and kept beating him. . . . Mrs. Schiff said she had a marvelous solution . . . and she said if Danny ever wets his bed again, put him in diapers and make sure they're the roughest and scratchiest kind.

Danny wouldn't call her mom. . . . He called her Jacqui and she hit him over and over again and Aaron held him down. And then she slapped him and beat him with her fist.[94]

Jacqui Schiff was cleared of a charge of battering one of her patients, but authorities shut down the Schiff Rehabilitation Project on September 1, 1971, citing "a serious and imminent threat to the lives, health, safety, and welfare of the patients treated and maintained" there.[95]

"People in Our House Are Not Allowed to Act Crazy."[96]

After being refused a license to practice in Ohio, Jacqui Schiff and her husband Morris moved to Alamo, California, and bought a two-story home with a guest house in back. They called the home the Cathexis Institute and began accepting referrals from local hospitals.

Contrary to the atmosphere at those hospitals, however, Cathexis was designed to run almost as an equal-opportunity village. The term "patient," if used at all, was downplayed.

The adults who lived in the guest house were simply referred to as "kids."

"I don't run or control," Jacqui Schiff told a grand jury in Contra Costa County, California in 1972. "Essentially, I'm part of the community."[97] The grand jury had convened to investigate the October 23, 1972 death of 17-year-old John Hartwell, the youngest of the Cathexis kids. His hands and feet had been bound and he was lowered into a bathtub of scalding hot water, where he remained for more than 20 minutes. The incident could have ended Schiff's budding career. Instead, it created barely more than a ripple.

John's troubles had become noticeable to his parents two years earlier. In testimony before the grand jury of Contra Costa County, Sara Hartwell said that around the time her son reached the 10th grade, he became moody and withdrawn. He stopped talking. His parents tried to get him to see a psychiatrist, but he wouldn't go.

"He felt anything that was establishment, anybody that was in this line of work didn't know anything," Sara Hartwell testified. "They were all stupid, worthless."[98]

The summer after 10th grade, John's condition worsened.

> He'd be sitting in a room with you, he'd suddenly look like he was seeing a terrible vision off in the distance. He started to walk with a funny-physically odd stance sort of hitched up on one shoulder. Then we really thought we had a problem, but we still couldn't get him to go and talk to the doctor. We finally got him to go, but once he was there he wouldn't talk.
>
> Then he started staying up all night long. He would prowl all around the house and you'd hear him laughing very bizarrely. He'd talk as if he had somebody

there . . . I mean, we were all nervous wrecks. We felt we had to lock our doors because he was acting so strange that we didn't know if he was going to burst in on us with a butcher knife or if he would hurt himself. Although he made no effort to do either of those things. It got to be an impossible thing. You can't have a person who acts that bizarre in your house. It ruins everybody else's life. So that's pretty much it.[99]

In January 1971, John Hartwell was committed to a residential psychiatric program for adolescents at Napa State Hospital in Orinda, California, where doctors gave him a diagnosis of paranoid schizophrenia. He fled several times, each time running away for a longer period of time. A psychiatrist advised the Hartwells that their only alternative might be to place their son in a locked ward.

Don and Judy Finer, a pair of social workers, had another idea. John did not seem to be improving at the hospital, they said, and a locked ward probably would only make things worse. About six weeks before being approached by the Hartwells, Judy Finer had looked at Cathexis and met with Jacqui Schiff. She was thinking about referring a female patient there. According to Sara Hartwell, Judy thought the place looked satisfactory, "and she had almost no other suggestions of places where somebody like John could go at that point."[100] Sara Hartwell agreed to do secretarial work for Schiff to defray expenses of $10 a day.

By all accounts, John was not a model patient. David Richman, a physician and psychiatric resident at Agnew State Hospital whom Schiff used as a consultant, told the grand jury that John had trouble accepting affection.

One of the things about the whole Schiff family is that

there's a great emphasis on caring, on loving, on nurturing. One of John's problems was that you try to be tender with him, if you try to be caring, he would see that as you're just trying to hurt him or you're just trying to manipulate him.[101]

Sara Hartwell told the grand jury that both her son and Jacqui Schiff told her of John's refusal to nurse with a baby bottle: "He told me they had been trying to get him to take a bottle, which is a thing she does with the kids. And that he didn't want to. He didn't want to regress is what she said."[102]

Regressing to one's "emotional age" is a key tenet in reparenting. Operating on the assumption that development has been stunted, therapists try to get the patient to "go back" to that time in order to "re-learn" or "re-decide" what it means to be safe and functional. For this purpose Schiff used diapers on many of her patients. The patients were expected to relieve themselves in the diapers instead of using the bathroom. Then the therapist would change the diapers.

During the early-to-mid 1970s, Jacqui Schiff was a force to be reckoned with in the ITAA. Reparenting was considered a hot commodity and many ITAA members who are still practicing today did part of their training under Schiff. As such, those deemed to need regressing to, say, age eight, could get away with jumping around and acting like eight year olds. Those who needed "cathecting" to infancy, however, were urged to defecate into diapers and have them changed. Some managed to wriggle out of this obligation, but many others complied.

What puzzled Sara Hartwell was the adult kids' ability to stop being kids at any moment:

And I've seen a couple of kids over there in a regressed situation, and they do, you know, go around in diapers and crawl on the floor, but they can snap in and out of it. . . . honestly, to me it's a complete mystery. I don't know whether those kids really think that they are babies at this time, or whether it's an act that they think they have to go into.[103]

A juror asked, "Why would they have to go into an act?"

"Maybe in order to please her so they can get on to something else," Sara Hartwell answered. "Because I can't imagine anybody who's almost an adult, even some of them are adults, being able to snap into this baby thing and really live it. But, you know, maybe they can."[104]

Near the end of May 1972, John ran away from Cathexis. This was nothing new. His mother continued to do secretarial work for Jacqui Schiff. Early in July, the sheriff from Corvallis, Oregon, called her. John had been found breaking into an old, abandoned farm, apparently looking for food. The sheriffs put him on a plane to San Francisco, where he was met by Jack and Sara Hartwell. They kept him at home for a week, without telling anybody, before deciding to return him to Cathexis.

John was placed under the semi-care of four or five other patients and staff who made sure that he dressed, bathed and ate on schedule. One of these patients assigned a caretaking role was a man named Carl Fjelle. On the week leading up to Monday, October 23, 1972, John had been acting strangely, threatening to run away. Plus, Carl said John had been "talking about weird stuff."[105]

When a grand juror asked what Carl meant by weird stuff, he replied, "You know, talking about things in the room."

"In other words, things in the room that weren't there?"

"Yeah, right," Carl testified. "And people would tell him to cut it out, because people in our house are not allowed to act crazy."[106]

Carl and John slept on bunkbeds in the guest house where the kids stayed. Carl on top, John on the bottom. Each night before they went to sleep, Carl would handcuff John's right arm to the lower bedpost. Doctor's orders, Carl said. The handcuffs were the standard metal kind and had been purchased at the Army Surplus store.

On the morning of October 23rd, Carl removed the handcuffs. Accounts differ slightly as to exactly what happened next. Aaron, who was not present at the time, testified that John had hit Carl in the face. Carl agreed, but said, "It was more a combination slap and hit."[107]

Carl admitted freely that this had made him angry. He told the grand jury that after being slapped or hit, he had pinned John's arms back on the bed and told him to cut it out, that people don't do that kind of thing around here. John did not respond. Then Carl and another patient named Jim Freund tried to get John's pants on, but he broke away and tried to run out of the room in his pajamas. So Carl and Jim handcuffed him again, this time with both hands behind his back. They managed to get the jeans on, left the pajama top and took him over to the house.

There Carl told Aaron what had happened. John had hit him, been giving him a hard time. "Then Aaron got angry and shook him," Carl testified.

Juror: What did he say to John, if anything?

Carl Fjelle: Okay. Again I don't remember the—

Juror: Approximately?

Carl Fjelle: "People aren't allowed to hit anybody." That kind a thing. Expressing a lot of anger at what he did and at the way he was functioning."[108]

Aaron remembered it differently:

I was a little bit angry at him, you know, but not a whole lot. It hadn't involved me. The main thing is I was interested in that he understand very clearly that he wasn't supposed to hit, you know, I yelled at him. But I yelled at him because John responds—you know, he responded to people yelling at him that sometimes he wouldn't respond to by just telling him.[109]

House rules dictated that patients keep themselves clean. Immediately after having forcefully told John that hitting people was not acceptable behavior, Aaron decided to take charge of John's bath or shower. He knew that Carl and John were upset with each other and figured he would be better able to control the situation and keep it from getting violent. He gave John a choice of taking a shower or a bath. According to Carl, "Aaron repeatedly told [John] that the bath would, you know, be worse because he would be, you know, tied."[110] Carl had never seen anyone tied up to take a bath before. But then John's behavior had been unusual.

John chose the bath. Within five minutes after having arrived at the main house, Aaron and Carl went to the first-floor bathroom with John, who was still in handcuffs. Carl described John at this time as "psychotic"—which under questioning he rephrased as "He looked really scared, he didn't look like he was with it. He looked like he really had mixed emotions."[111]

Whatever his mental state, John had never lost the ability to understand and converse. Once they arrived at the bath-room, Aaron told John that he would have to take his bath in restraints. Then he sent Carl off to get a box of Perform detergent. The handcuffs had been removed in order for John to undress. Aaron took a length of rope which was already in the bathroom and tied John's hands behind his back. He looped the same rope around John's waist and tied his ankles together so that his knees would be flexed. Aaron said he tied him that way so that John wouldn't be hitting him or trying to hit him while Aaron was bending over him in the tub.

"He was very impulsive," Aaron told the grand jury. "You know, one moment he would be standing there, the next moment he would be doing something, threatening."[112]

After Carl handed the detergent through the door, Aaron sent him off to eat breakfast. He turned on both hot and cold faucets in the bathtub, and put his hand under the tap to test the water, once.

Fifteen minutes later Carl was still in the kitchen when someone sent word that Aaron needed him to get a red pitcher from the supply closet. When he entered the bathroom, Carl said John had beads of sweat on his face, and that "he was kind of reddish-white . . . it's kind of hard to explain. . . . Aaron, took the pitcher, dipped it in the water, and poured it over John's body four or five times,"[113] Carl guessed.

Aaron told John it would be his responsibility to clean up the bathroom. Then Aaron left. John had been in the tub for approximately 20 minutes. Carl, who was now in charge, reached into the water to undo John's restraints. He immediately pulled his hands back out. The water was uncomfortably hot.

Carl reached in again and untied the rope. Then he lifted John out of the tub, and that was when he began to appreciate the situation. There was no skin on John's hands or on his feet. Instead, that skin was on the bathroom floor.

"But it looked worse than that. It wasn't a sunburn color, it was like a brownish skin color. It was red around the buttock area." John's hands and feet were bleeding.

"God, you must be in pain!" Carl said.

"Yes, I am in pain," John answered.[114]

At the foot of the stairs, Jacqui and Aaron Schiff were talking, Aaron telling his mother which of the kids' cars they could use that day and so on, when they heard a loud thump. Aaron looked both ways and then Jacqui said, "I think that came from the bathroom."[115] While he went to the bathroom, Jacqui checked the dining room, where some of the kids were eating. She thought it was probably John acting up again.

A moment later, Jacqui recalled, Aaron appeared at the kitchen door. He looked really upset.

"There's something the matter with John's skin,"[116] Aaron said.

When Jacqui saw John, it looked to her as if he had been burned. She told Aaron to go get some clean blankets and get him to the hospital right away.

Carl remembered that Aaron had come into the bathroom right after John had fallen. As they lifted him to his feet, the magnitude of what had happened began to weigh down on Carl, who testified:

So we picked John up and I said, "Oh, look!" I was like freaking out with what I saw. It looked really—you know. And [Aaron] said something like, "You don't do that, you've got to act responsibly." He wanted me to get to a point where I would be responsible and not zap myself out by looking at him. The point was that I should really—like Aaron was really effective in getting the blankets around John, carrying him out and putting him in the car . . . Like Aaron, I believe, acted responsibly, you know, when he saw what happened.[117]

"Being effective" and "acting responsibly" were standards the Schiff children were expected to maintain. It was the price of their living in a community. Aaron was well on his way to becoming a therapist. He was very responsible. John, on the other hand, had resisted treatment at every turn. He would not take a baby bottle. He was always running away, he had eluded authorities once for six weeks and he had hit people.

David Richman explained the mindset of the paranoid schizophrenic to the grand jury: "They think you're going to hurt them, so instead of waiting for you to hurt them, what they are going to do is to hurt you. It's kind of like the best defense is a good offense, that kind of strategy."[118]

But according to Sara Hartwell, before going to Cathexis John had never acted violently. Only once had she ever seen her son hit anybody. That was during one of the times John had run away and was staying at home. The people at Cathexis thought it would be a good idea for John's father to spank him. Sara Hartwell testified:

And this is one of their methods, they think spanking is really good. I guess this is going along with treating them like little kids. But my husband is not the type who really goes in for this kind of thing. But they really—well, finally Jack did spank him and I would say, you know, that really got John all stirred up. And John slugged him just once, he hit him really hard on the side of the face. This was a blow that was unexpected so it really got him and just knocked him . . . But he did not as a matter of normal events go around hitting anybody.[119]

John had spent a lot of time at home. He had siblings, and siblings sometimes hit each other. But the only time his mother had seen John hit anyone was after his father spanked him at the Schiff's behest. Other than that, she said, "He just plain was not violent."[120]

Cathexis was another matter. Everyone who testified before the grand jury said that John always had at least a rope around his waist. If Dr. Richman is right about some schizophrenics, he still did not address how some patients may have good reason to think they will be hurt.

This seems ironic, given that Cathexis was built around freedom. At a time when institutionalizing schizophrenics implied warehousing and hopelessness, Jacqui Schiff said many if not most of these people were salvageable, and that she could cure them at a much lower cost than hospitals and without medication. Today, her adopted sons Aaron, Eric and Shay are all productive members of society. No doubt she has many more such stories. But freedom at Cathexis had to be earned. It had to be tempered with responsibility. Those who did not act responsibly had to be taught.

John was taken to a local hospital, where he remained overnight. The next day he was transferred to the burn unit at St. Francis Hospital in San Francisco, where he was diagnosed with deep second-degree burns and spotty third-degree burns covering 70% of his body. Jack and Sara Hartwell were reached in Carmel, California, where they had gone for the weekend. Upon learning of the accident, they headed for San Francisco, unaware of the details surrounding their son's injury.

To Joan Wexler, the atmosphere around the Schiff house

seemed a little quieter than usual. Joan also had a schizophrenic son at Cathexis, David Hoffer, for whom traditional methods had not worked. Like Sara Hartwell, she had been working for Jacqui to help pay for his therapy. Around noon on October 23rd, Joan was delivering some vegetable bins she had purchased for the kitchen.

When she asked who was in charge that day, someone told her Aaron Schiff. Joan wanted to be reimbursed for the vegetable bins. When she asked where Aaron was, she was told he was upstairs with Jacqui. The way it was said sounded as though something serious was in the air. At one o'clock, a group meeting was called. It seemed to Joan as though a lot more people were in attendance than normal. There were people standing in back of people.

Jacqui Schiff entered and the room got quiet. She opened by asking if everyone knew what had happened that morning. Since Joan had been at the market, she spoke up and said, no, she didn't know what had happened. Jacqui explained that John had been badly burned.

"And I remember that particularly," Joan said, "because she did not use the word scalded, she used the words 'badly burned.' "

"I asked her, 'How was he burned?'

She said, 'In a bathtub.' Then she proceeded to just sort of say that he had been very badly burned and had been taken to the hospital."[121]

A new water heater had been installed about 10 days earlier. There was a lot of speculation regarding the fact that a female patient named Ann was taking a shower in the upstairs bathroom while John was taking his bath downstairs. Had that caused the water in the tub to be hotter? Later, Jacqui would tell the grand jury that a mentally disabled patient who liked to create mischief was seen near the thermostat before the accident. At any rate, someone had set the temperature as high as it would go.

Carl was sitting directly across from Joan at the meeting. To Joan, he seemed very upset:

> And he said that he couldn't understand it at all, because he said when he came into the bathroom, he said he knew something was wrong immediately . . . He said that John was hyperventilating. He was in the bathtub and he was hyperventilating . . . And Carl just kept repeating, "I don't understand why you couldn't have known, you know, I could tell something was wrong."[122]

Carl confirmed that he was really angry with Aaron for not testing the water except once, when he had stuck his hand under the tap.

When a jury member asked Carl if he had connected the anger Aaron had shown earlier with John's scalding in the tub, Carl answered, "That's what I was thinking about first. But that's not a realistic situation. Like I know Aaron personally well enough to know he wouldn't do anything like that."

"But you did connect that anger that you saw in Aaron and the incident at first?" the juror asked.

"Yeah," Carl said. "But that's really a stupid thing to think. Aaron is not that kind of a guy."[123]

Joan Wexler testified:

> And then Jacqui looked around again and asked if anyone else had anything they wanted to ask. And a boy that I don't know the name, the last name of the young man, he's called Jim, he was looking very upset.

In fact, I remember particularly he was red in the face as though this was something that he was going to have to say, but he didn't really want to say it. But he was very upset. And he said that he felt that Aaron had been very, very angry because of what had occurred before the bath was given.[124]

Jim Freund had slept in the same room with John and Carl. He had helped Carl put on John's jeans, during which time John had tried to run. When a grand juror asked Jim if he had said anything in the group about Aaron seeming angry that morning, Jim said yes, he had told the group that Aaron had seemed angry. Jim also confirmed seeing Aaron push or shove John in the sitting room—when as other testimony had indicated John was handcuffed—hard enough for John's head to hit the wall.[125]

By all accounts, Aaron expressed sorrow at the meeting about what had happened. He said he should have tested the water properly. To Joan Wexler, Aaron seemed not only upset but confused, she testified:

And people sort of—I'm having a hard time finding words to describe how you should shut some people up. But the impression I got is that these two young men, Carl and Jim, were being hushed, you know, "Don't say any more," kind of thing, "Because you have already said that and Aaron has already admitted his negligence," you know.[126]

Sara Hartwell noticed the same dynamic. When a juror asked her if she had seen Joan Wexler's son David tied to a chair, she responded:

I only saw him once in a chair. I don't know how long he spent in it. And I saw people with their hands tied behind their backs. And a boy named Mike Thomas was one who went around frequently blindfolded and gagged, and I was never able to understand that. But whenever you asked anybody what was going on, Jacqui is very good at dropping the subject and getting on to something else. So she would never tell me. And the other kids aren't allowed to talk to you. And if you ask questions, you are being—there's a term which I can't recall that they use, but you don't question what's going on, that's considered bad form.[127]

On Wednesday, two days after the accident, Jacqui Schiff phoned Sara. As Sara remembered the conversation, Jacqui began by saying she felt very badly about what had happened.

> And she told me this long involved story about how Aaron had tested the water and that somehow when he tested it, it was all right. And then they couldn't understand how it happened, but it was hotter than they thought. But that John made no outcry. Jacqui's very words [were], "There was no commotion."
> So then I said to her, "Well, was he tied up?" because John had told me that he was. And there was a very long silence on the phone. And then in a really very faint voice she said, "Yes."[128]

The timing of the injury was also tragic. About a week before the incident, Jack and Sara Hartwell had decided to remove him from Cathexis. Sara had been reporting what she had seen there: Adults who seemed normal most of the time living under very strict rules, being tied up and having to apologize immediately for rule infractions or stand in the corner until they were ready to apologize. And John did not seem any better for having been there. If anything, he was worse.

Dr. Richman, who had authorized the restraints, said he thought John had improved at Cathexis. When asked if a psychotic person might not be able to feel pain, Richman answered that "it's not uncommon for someone who is psychotic to have difficulty discriminating pain, difficulty discriminating temperature. It's something that people don't really understand, but it happens."[129]

According to Lawrence Foster, a plastic surgeon who treated John Hartwell at St. Francis Hospital, John felt plenty of pain during the last 30 days of his life and was able to communicate that pain. Dr. Foster said it was unusual that all of the fingernails on John's left hand had fallen off within 24 hours after the burn, as did several fingernails on the right hand. This was uncommon for second-degree burn patients. Foster attributed the cause to the length of time John was immersed in the water, which he estimated at around 150 degrees or more. Caucasians normally can't tolerate water hotter than 120 degrees, Foster said. John's second-degree burns eventually converted to third-degree, meaning that all of the affected skin died. Had he survived, he would have had to undergo massive skin grafts.

Aaron Schiff pleaded guilty to involuntary manslaughter. The charge was later reduced to misdemeanor child abuse.

Two weeks after the accident, Joan Wexler got a phone call. Jacqui had been to Sacramento, California and been denied a license to care for patients as ill as David. The Wexlers transferred their son to Napa State Hospital.[130] In 1980, David died of cancer.

"It's incredibly fresh after 20 years," Wexler said during an interview in 1992. "For a long time I couldn't talk about that place at all. Then as I came to understand all of the ramifications, I came to see it as kind of a weird cult."[131] In the 10 weeks she was around Cathexis, Wexler saw most of the things that would haunt Jacqui Schiff's career first-hand, including adults crawling around in diapers; Jacqui nursing an adult woman at her breast; her son, David, tied to a chair and force-fed a tasteless baby food concoction called Sustagen, designed to provide nutrients without any of the pleasure of eating; people being barricaded under the coffee table while others shot questions at them; and being stood in the corner herself any time she questioned these practices.

"I personally was on the floor one day," Wexler said, "and was given the task of diapering grown female people. Each and every day I was realizing I had to get out of there."

So why did she stay 10 weeks?

"The only word I can use for it is desperation,"[132] Wexler said.

Had Aaron really exorcised his "werewolf parent"? Could the water heater accident have happened to anybody? Alan Jacobs suggests a relationship between the Cathexis atmosphere, in which Aaron had played an integral role, and the death:

> The implication is clear. Jacqui Schiff was not above resorting to drastic, even violent methods imposing her particular doctrinal approach . . . the logic of the end justifies the means dominates this treatment approach. It is a dangerous position, for one never knows what one is implanting in the human psyche. Whatever one accomplishes in this way will reap unknown and possibly disastrous results. Violence begets violence.[133]

After California authorities refused to renew her license in Alamo, Schiff moved to Oakland, California and set up a Cathexis Institute there. Two years after Hartwell's death and four years after publishing *All My Children*, the ITAA presented Jacqui and Aaron Schiff with its highest honor, the Eric Berne Memorial Scientific Award.

The association's leadership had second thoughts in 1978, however, after former patients testified before an ethics committee of being beaten with whips and paddles, tied to couches and chairs for days at a time, barricaded under tables and called "disgusting pigs," force-fed the Sustagen gruel until they vomited and left to sit in their own bodily wastes.

Psychologist Harry Boyd, who chaired that ethics committee investigation, recalled the speculations offered in the defense. "They believed in what they were doing," Boyd said. "They thought the violations were worth it considering the alternatives. I can recall Jacqui saying if we punish someone in a closet, that beats the hell out of warehousing them and drugging them for 20 years."[134]

The Schiff residences in Fredericksburg, Virginia and Alamo, California had been sealed environments. As a pioneer, Schiff had no peers, hence no peer review. Among her devotees, anything was possible.

Boyd remembers: "One of the contentions was that the water wasn't too hot, Aaron had checked it. The death was self-induced—he had simply willed himself to boil."[135]

Schiff was stripped of her ITAA membership. She moved to Bangalore, India, where she started Cathexis Europe. The Cathexis Institute in Oakland continued to be run by Schiff trainees until 1988. John Thattil, a Catholic priest who worked at the Bangalore home in the early 1980s, saw Schiff leading patients into a closed room, out of which then filtered cries of pain. Patients later told him they had been beaten with a five-stranded whip.

"I did not see them beaten," Thattil recalled, "but I heard them crying, and afterwards I asked them what had happened and this is what they said."[136]

Psychologist Carlos Welsh, who worked with Schiff from 1979 to 1984, had a different impression. "She was a very gifted and committed person," said Welsh, who in 1992 was still working at the Bangalore clinic, now called Atma Shakti Eiyala. Many of the Indians and Europeans who came to the clinic were "highly disturbed," he said, and Schiff "had a real sensitive way of understanding psychotic people."[137]

Welsh acknowledged that Schiff sometimes hit or slapped patients, but said this kind of contact was often initiated by patients themselves. "They'd say, 'Mommy, give me a whack because that's the only way I can learn.' It was always a therapeutic approach. A whip would be appalling. Everything she did was therapeutic."[138]

"The Strange Babies of Small Heath"[139]

Schiff left India in 1984 to obtain treatment for her multiple sclerosis in the United States. In 1985 she moved to England and set up a residential Cathexis clinic in Small Heath, a subdivision of Birmingham, along with former prison psychologist Jenny Robinson. Schiff had reparented Robinson in Bangalore, consistent with her belief that the only way to learn the method was to undergo it.[140]

According to an article in the *Weekend Guardian*, the two had a parting of ways after "serious differences of opinion and practice" arose between them. Specifically, Robinson objected to the "heavy-handed" physical methods Schiff was using on the patients who lived there.[141] Schiff withdrew from the clinic and rescinded permission for

Robinson to use the name Cathexis.

With Schiff out of the picture, Robinson's home in Shropshire still managed to attract its share of unwanted publicity. An investigation spurred by a citizen's complaint to Shropshire's social services department resulted in a demand that Robinson cease the following practices: standing patients in the corner; withholding mail; and the use of ropes to connect staff and patients in an "umbilical" bond. The home complied with the city's demands,[142] but negotiated that velcro linkages be permitted in place of the ropes. The point, they insisted, had never been restraint, but connection and security.[143]

The investigation came about after Mark Stein, a local government officer in Manchester, and his partner visited the home in October 1990 to see a friend who had been living there for two years. It was Stein's fourth visit and he was becoming concerned. The friend, "Claire" (a pseudonym adopted by the *Guardian*), had checked into the home in August 1988 for depression. Since then she had withdrawn from a once-active social circle and put her home up for sale.

But it was the plight of another patient that perturbed Stein the most: A woman being remanded to the corner for 24 hours straight. The woman was allowed to sit down during the night but not to sleep. He began to conduct what he called an investigation.[144] Defenders of the home called it a crusade.

Stein claims to have taped an interview with trainee therapist Caroline Jones saying, "We've got people here who wouldn't ever be conventionally diagnosed as schizophrenic. . . it really is just a term that we use to help us in helping people understand their problems."[145] This kind of statement, coupled with the alleged corner incident and

Robinson's acknowledgment that in five years, only four patients had "graduated" from the home,[146] triggered intense media interest, particularly after the home moved from Shropshire to Birmingham in June 1991 and applied for registration with Birmingham Social Services. By now it had become known simply as "Trident," after its regulatory body, Trident Housing Authority.

The Evening Mail led the charge with an August 15, 1991 investigative report titled, "The Strange 'babies' of Small Heath. Robin Jones reported:"

> Women and young mothers have been told to act like babies during controversial therapy at a Birmingham clinic. Treatment is said to include wearing nappies and crawling around on all fours, making baby noises and sucking milk from bottles . . . while tied to psychotherapists by short lengths of rope.[147]

One month after the *Mail*'s exposé appeared, the Birmingham city council refused to grant Trident's registration as a psychotherapy clinic. The council argued that because the therapy was residential, long-term and intensive, Trident should apply to the health authority for registration as a nursing home, a move that would have placed Trident under strict medical supervision.

Trident immediately appealed the decision. The outcome was critical because without the registration, weekly social security payments of £170 per patient would cease.[148]

In November 1991, the weekend before the city council was to decide the appeal, the *Guardian* entered. Reporter Edward Pilkington claimed the high road, part of which entailed taking a shot at the "Strange Babies" series by Robin Jones:

On August 15, prompted by Stein, the *Birmingham Evening Mail* carried a four-page blockbuster on "The Strange 'babies' of Small Heath." "Women told to crawl and wear nappies," it claimed under its strap-line, "The paper that cares." After rehearsing Mark Stein's allegations the *Mail* said, "We draw no conclusions. But we do pose one simple question: do you think this is the way to treat human beings?"[149]

Pilkington's lengthy story could rightly boast of two advantages—a more in-depth discussion of schizophrenia than provided by the *Mail,* and the fact that he succeeded in getting interviews with residents, providing a rare glimpse of Trident life:

> Eight people in a room. Sitting in silence on pink cushions holding hands. Their faces lowered, eyes half shut. Perhaps they are about to chant. Or raise the roof with a primeval scream.
>
> A young woman with her hair swept back takes a deep breath, looks up, and says, "I feel all right. But a bit scared and excited that the *Guardian*'s here." There is a collective sigh as the group expresses its accord. "I feel a bit scared that Mum's not here," says her neighbour in a baggy white T-shirt. Heads nod. A man with a hunted look in his eyes says, "Yesterday I felt jealousy and anger when Mum told me not to eat pudding late at night."[150]

The article tells the story of a schizophrenic man, Neil, whose experience with conventional medicine was so abysmal he committed suicide, and whose father believes the only good treatment Neil received was during the four months he spent at Trident (before being released by Robinson for not being "motivated"). The *Guardian* story concludes on a note that is as passionate as the *Mail*'s treatment was sensational: "What is clear is that it is not a cult, despite Mark Stein's protestations. And when Birmingham hears Trident's appeal for registration this Wednesday it should rule that the project stay open."[151]

The Birmingham City Council postponed a decision on the appeal in order to review voluminous documents submitted by both sides, including Trident's own report describing its guiding theory and practices. Jenny Robinson, the report's author, begins with a brief description of her professional background and training, including two years in Bangalore, India, using transactional analysis methods with "severely disturbed young adults."

"I was very impressed with what I saw and became a trainee in order to learn their methods," Robinson writes. "Following this I was involved in a small group of professional people seeking to establish a similar project in England."[152]

Jacqui Schiff's name does not appear anywhere in the 23-page report, despite the fact that it was Schiff who had invented the techniques that had impressed Robinson in India, who had reparented Robinson over a two-year period and who had then joined forces with her to set up Cathexis in Shropshire. Whatever the influences were or were not, Trident provided a highly structured environment, described by Robinson:

> When a new resident first arrives he or she often comments on the fact that there are many rules. These were formulated and are revised and added to when necessary by the whole community. There is a reason

behind each one. They provide a framework for the individual in that they tell him or her what to do, when to do it and, if appropriate, how. Collectively they are referred to as "the structure."[153]

She also provides an example of misbehavior and how it might be dealt with:

> When a resident behaves irresponsibly sanctions are not appropriate. The goal is to understand why he or she has done this and to find a way of responding that will assist the individual in solving the problem that lies behind the behaviour. So, for example, if someone breaks the rule about the care of sharp knives and leaves one in the washing up water for someone else to find, this may be intended as a threat to frighten the person washing up. A demand would then be made on the person to explain why he or she wanted to threaten the individual and set up a protected situation where both can talk it out and solve the problem in a socially acceptable way.[154]

At least three conclusions seem possible from the above: a) That Robinson regarded verbal confrontation as qualitatively different from a sanction; b) That definitions for schizophrenic and threatening behavior employed at Trident were relatively liberal ones; and, c) That Robinson was anxious to distance her version of reparenting from its founder, Jacqui Schiff.

Over the objections of Britain's National Schizophrenia Fellowship, Birmingham granted Trident a registration in February 1992, ending eight months of turmoil. Yet of all the hearings, broadcasts, documents and coverage of Trident in the British press, nothing defined the controversy more starkly than the following quote, obtained in an interview by the *Evening Mail*: "People have ways of defending against things that they do not want to hear," said Mrs Schiff. "If they are emotionally or physically exhausted, they are not going to have the energy to do that."[155]

Reparenting Changes Its Name

The distancing of Jenny Robinson from Schiff mirrors what has been happening in the United States since Schiff lost her ITAA membership in 1978. For nearly two decades, therapists who were trained in reparenting—many by Schiff—have been distancing themselves from their onetime mentor while retaining many of her methods. In particular, Schiff's central metaphors of cathecting to infancy and her use of harsh verbal or even physical confrontation survived well into the late 1980s and have been the basis for several successful lawsuits in the 1990s.

Today, many therapists who do "corrective parenting" claim their work bears little resemblance to reparenting. But a 1987 doctoral thesis by Susan Smith of Sierra University, built around a survey of 267 therapists known to be doing "regressive work" noted, "Regressive Work is closely associated with the reparenting model of therapy; and it was my impression that the respondents often answered questions about Regressive Work from a reparenting frame of reference."[156]

Moreover, much of the information returned by the 134 answering therapists would shock the average consumer. As recently as 1987:

- 22% of the therapists acknowledged spanking some of their regressed clients.

- 82% punished clients by standing them in a corner.
- 7% "breast-fed" clients.[157]

To explore the alleged sexual, emotional and financial abuses stemming from reparenting and corrective parenting in the United States today would literally require another book.

A Journey of Reparenting

Toward the conclusion of his "Finishing Business With Mother" workshop in 1992, Bradshaw made these comments:

> *As we begin, then, this new journey, it's a journey of reparenting. Now, I want to be clear about what I mean by "reparenting". There are models of reparenting where you literally have people, ah—Jacqui Schiff did a very famous kind of reparenting where she had children live with her—and, literally, over a period of years, did reparenting. There are some very good people in the field who do this kind of reparenting. I have some reservations about it, because it means a commitment to someone for a very, very long time. And I would rather think about—at least, my style of reparenting—is reparenting my own inner child.*[158]

Bradshaw's comments that Schiff "did a very famous kind of reparenting" and then his saying he "[has] some reservations about it, because it means [making] a commitment to someone for a very, very long time," reads like a citation for doing 45 miles per hour in a 35-mile-per-hour zone.

Reparenting and dependency are so intertwined that

one would have to question why he would use the term as something a person could do by himself.

These are not 100-year-old apparitions or conjectures. This is patient after patient in the 1980s and 1990s with the same complaint. They went to a therapist who told them they had a number of unresolved issues—none of which were ever what they seemed. They became attached to doing the work, regressing in age, sucking on baby bottles and honoring their mom contracts. And doing "accountability work" if they so much as came down with a cold; or past-life work, or remembering-conception work; or nude rebirthing sessions in hot tubs with their therapists. They became so attached that many of these former patients expired their insurance policies and then ran out of cash.

Be a Kid Again

It is surprising that the only person Bradshaw discussed in his comments was Jacqui Schiff. Although reparenting is generally not done today, an exception would be Alfred and Jeanne Wiger, who operated the Center for Creative Living (CCL) in St. Paul, Minnesota.

I talked to Jeanne Wiger briefly, and I did not get the impression a person had to be off-the-wall crazy to go to them for therapy. So I was a little surprised to see in the CCL literature that handcuffs, ropes and other forms of restraint were being advocated as "non-punitive ways in which people can safely discharge anger."[159]

The Center was closed down in 1987 after a female patient filed a lawsuit against Alfred Wiger for sexually exploiting his role as a therapist. The Wiger "family" moved to Stillwater, Minnesota, but would settle one more lawsuit over the St. Paul residence, also by a former female patient against Alfred Wiger. That complaint, filed in Dakota County

District Court, was settled in 1992. It alleged that from 1980 through 1987, Wiger sexually assaulted Joyce Sankey, and that throughout this seven-year period Sankey "was emotionally dependent on defendants and believed that the sexual contacts were for the purpose of therapy." [160]

Elizabeth Carlson, 39, tells what it has been like since her mother joined the Wiger family 20 years ago:

> My mom had eight kids. The demands on her were great. Suicide was a mode she would either talk about or try to act out. I've seen her stick her head in the gas oven. Then she said she was going to ingest poison after her youngest turned eighteen. So when she went (to reparenting) we did question the fact that it was a cult. But we said, well, at least she's not dead and we don't have to see her in a graveyard over the holidays. At least we have a small portion of her here.
>
> My mom went to see the Wigers around six months after the divorce. One night she called and said she needed to stay the night, she couldn't drive home. My younger sister was thirteen or fourteen at the time. My mom's basically been with the Wigers ever since. Right now she lives with them in Stillwater. The house has seven bedrooms and six baths. The adults live as kids.
>
> It seems to me and my other siblings that in the process of being reparented, the idea is to come around full circle and say, "Okay, I'm taking care of my life." At some point you have to come back to a reality base and say, "I'm a mother and a grandmother of twelve." There was a two- to-three-year period when she was stuck on being three years old. My brothers and sisters would kid around and say, "Hasn't she been three for three or four years now?"

As far as her own parenting goes, she wasn't the best. She was abusive. But she basically has no memories except that she would have put June and Ward Cleaver to shame. The way she's cut off from us makes it difficult. When my grandmother died a year ago, several of my sisters broke down crying talking about how difficult it has been to explain it to their kids. They are getting old enough to start saying, "Well, if this was my grandmom, then it was my mom's mom, and why didn't she go to her own mom's funeral? Why didn't she go to her dad's funeral before that?"

Now she's in her late 60s, and the Wigers are still her parents. They're in their early 60s. It's so weird to hear her call these people mom and dad. My mom is also reparenting other people. One day she told me she was going to have this garage sale, to help some kids get to camp. I thought she was talking about children. I went to the garage sale. I saw my mom and waved. And then three or four women about ten years older than I am ran out and came jumping around me saying, "Oh, your mom is my mom and isn't it wonderful?" And, "You've got the best mom in the world and I've got her, too! Isn't it great?" The camp was for the adults—something about being able to experience a cabin life and play in the sand with Jeanne and Al as Mom and Dad.

Al has talked to me about spanking. Jeanne has talked to me about bottle feeding, bathing and rebirthing in a gigantic pool they have. I've never seen any of it first-hand. I don't know Al and Jeanne well and I don't care to. One day my mom came over to my sister's house to get something. She had somebody with her. They had on these handcuff things, like a belt or a hoop with something that runs through the center of the belt. And my mom said, "Oh, don't worry, they need to be restrained, they feel safe." My sister was appalled that people were going to be with her while in handcuffs, having her children there to see that. I've asked her about the sexual abuse allegations directed at Al Wiger, but whenever I bring it up she says, "I know nothing about it."[161]

There still is a lot more to say about long-term, short-term, "spot" and "corrective" parenting and reparenting, some of it favorable. But maybe it's all moot. Could the possibility of overly dependent relationships and vulnerability to exploitation be one or two of Bradshaw's reservations? If one of the dangers involves losing one's capacity for independent judgment the more this dependency increases, it is possible that people may not know how to distinguish between a potentially helpful reparenting relationship and a potentially destructive one.

Recovery and Reason

In *Healing the Shame That Binds You*, Bradshaw writes:

> For me the reading and teaching of philosophy was a way out of my feelings. When I was reading the *Summa Theologiae* of Thomas Aquinas or Emmanual Kant's *Critique of Pure Reason* or Wittgenstein's treatise on logical positivism, I could completely mood alter my toxic shame.[162]

This passage comes under the heading, "Thought Addiction." It is not an indictment against the study of philosophy (which Bradshaw allows is "not harmful"). But it would seem to cast a vote in favor of not trusting the relationship between language and knowledge, at least insofar as such study might be mood-altering—perhaps even for the people who devote their lives to untangling these sorts of ambiguities.

Elsewhere in *Healing the Shame*, Bradshaw blames cultural attitudes justifying child abuse on archaic societal systems in which parents held power in the home equivalent to that of monarchs and kings. Such beliefs, he contends, "are pre-democratic and pre-Einsteinian. They presuppose a world of eternal laws, a *Deus Ex Machina* view of the world. This was the world of Newton and Descartes. Such a worldview has been refuted many times over."[163]

If Descartes were alive to defend himself, he might direct Bradshaw and the reader to one of his "principles for thinking," such as the explanation for "why we may doubt of sensible things— . . .because we know that our senses have before deceived us, and that prudence directs us not to trust too much in what has even once deceived us."[164]

This chapter has covered some of the extreme dangers of regressing adults to the status of compliant children. Given the harm that can come about by age regression techniques and the risks of encountering bad therapists who use them, one might well ask some of the following questions:

Is now really the best time to seek a cure for thought addiction? Would it really hurt anyone if we trusted a little more in ourselves as reasoning adults, and a little less in professional parent figures who would interpret life's ambiguities on our behalf? And who benefits from that kind of blind trust, who suffers most when it has been misplaced?

Conclusion:
Whither Goes Recovery?

The movement's march from recovering alcoholics to recovered memories has been slowed by recent developments. First, the tide of public opinion has turned away from the uncritical acceptance of survivor stories, no matter how deeply buried or long endured they are said to be. Though it took several years, advocates for the accused have succeeded in impressing upon Americans that there is another side to the story, a side that may render the phenomenon of recovered memory even more tragic than first imagined.

While most experts acknowledge the possibility that some traumatic incidents can be repressed, the assertion that years of continued sexual abuse can be forgotten has yet to be scientifically proved. Meanwhile, evidence that humans can produce false memories has increased over recent years. The result has been a shifting definition of what it means to "err on the safe side." This phrase was once used by recovery-oriented therapists to explain why they encouraged their patients to recall long-hidden memories. That others (and the patient herself) might suffer unnecessarily if these "re-called" incidents never happened seemed irrelevant, un-likely and not the therapist's concern.

A flood of investigative media coverage, as well as several sizeable judgments against therapists in lawsuits brought by former patients, has helped remove this attitude of indiffer-ence. Today, erring on "the safe side" means examining the substance and background of each previously buried allega-tion of abuse. This entails taking into account the fertile soil that still exists for false recall in the form of popular books and films; inflated statistics of the prevalence of abuse; therapists using suggestive techniques; and a network of survivors and hardcore feminists who regard the memory issue as one more example of society's unfairness to women.

It may be helpful to remind the reader of what this book has not said. It has not said that the recovery movement, beginning with alcoholism and expanding to all varieties of family dysfunction, is solely responsible for the outbreak of very questionable memories of sexual abuse. It has, how-ever, emphasized that recovery is a series of interconnected subjects beginning with addiction and mental health, but encompassing unique ideas about family and spirituality powerful enough to influence an entire culture. One cannot address any part of recovery without soon encountering a larger connected body of ideas whose end appears almost limitless.

The idea of survivor spirituality seemed to include a kind of deification of children—their innocence, honesty and pu-rity. Skeptics of a witch-hunt, whose victims included day-care workers, were told in confident tones that "children don't lie" about abuse. But questioning adults can signal the "right" answers about events that may not have occurred, and children—like adults—respond to these cues. The '80s and '90s have seen many people imprisoned as the result of testimony tainted by investigator bias. Suddenly, their "spirituality" began to look reckless and vindictive.

Meanwhile, treatment centers based on AA concepts routinely advised their patients to find a Higher Power or take a "moral inventory," untroubled by the contradiction between giving such advise and providing insurance-funded treatment for medical diseases. In the late 1980s, book authors with varying credentials searched for underlying "causes" of addiction and found them in dysfunctional families, low self-worth, or that "hole in the soul" they sometimes called codependency.

By the time recovery stars and their book-buying readers became curious about the causes of codependency, their field was ripe for new discoveries. HMOs and other cost-cutting, managed care organizations were transforming health care, and one of the first programs to be cut was the automatic 28-day stay in a treatment center. A wave of bankruptcies heralded the emergence of a new recovery concept called original trauma. That prospective patients could not remember this trauma, which often included years of rape and sometimes participation in heinous criminal acts, could be presented as all the more reason to dig deeper. With recovered memory came an even more fervent attachment to spirituality as a refuge from the unbelieving family.

But then, how could recovery from alcoholism or incest not incorporate spirituality, given that recovery is and has always been a movement? Movements offer meaning and the keys to a new identity. How can one not be influenced over time by such self-encompassing labels as addict, bulemic, or survivor, reiterated with each new comment—"Hi, I'm still John and I'm still an addict." The subtleties of these mass-produced identities and group-supplied descriptions for who we really are involves a kind of re-learning of the world. The intimacy of shared beliefs, along with the reassurance of others to stay introspective and keep "working their issues," have no doubt helped many people to understand themselves better.

But when support becomes control, when spirituality becomes fundamentalism, when medical-sounding diagnoses take the place of reasoned argument and people either understand the truth or are "in denial" of it, then this frequently admirable recovery movement has slipped a gear.

That, of course, is exactly what happened in the late 1980s as the well-intentioned machinery of broader recovery, through overreach and exploitation, began to breakdown despite the efforts of AA's founders to protect its organization from outside interests. Yet the original principle of "one alcoholic helping another" remained unbroken and sound, and continues to supply meaning for thousands of 12-step groups and other groups around the world. That is worth remembering—even emulating.

The recovery era was one of rapid expansion followed by a partial collapse, a thinning down and a rebuilding. Its motives, I believe, were good. Its excesses were both ideological and financial, characterized by compassion and the zeal of a developing movement. Its leaders sought not so much to help sick people get well as to elevate wellness beyond the mundane—to a serene and spiritual place. That to elevate wellness necessarily meant to shrink it, while expanding the dominion of disease, has not been the kind of problem recovery experts find troubling. Instead, they have hailed each new wave of pathologizing description—whether of sex addiction, codependency, covert incest or recovered memory—as an important discovery and capitalized on it through books, tapes, workshops and treatment services.

In considering recovery's impact on the culture, it is important to remember that this movement continues to give emotional support and advice to peole who need it. As the commercial success of recovery appears past its peak, its essential core of "one addict helping another" will remain. The less fortunate aspects—overreach and arrogance, religiosity and contempt for the masses, hucksterism and emotional manipulation—will reappear in the form of some new movement. Like recovery, the new movement will carry as one of its features an attack on methods of analysis and reasoning that would expose its weaknesses. Its articulate leaders will answer questions confidently, with a sense of finality made believable by "new discoveries" the movement will announce about the human condition. Thousands will join up to be saved, claimed, redeemed or re-dreamed according to the new vision.

If the purveyors of the new truths in the next great social movement are like their counterparts in the old, they will manage to demonize all questions, criticisms and doubts lodged against them. Words that have been used in the past—sin, addiction, disease, denial—may or may not be resurrected. Some catch phrase or combination of phrases will emerge, however, and their purpose will dismantle dissent. By discouraging analysis, criticism and dissent, marketers of the next great scheme to heal humanity can present their ideas as established fact, as opposed to a set of highly controversial claims.

When someone completely disregards Western standards of evaluating a truth claim, there is always a price to pay down the road. Some of these standards are reflected in the questions one might ask of the new claim, such as: Is the claim internally consistent; do its parts interact with each other or do they contradict each other? Are the particulars of the claim verifiable or checkable against any outside data? Do the parts of the new claim hang together in a coherent whole? These are the questions that ought to be asked whenever someone sets out to "heal the human condition." Not: "Will it be popular?" or "Will it sell?" And not: "Does believing in the truth claim seem to help people?"

When sales determine which mental health ideas are considered legitimate, harm to consumers is inevitable. The "spiritual foundation" of AA and other 12-Step groups has always been anonymity, which sanctifies the act of seeking help for a problem or a disease. Anonymity is a kind of guarantee. Is says that if you bring your problem to another alcoholic or drug addict, you will be given a safe place to begin healing. Who you are on the outside is not important. As an organizational principle, anonymity implies separation from the pursuit of profit, or from anything else that would interfere with the group's "primary purpose . . . to carry the message to the addict who still suffers."

But profit-making institutions found their way to 12-Step groups long ago, and have been exploiting the connection ever since. This book has been an attempt to document the profit-making end of self-help and recovery. My hope is that society will learn from the recovery movement without repeating some of its worst errors.

Reference Notes

Chapter 1

1 Meacham, A. (1990, August). Drinking has been opposed since colonial days. *The U.S. Journal of Drug and Alcohol Dependence, 14(8)*.

2 Ibid., 12.

3 Ibid., 1.

4 Meacham, A. (1990, August). 30 lashes proposed for drug peddlers. *The U.S. Journal of Drug and Alcohol Dependence, 14(8)*, 12.

5 Meacham, A. (1990, August). Are we in a 'New Temperance' mood? *The U.S. Journal of Drug and Alcohol Dependence, 14(8)*, 12.

6 O'Connell, T. (1988, January). Public is smarter about addictions—Gallup. *The U.S. Journal of Drug and Alcohol Dependence, 12(1)*, 1-20.

7 Zimmerman, R. (1987, March). APA agrees to new criteria for A & D dependence. *The U.S. Journal of Drug and Alcohol Dependence, 11(3)*, 1-10.

8 Ibid., 10.

9 Meacham, A. (1987, July). AMA declares all drug dependencies diseases. *The U.S. Journal of Drug and Alcohol Dependence, 11(7)*, 1-20.

10 Ibid., 20.

11 Bromley, J. (1987, June). Interview by author.

12 *Dorland's* Illustrated *Medical Dictionary* (28th ed.). (1906). Philadelphia: W.B. Saunders Company.

13 Esterly, R. (1987, June). Interview by author.

14 Dole, V.P. (1980, December). Addictive Behavior. *Scientific American*, 138-154.

15 Rodgers, J.E. (1994, September/October). Addiction: A Whole New View. *Psychology Today*, 33-38.

16 Ibid., 34.

17 Erickson, C. (1994). Interview by author.

18 Ibid.

19 Washton, A.M. (1987, August). Face of addictions changed by cocaine abuse problem. *The U.S. Journal of Drug and Alcohol Dependence, 11(8)*, 8.

20 Ibid.

21 Ibid.
22 Flavin, D. (1991). *Alcoholism: Is it Really a Disease?* Paper presented at the 22nd Annual Medical/Scientific Conference sponsored by the American Society on Addiction Medicine, Boston, MA.
23 Ibid.
24 Ibid.
25 Ibid.
26 Schneider, M.A. (1987, September). Alcoholism—still the giant. *The U.S. Journal of Drug and Alcohol Dependence, 11(9)*, 9.
27 Ibid.
28 Ibid.
29 McClellan, K. (1987, August). EAPs vary in emphasis. *The U.S. Journal of Drug and Alcohol Dependence, 11(8)*, 9.
30 Ibid.
31 Culhane, C. (1987, December). Congressmen charge: Administration ignores drug act. *The U.S. Journal of Drug and Alcohol Dependence, 11(12)*, 1-4.
32 Besteman, K. (1987, February). Budget reflects real priorities. *The U.S. Journal of Drug and Alcohol Dependence, 11(2)*, 9.
33 Culhane, C. (1987, February). Disputed "cuts" cloud Reagan budget. *The U.S. Journal of Drug and Alcohol Dependence, 11(2)*, 1-21.
34 Ibid., 21.
35 Ibid.
36 Culhane, C. (1987, August). Kennedy plan assailed: Bill could kill treatment benefits. *The U.S. Journal of Drug and Alcohol Dependence, 11(8)*, 1-4.
37 Besteman, K. (1987, August). Insurance bill omits addictions coverage. *The U.S. Journal of Drug and Alcohol Dependence, 11(8)*, 17.
38 Meacham, A. (1987, September). Media fights drugs for free. *The U.S. Journal of Drug and Alcohol Dependence, 11(9)*, 1-2.
39 Ibid., 2.
40 Meacham, A. (1990, August). Are we in a 'New Temperance' mood?, 1.
41 McVernon, J. (1987, November). Recent Developments Memo. *The U.S. Journal of Drug and Alcohol Dependence, 11(11)*, 8.
42 Ibid.
43 Lang, S.S. (1991, January 20). When Women Drink. <*Parade*>, pp.18+. (From <Alcohol 1991> [Sirs Researcher CD-ROM Fall 1997, Art. No. 86]. Boca Raton, FL: SIRS, Inc. [Producer and Distributor].)
44 Blume, S. (1987, December). Women drinkers face triple stigma. *The U.S. Journal of Drug and Alcohol Dependence, 11(12)*, 9.
45 Gordis, E. (1987). Accessible and affordable health care for alcoholism and related problems: Strategy for cost containment. *Journal of Studies of Alcohol, 48*, 579-85.
46 Rodgers, J.E. (1994, September/October). Addiction: A Whole New View. *Psychology Today*, 33-38.
47 Ibid., 34.
48 Ibid., 34-35.
49 Ibid., 35.
50 Ibid., 38.

51 Ibid., 35.

52 Ibid., 36.

53 Ibid.

54 Fingarette, H. (1988). *Heavy Drinking: The Myth of Alcoholism as a Disease.* Berkeley, CA: University of California Press, 125.

55 Ibid., 126.

56 Ibid.

57 Wallace, J. (1989). Alcoholism & Treatment: A Critical Analysis of the Rand Report. In *John Wallace: Writings.* Newport, RI: Edgehill Publications, 267-275.

58 Fingarette, H. (1988). *Heavy Drinking,* 126.

59 Ibid., 128.

60 Creager, C. (1994, August). A Tree Grows in Wyoming: Colleagues plant a living memorial to Mary Pendery. *Professional Counselor,* 31.

61 Maltzman, I. (1994, August). Who killed Mary Pendery? *Professional Counselor,* 31-32.

62 Ibid., 31.

63 Ibid., 32.

64 Ibid., 31.

65 Hester, R. (1990, January). Interview by author.

66 McCrady, B. (1990, January). Interview by author.

67 Ibid.

68 Hester, R. (1990, January). Interview by author.

69 Ibid.

70 Meacham, A. (1990, March). Wrestling with concepts. *The U.S. Journal of Drug and Alcohol Dependence, 14(3),* 4.

71 Hester, R. (1990, January). Interview by author.

72 Kishline, A. (1996, January/February). A Toast to Moderation. *Psychology Today,* 53-56.

73 Korcok, M. (1987, October). PPS exemptions end: It's final—field must comply with DRGs. *The U.S. Journal of Drug and Alcohol Dependence, 11(10),* 1-19.

74 Miller, M.E. (1987, June). 11,000 patients surveyed, Payor charges vary: National study reveals inpatient treatment costs. *The U.S. Journal of Drug and Alcohol Dependence, 11(6),* 1-20.

75 Korcok, M. (1987, October). PPS exemptions end, 19.

76 Korcok, M. (1987, August). Letter of opposition says field groups seek exemption from new DRGs. *The U.S. Journal of Drug and Alcohol Dependence, 11(8),* 1-20.

77 Ibid., 4.

78 Rothman, S. (1990, February). Treatment field to grow in '90s. *The U.S. Journal of Drug and Alcohol Dependence, 14(2),* 1-7.

79 Korcok, M. (1987, August). Letter of opposition, 20.

80 Korcok, M. (1995, September). Interview by author.

81 Zimmerman, R. (1991, April). Betty Ford Center Conference—Expert: Field must restrict power of managed care. *The U.S. Journal of Drug and Alcohol Dependence, 15(4),* 14.

82 Ibid.

83 Wegscheider-Cruse, S. (1981). *Another Chance: Hope and Health for* *the Alcoholic Family.* Palo Alto, CA: Science and Behavior Books, 104.

84 Ibid., 123.

85 Ibid., 116.

86 Ibid., 140.

87 Ansbacher, H., & Ansbacher, R. (Eds.). (1956). *The Individual Psychology of Alfred Adler: A Systematic Presentation in Selections from His Writings.* New York: Basic Books, 378.

88 Ibid.

89 Wegscheider-Cruse, S. (1981). *Another Chance,* 115.

90 Ansbacher, H., & Ansbacher, R. (1956). *The Individual Psychology of Alfred Adler,* 379.

91 Ibid.

92 Ibid., 380.

93 Ibid.

94 Wegscheider-Cruse, S. (1981). *Another Chance,* 125.

95 Ansbacher, H., & Ansbacher, R. (1956). *The Individual Psychology of Alfred Adler,* 378.

96 Wegscheider-Cruse, S. (1981). *Another Chance,* 125.

97 Woititz, J. (1983). *Adult Children of Alcoholics.* Deerfield Beach, FL: Health Communications, Inc., 55.

98 Ibid., 24, 55.

99 Ibid., 39, 68.

100 Ibid., 30, 62.

101 Ibid., 28, 59.

102 Beattie, M. (1992). *Codependent No More: How to Stop Controlling Others and Start Caring for Yourself* (2nd Ed.). Center City, MN: Hazelden Educational Materials, 53.

103 Ibid., 43-44.

104 Ibid., 50.

105 Ibid., 46.

106 Ibid., 52.

107 Ibid., 46.

108 Ibid.

109 Ibid.

110 Larsen, E. (1983). *Basics of Co-dependence.* Brooklyn Park, MN: E. Larsen Enterprises.

111 Whitfield, C.L. (1984). Co-Dependency—An Emerging Problem. In *Co-Dependency.* Deerfield Beach, FL: Health Communications, Inc., 47.

112 Wegscheider, S. (1984). Co-Dependency: The Therapeutic Void. In *Co-Dependency.,* 1-4.

113 Ibid.

114 Schaef, A.W. (1986). *Co-dependence: Misunderstood—Mistreated.* San Francisco: HarperSanFrancisco, 48-59.

115 Schaef, A.W. (1987). *When Society Becomes an Addict.* New York: Harper & Row, Publishers, 15.

116 Ibid., 13.

117 Schaef, A.W. (1990). *Laugh! I Thought I'd Die (if I Didn't): Daily Meditations on Healing Through Humor.* New York: Ballantine Books.

118 Subby, R. (1987). *Lost in the Shuffle: The Co-dependent Reality.*

Deerfield Beach, FL: Health Communications, Inc., 31.

119 Ibid., 43.

120 Miller, J.K. (1987). *Sin: Overcoming the Ultimate Deadly Addiction.* San Francisco: Harper & Row, Publishers, 62.

121 Ibid.

122 Ibid., 62-63.

123 Ibid., 44.

124 Seidler, G., & Vegso, P. (1987, March/April). From the Publisher: ACoAs—A Flash in the Pan? *Changes: For and About Children of Alcoholics, 2(2),* 6.

Chapter 2

1 Lerner, R. (1986, July/August). Affirmations for Self-Healing. *Changes: For and About Children of Alcoholics, 1(4),* 9.

2 Bowden, J., & Gravitz, H. (1987, May/June). Genesis: Awakening Your Spiritual Relationship to Self and the World. *Changes: For and About Children of Alcoholics, 2(3),* 8-42.

3 Woititz, J. (1987, November/December). Ask Jan. *Changes: For and About Children of Alcoholics, 2(6),* 16-50.

4 Seidler, G., & Vegso, P. (1987, January/February). From the Publisher: Happy New Year. *Changes: For and About Children of Alcoholics, 2(1),* 4.

5 O'Connell, T. (1988, November). Northeast conference: Scope broadens in addictions field. *The U.S. Journal of Drug and Alcohol Dependence, 12(11),* 2.

6 Ibid.

7 Ibid.

8 Ibid.

9 Ibid.

10 Bradshaw, J. (1988). *Bradshaw On: Healing The Shame That Binds You.* Deerfield Beach, FL: Health Communications, Inc., 15.

11 Meacham, A. (1988, September/October). Bradshaw Delivers Universal Message. *Changes: For and About Children of Alcoholics, 3(5),* 7.

12 Woititz, J. (1987, June 4-7). *Intimacy: An Informal Dialogue.* Lecture/Discussion at The 3rd Annual Western Conference on Alcoholism and the Family: *Adult Children Across Generations,* sponsored by *The U.S. Journal of Drug and Alcohol Dependence,* Oakland, CA.

13 Ibid.

14 Wegscheider-Cruse, S. (1987, March 1-4). Presentation given at The 3rd Annual National Convention on Children of Alcoholics, sponsored by *The U.S. Journal of Drug and Alcohol Dependence,* Orlando, FL.

15 Meacham, A. (1987, May/June). 1,300 Celebrate at Children of Alcoholics Conference. *Changes: For Adult Children of Alcoholics, 2(3),* 7, 48-49.

16 Sanford, L. (1987, March 1-4). Presentation given at The 3rd Annual National Convention on Children of Alcoholics.

17 Ibid.

18 Ibid.

19　Meacham, A. (1987, July/August). Interview with Wayne Dyer: Recovery Without Limits. *Changes: For and About Children of Alcoholics, 2(4)*, 6-49.

20　Ibid., 48.

21　Ibid.

22　Peele, S. (1989). *Diseasing of America: Addiction Treatment Out of Control.* Boston: Houghton Mifflin Company, 93-94.

23　Ibid.

24　James, W. (1902). *The Varieties of Religious Experience: A Study in Human Nature.* New York: The Modern Library.

25　Meacham, A. (1990, October). Biochemical controversy: Jury's still out on the role played by TIQs. *The U.S. Journal of Drug and Alcohol Dependence, 14(10)*, 14.

26　Ibid.

27　Ibid.

28　Ibid.

29　Ibid.

30　Ibid.

31　Meacham, A. (1991, May). New study questions ACA traits but clinicians ask for more proof. *The U.S. Journal of Drug and Alcohol Dependence, 15(5)*, 1-10.

32　Woititz, J. (1983). *Adult Children of Alcoholics.* Deerfield Beach, FL: Health Communications, Inc., 24-50.

33　Meacham, A. (1991, May). New study questions ACA traits, 1.

34　Ibid., 10.

35　Laign, J. (1991, May). Behind the Scenes: Landmark book still shines. *The U.S. Journal of Drug and Alcohol Dependence, 15(5)*, 4.

36　Ibid.

37　Carnes, P. (1988, September 19-20). Presentation given at The Second Annual Conference on Sexual Compulsivity, Minneapolis, MN.

38　Meacham, A. (1988, October). Sexual compulsivity: A new field defines itself. *The U.S. Journal of Drug and Alcohol Dependence, 12(10)*, 17.

39　Ibid.

40　Carnes, P. (1988, September 19-20). Presentation given at The Second Annual Conference on Sexual Compulsivity.

41　Levine, M.P., & Troiden, R.R. (1988, August). The Myth of Sexual Compulsivity. *The Journal of Sex Research, 25(3)*, 347-363.

42　Ibid., 354.

43　Ibid.

44　Ibid., 361.

45　Ibid., 360.

46　Ibid., 361.

47　Troiden, R.R. (1988). Interview by author.

48　Ibid.

49　Meacham, A. (1988, October). Sexual compulsivity, 17.

50　Stamas, D.T. (1981). *The Trap Map: How to Trap the Alcoholic to Recovery.* Lombard, IL: Eureka Alcoholism Publishers, 5-6.

51　Okene, J. (1988, September 22-25). Speech given at The First National

Conference on Nicotine Dependence: *Diagnosis, Treatment, and Smoke Free Issues*, sponsored by the American Medical Society on Alcoholism and Other Drug Dependencies, Minneapolis, MN.

52 Meacham, A. (1989, August/September). Thomas Szasz: The Politics of Addiction. *FOCUS: Educating Professionals in Family Recovery, 14(4)*, 20-37.

53 Szasz, T.S. (1970). *The Manufacture of Madness: A Comparative Study of the Inquisition and the Mental Health Movement.* New York: Dell Publishing Co., Inc., 137-159.

54 Ibid., 140.

55 Ibid., 140-143.

56 Ibid., 154.

57 Ibid., 141.

58 Meacham, A. (1989, August/September). The Politics of Addiction, 20-37.

Chapter 3

1 Meacham, A. (1991, March). Unconstitutional: Courts rule on forced AA attendance. *The U.S. Journal of Drug and Alcohol Dependence, 15(3)*, 1-11.

2 Ibid., 11.

3 Ibid.

4 Ibid.

5 Ibid.

6 Ibid.

7 Ibid., 1.

8 Ibid., 11.

9 Ibid.

10 Ibid., 1.

11 Ibid.

12 Ibid., 1-11.

13 Ibid., 11.

14 Tillich, P. (1965). *Ultimate Concern.* New York: Harper & Row, Publishers.

15 Irwin, K. (1989, March). Interview by author.

16 Stark, R., & Bainbridge, W.S. (1985). *The Future of Religion: Secularization, Revival and Cult Formation.* Berkeley, CA: University of California Press, 23.

17 Ibid., 22.

18 Ibid., 29.

19 Wallace, J. (1989). *John Wallace: Writings.* Newport, RI: Edgehill Publications, 231.

20 Ibid.

21 Stark, R., & Bainbridge, W.S. (1985). *The Future of Religion*, 8.

22 Ibid., 6.

23 *Alcoholics Anonymous: The Story of How Many Thousands of Men and Women Have Recovered from Alcoholism.* (3rd ed.) (Also known as *The Big Book*). (1976). New York: Alcoholics Anonymous World Services, Inc., 83-84.

24 Ibid., 564.
25 Ibid., 83-84.
26 Hassan, S. (1988). *Combatting Cult Mind Control.* Rochester, VT: Park Street Press, 200-201.
27 *Lois Remembers.* (1979). New York: Al-Anon Family Group Headquarters, Inc., 113.
28 Pendergrast, M. (1995). *Victims of Memory: Incest Accusations and Shattered Lives.* Hinesburg, VT: Upper Access, 474.
29 Meyer, J. (1989). Interview by author.
30 Meyer, J. (1997). Interview by author.
31 Galanter, M. (1990, May). Cults and Zealous Self-Help Movements: A Psychiatric Perspective. *American Journal of Psychiatry, 147(5),* 546.
32 Ibid.
33 Ibid.
34 Ibid., 543.
35 Ibid.
36 Ibid., 547.
37 Ibid., 543.
38 Deikman, A.J. (1990). *The Wrong Way Home: Uncovering the Patterns of Cult Behavior in American Society.* Boston: Beacon Press, 48.
39 Ibid., 9.
40 Ibid., 8.
41 Ibid., 7.
42 Wilson, B. (1967). *As Bill Sees It: The A.A. Way of Life...Selected writings of A.A.'s co-founder.* New York: Alcoholics Anonymous World Services, Inc., 199.
43 Ibid., 38.
44 Perera, S.B. (1986). *The Scapegoat Complex: Toward a Mythology of Shadow and Guilt.* Toronto, Canada: Inner City Books, 16-17.
45 Ibid., 19.
46 Ibid.
47 Ibid.
48 Ibid., 20.
49 Ibid., 20-21.
50 Ibid., 29.
51 Peele, S. (1989). *Diseasing of America: Addiction Treatment Out of Control.* Boston: Houghton Mifflin Company.
52 Kobler, J. (1973). *Ardent Spirits: The Rise and Fall of Prohibition.* New York: G.P. Putnam's Sons, 2.
53 Ibid.

Chapter 4

1 Kaminer, W. (1992). *I'm Dysfunctional, You're Dysfunctional: The Recovery Movement and Other Self-Help Fashions.* Reading, MA: Addison-Wesley, 30-31.
2 Whitfield, C.L. (1995). *Memory and Abuse: Remembering and Healing the Effects of Trauma.* Deerfield Beach, FL: Health Communications, Inc., 207.

3   Ibid.
4   Ibid.
5   Ibid.
6   Whitfield, C.L. (1990). *A Gift To Myself: A Personal Workbook and Guide To Healing My Child Within.* Deerfield Beach, FL: Health Communications, Inc., 5.
7   Kaufmann, W. (Ed.) (Trans.). (1956). *Existentialism from Dostoevsky to Sartre.* New York: The World Publishing Company, 274-275.
8   Meacham, A. (1988, March/April). A Travelogue with M. Scott Peck, M.D. *Changes: For and About Children of Alcoholics, 3(2),* 20-42.
9   *Dr. Bob and the Good Old Timers: A biography with recollections of early A.A. in the Midwest.* (1980). New York: Alcoholics Anonymous World Services, Inc., 331.
10   Kaminer, W. (1992). *I'm Dysfunctional, You're Dysfunctional,* 94.
11   Jaffe, A. (Ed.). (1979). *C.G. Jung: Word and Image.* Princeton, NJ: Princeton University Press, 228.
12   Berger, P.L., & Luckmann, T. (1966). *The Social Construction of Reality: A Treatise in the Sociology of Knowledge.* Garden City, NY: Doubleday & Company, Inc., 157.
13   Ibid., 160.
14   Ibid.
15   *Alcoholics Anonymous: The Story of How Many Thousands of Men and Women Have Recovered from Alcoholism.* (3rd ed.). (Also known as *The Big Book*). (1976). New York: Alcoholics Anonymous World Services, Inc., 568.
16   Ibid.
17   Ibid., 567.
18   Stein, H. (1985, Fall). Alcoholism as a Metaphor in American Culture. *Family Medicine,* 995.
19   Ibid., 996.
20   *Alcoholics Anonymous* (3rd. ed.)., 59.
21   Ibid.
22   Ibid.
23   Ellis, A. (1963). *Reason and Emotion in Psychotherapy.* New York: Lyle Stuart, 138.
24   Bradshaw, J. (1995). *Family Secrets: What You Don't Know Can Hurt You.* New York: Bantam Books, xvii.
25   Ibid.
26   Ibid., xviii.
27   Ibid.
28   Ibid., xiv.
29   Ibid.
30   Peele, S. (1989). *Diseasing of America: Addiction Treatment Out of Control.* Boston: Houghton Mifflin Company, 151.
31   Ibid., 167.
32   Ibid., 168.
33   Ibid., 140.
34   Ibid.
35   Schaler, J.A. (1989, July). Is addiction treatment 'fundamental'? *The*

U.S. Journal of Drug and Alcohol Dependence, 13(7), 5.

36 Wallace, J. (1989). *John Wallace: Writings.* Newport, RI: Edgehill Publications, 214, 350.

37 Royce, J.E. (1995, July 29). Alcoholics cannot learn to be "social" drinkers. [reprint] *Seattle Post-Intelligencer.*

38 Ibid.

39 Peele, S. (1989). *Diseasing of America,* 77.

40 Ibid.

41 Ibid.

42 Wallace, J. (1989). *John Wallace: Writings,* 120.

43 Peele, S. (1989). *Diseasing of America,* 78.

44 Ibid.

45 Royce, J.E. (1995, July 29). Alcoholics cannot learn to be "social" drinkers.

46 Peele, S. (1989). *Diseasing of America,* 78.

47 Ibid., 77-78.

48 Ibid., 78.

49 Ibid.

50 Ibid.

51 Ibid.

52 Ibid.

53 Ibid.

54 Ibid.

55 Ibid.

56 Meacham, A. (1989, February). Sobells continue to try out moderation therapies. *The U.S. Journal of Drug and Alcohol Dependence, 13(2)*, 10.

57 Bissell, L., & Royce, J.E. (1987). *Ethics for Addiction Professionals.* Center City, MN: Hazelden Foundation, 35-36.

58 Ibid., 36.

59 Ibid., 36.

60 Hassan, S. (1988). *Combatting Cult Mind Control.* Rochester, VT: Park Street Press, 200.

61 Bissell, L., & Royce, J.E. (1987). *Ethics for Addiction Professionals,* 36.

62 Hassan, S. (1988). *Combatting Cult Mind Control,* 200.

63 Berger, P.L., & Luckmann, T. (1966). *The Social Reconstruction of Reality,* 158.

64 Bradshaw, J. (1988). *Bradshaw On: Healing The Shame That Binds You.* Deerfield Beach, FL: Health Communications, Inc., 67.

65 Ibid., 66.

66 Kellogg, T., & Harrison, M. (1991). *Finding Balance: 12 Priorities For Interdependence And Joyful Living.* Deerfield Beach, FL: Health Communications, Inc., 107-124.

67 Ibid., 108.

68 Ibid.

69 Ibid., 116.

70 Ibid., 117.

71 Schaef, A.W. (1989). *Escape From Intimacy: The Pseudo-Relation-*

ship Addictions—Untangling the 'Love' Addictions: Sex, Romance, Relationships. San Francisco: Harper & Row, Publishers, 150, 155.

72   Bradshaw, J. (1988). *Bradshaw On: Healing The Shame That Binds You,* 66.

73   Meacham, A. (1993, April). Presumed Guilty. *Changes: The Magazine for Personal Growth, 8(2),* 80-81.

74   *How It Works: Big Book Selections—The Promises.* (1997, August 22). [On-line]. http://members.aol.com/powerless/HOW.htm#4

75   Bufe, C. (1991). *Alcoholics Anonymous: Cult or Cure?* San Francisco: See Sharp Press, 35-36.

76   Lifton, R.J. (1986). *The Nazi Doctors: Medical Killing and the Psychology of Genocide.* New York: Basic Books, 474.

77   Canetti, E. (1962). *Crowds and Power.* New York: The Noonday Press, 61.

Chapter 6

1   Fabius, R., Anhbach, N., & Terry, L. (1997). *Major Trends in Health Care Delivery.* The Forum on Health Care Delivery. [On-line]. http://www.acpe.org/Forums/delivery.html

2   *Managed Care as a Percentage of Total Medicaid.* (1996, October). HCFA. [On-line]. http://www.hcfa.gov/medicaid/pctoftot.htm

3   Thomas, R. (1993, October 4). Special Report: 'A Walk in Space'. *Newsweek,* 46.

4   Ibid.

5   Goodman, J.C., & Musgrave, G.L. (1992). *Patient Power: Solving America's Health Care Crisis.* Washington, D.C.: Cato Institute, 104.

6   Ibid., 103.

7   Meacham, A. (1990, February). Insurance guidelines aim to cut costs. *U.S. Journal of Drug and Alcohol Dependence, 14(2),* 11.

8   Ibid.

9   Ibid.

10   Rothman, S. (1990, December). Holidays bring sadness, hope. *U.S. Journal of Drug and Alcohol Addictions, 15(12),* 1, 14.

11   Gerstein, D.R., & Harwood, H.J. (Eds.). (1990). *Treating Drug Problems: A Study of the Evolution, Effectiveness, and Financing of Public and Private Drug Treatment Systems.* Washington, D.C.: National Academy Press, 20.

12   Ibid.

13   Ibid.

14   Rothman, S. (1990, December). Holidays bring sadness, hope., 1, 14.

15   Miller, M.E. (1997, June). National study reveals inpatient treatment costs. *The U.S. Journal of Drug and Alcohol Dependence, 11(6),* 1.

16   Ibid.

17   Meacham, A. (1990, December). Treatment and managed care: an uneasy mix. *U.S. Journal of Drug and Alcohol Dependence, 15(1),* 1, 16.

18   Ibid.

19   Lipton, D.S. (1995, November). *Series NIJ Research Report: The*

Effectiveness of Treatment for Drug Abusers Under Criminal Justice Supervision. U.S. Department of Justice. [On-line]. http://www.ncjrs. org/txtfiles/drugsupr.txt

20 "Heal the Pain", Centerpoint. (1993, June). [Advertisement]. *Changes: The Magazine for Personal Growth, 8(4)*, 54.

21 The Rader Institute. (1992, April). [Advertisement]. *Changes: For People in Recovery*, 8.

22 Ibid.

23 "Are you sick and tired of Food Controlling your Life?", Glenbeigh Health Source. (1993, April). [Advertisement]. *Changes: The Magazine for Personal Growth, 8(2)*, 13.

24 "Do you wear the mask of normal?", Charter Lake Hospital. (1991, September/October). [Advertisement].*Changes: For and About Adult Children*, 40.

25 Ibid.

26 Meacham, A. (1990, December). Treatment and managed care, 16.

27 Kuhn, T.S. (1962). *The Structure of Scientific Revolutions.* Chicago: University of Chicago Press, 24.

28 Carnes, P.J. (1991). *Don't Call It Love: Recovery from Sexual Addiction.* New York: Bantam Books, 76.

29 Seipel, T. (1992, September 6). Bond of therapy turns bitter after love affair. *The Denver Post*, pp. 1C, 9C.

30 Ibid.

31 Ibid.

32 Ibid.

33 Anderson, J. (1993). Co-owner details renovations under way at hot springs during fund- raising concert. *The Montana Standard.*

34 Whitfield, C. L. (1991). *Co-Dependence: Healing the Human Condition: The New Paradigm for Helping Professionals and People in Recovery.* Deerfield Beach, FL: Health Communications, Inc., 209.

35 Wegscheider-Cruse, S. (1989). *Another Chance: Hope and Health for the Alcoholic Family.* (2nd ed.). Palo Alto, CA: Science and Behavioral Books, Inc., 9.

36 Horgan, J. (1991, May). Profile: Reluctant Revolutionary. *Scientific American, 264(5)*, 40-49.

37 Ibid.

38 Laign, J. (1991, September/October). John Bradshaw: "I'm Not Drinking Again!" *Changes: For and About Adult Children*, 26-29.

39 Ibid., 29.

40 Meacham, A. (1988, March/April). The Re-Emergence of Suzanne Somers. *Changes: For and About Adult Children of Alcoholics, 3(2)*, 18, 50-53.

41 Meacham, A. (1993, February). Doggone It, People Like Him! *Changes: The Magazine for Personal Growth, 8(1)*, 30-31, 50.

42 Wassil-Grimm, C. (1995). *Diagnosis for Disaster: The Devastating Truth About False Memory Syndrome and Its Impact on Accusers and Families.* Woodstock, NY: The Overlook Press, 289.

43 Ibid., 289-290.

44 Ibid., 290-291.

45 Fick, P.M. (1995). *The Dysfunctional President: Inside the Mind of Bill Clinton.* Secaucus, NJ: Birch Lane Press, 222.

46 Ibid.

47 Ibid.

48 Ibid., 223.

49 Collins, N. (1995, November). A Legacy of Strength and Love. *Good Housekeeping*, 113-115, 200.

50 Ibid.

51 Ibid.

52 Ibid.

53 Fick, P.M. (1995). *The Dysfunctional President*, 222.

54 Wegsheider-Cruse, S. (1988, November 10-12). Speech given at the First Regional Conference on Codependence and Intimate Relationships: *Facing the Realities in Recovery*, sponsored by Health Communications, Inc., Clearwater, FL.

55 Meacham, A. (1987, May/June). 1,300 Celebrate at Children of Alcoholics Conference. *Changes: For Adult Children of Alcoholics, 2(3)*, 7, 48-49.

56 Wegsheider-Cruse, S. (1988, November 10-12). Speech given at the First Regional Conference on Codependence and Intimate Relationships.

57 Ibid.

58 Ibid.

59 O'Hanlon, W.H., & Weiner-Davis, M. (1989). *In Search of Solutions: A New Direction in Psychotherapy.* New York: W.W. Norton & Company, 32-33.

60 Ibid., 33.

61 Teodo, P. (1990, Fall). Interview by author.

62 Kelly, L. (1990, Fall). Interview by author.

63 Meacham, A. (1990, December). Treatment and managed care: an uneasy mix.

64 Kelly, L. (1990, Fall). Interview by author.

65 Ibid.

66 Hughes, (1990, Fall). Interview by author.

67 Ibid.

68 Kriha, C. (1990, Fall). Interview by author.

69 Rothman, S. (1990, April). Rehabs change hands in corporate buyouts. *The U.S. Journal of Drug and Alcohol Dependence (14)4*, 1, 16.

Chapter 7

1 Meacham, A. (1990, December/1991, January). Co-dependency at the Crossroads. *FOCUS: Educating Professionals in Family Recovery, 13(6)*, 16-17, 36-38.

2 Laign, J. (1989, October). Conference spotlights co-dependency. *The U.S. Journal of Drug and Alcohol Dependence, 13(10)*, 1.

3 Meacham, A. (1990, December/1991, January). Co-dependency at the Crossroads.

4 Ibid., 36.

5 Subby, R. (1990, August). Interview by author.

6   Meacham, A. (1990, December/1991, January). Co-dependency at the Crossroads.
7   Whitfield, C. (1990, August). Interview by author.
8   Meacham, A. (1990, December/1991, January). Co-dependency at the Crossroads, 36.
9   Cruse, J. (1990, August). Interview by author.
10 Meacham, A. (1990, December/1991, January). Co-dependency at the Crossroads, 36.
11 Kellogg, T. (1990, August 26-29). [Panel Discussion]. The Second Annual National Conference on Co-Dependency: *Discover the Miracles: Strategies for Healing in Recovery*, sponsored by the *U.S. Journal of Drug and Alcohol Addictions* and *FOCUS* magazine, Scottsdale, AZ.
12 Cruse, J. (1990, August 26-29). [Panel Discussion]. The Second Annual National Conference on Co-Dependency.
13 Meacham, A. (1990, December/1991, January). Co-dependency at the Crossroads, 36.
14 Ibid.
15 Ibid.
16 Ibid.
17 Miller, K. (1990, August). [Panel Discussion]. The Second Annual National Conference on Co-Dependency.
18 Meacham, A. (1990, December/1991, January). Co-dependency at the Crossroads.
19 Ibid.
20 Ibid., 37.
21 Ibid.
22 Cruse, J. (1990, August). [Panel Discussion]. The Second Annual National Conference on Co-Dependency.
23 Gorski, T.T. (1990, December/1991, January). We Need Non-Spiritual Options. *FOCUS: Educating Professionals in Family Recovery*, 17, 45-46.
24 Whitfield, C.L. (1991). *Co-dependence: Healing the Human Condition—The New Paradigm for Helping Professionals and People in Recovery.* Deerfield Beach, FL: Health Communications, Inc., 235.
25 Ibid.
26 Ibid.
27 Meacham, A. (1990, December/1991, January). Co-dependency at the Crossroads.
28 Szasz, T.S. (1970). *The Manufacture of Madness: A Comparative Study of the Inquisition and the Mental Health Movement.* New York: Dell Publishing Co., Inc., 85.
29 American Psychiatric Association. (1987). *Diagnostic and statistical manual of mental disorders.* (3rd ed.). Washington, D.C, 247-248.
30 Ibid., 250.
31 Ibid.
32 Ibid.
33 Ibid.
34 Ostrover, C.T. (1991, August/September). Promoting Therapy. *FO-*

CUS: Educating Professionals in Family Recovery, 14(4), 17.
35 Ibid.
36 Ibid.
37 Ibid.
38 Haaken, J. (1993, Winter). From Al-Anon to ACOA: Codependence and the Reconstruction of Caregiving. *Signs, 18(21)*, 321-345.
39 Ibid.
40 Newman, J.H., Turner, F.M. (Ed.). (1996). *The Idea of a University*. London: Yale University Press, 84.
41 Ibid., 85.
42 Co-Dependency: CN ED 416. (1994). [Course Syllabus]. Pennsylvania State University.
43 Ibid.
44 Babcock, M. (1991, August/September). The Co-dependency Clash: Who Are the Real Co-dependents? *FOCUS: Educating Professionals in Family Recovery, 14(4)*, 28, 44-45.
45 Ibid.
46 Ibid.
47 Ibid.
48 Ibid.
49 Ibid.
50 Meacham, A. (1990, December/1991, January). Co-dependency at the Crossroads.
51 Ibid.

Chapter 8
1   Nick and Holly. (Personal communication, 1993, June).
2   Hannah. (1993, June). Interview by author.
3   Nick and Holly. (Personal communication, 1993, June).
4   Russell, D.E.H. (1986). *The Secret Trauma: Incest in the Lives of Girls and Women*. New York: Basic Books, Inc., 69-71.
5   Gilbert, N. (1994, March/April). Miscounting Social Ills. *Transaction: Social Science and Modern Society, 31(3)*, 21.
6   Ibid.
7   Ibid., 22.
8   Kurzweil, E. (1994, March/April). Did Freud Commit Fraud? *Transaction: Social Science and Modern Society, 31(3)*, 35.
9   Gray, P. (1993, November 29). The Assault on Freud. *Time, 142(23)*, 49.
10 Holmes, D.S. (1990). The Evidence for Repression: An Examination of Sixty Years of Research. In J.L. Singer (Ed.), *Repression and Dissociation*. Chicago: University of Chicago Press, 96.
11 Meacham, A. (1993, April). Presumed Guilty. *Changes: The Magazine for Personal Growth, 8(2)*, 71-78.
12 Ibid.
13 Ofshe, R. (1995, October). Interview by author.
14 Gray, P. (1993, November 29). The Assault on Freud. *Time, 142(23)*, Cover.
15 Ibid., 51.

16 American Medical Association House of Delegates. (1994). *Report of the Council on Scientific Affairs.* (CSA Report 5-A-94). Yank D. Coble.

17 Tennessee Court of Appeals in a Case of First Impression, Declines to Apply Discovery Rule to Toll Statute of Limitations in Repressed Memory Case. (1996, March 1). *FMS Foundation Newsletter, 5(3),* 9.

18 Bass, E., & Davis, L. (1988). *The Courage to Heal: A Guide for Women Survivors of Child Sexual Abuse.* New York: Harper & Row, Publishers, 22.

19 McHugh, P. (1993, April). Speech given at False Memory Syndrome Foundation Conference.

20 Fredrickson, R. (1992). *Repressed Memories: A Journey to Recovery from Sexual Abuse.* New York: Simon and Schuster, 48-51.

21 Beattie, M. (1992). *Codependent No More: How to Stop Controlling Others and Start Caring for Yourself.* (2nd ed.). Center City, MN: Hazelden Educational Materials, 52.

22 Fredrickson, R. (1992). *Repressed Memories,* 49.

23 Beattie, M. (1987). *Codependent No More,* 44.

24 Fredrickson, R. (1992). *Repressed Memories,* 50.

25 Ibid., 49-50.

26 Loftus, E. (1991). *Witness for the Defense: The Accused, the Eyewitness, and the Expert Who Puts Memory on Trial.* New York: St. Martin's Press, 22-24.

27 Van Derber-Atler, M. (1993, February 13). Speech given at A Symposium On Relationships: *People Coming Together in the 90s,* sponsored by the Joan E. Childs Institute, North Miami Beach, FL.

28 Meacham, A. (1993, April). Roseanne Arnold's Shocking Story: Her parents deny that they abused her. *Changes: The Magazine for Personal Growth, 8(2),* 74-75.

29 Van Derber-Atler, M. (1993, February 13). Speech given at A Symposium On Relationships.

30 Ibid.

31 Ibid.

32 Ibid.

33 Lawrence, V. (1993, June). Interview by author.

34 Limitations other than for the recovery of real property shall be commenced as follows, Florida Statutes Annotated. Section 95.11 (1994).

35 McHugh, P. (1992). Presentation given at False Memory Syndrome Foundation meeting, Philadelphia, PA.

36 Ibid.

37 Fredrickson, R. (1992). *Repressed Memories,* 173.

38 Stout, G. (1993, April). Interview by author.

39 Pittman, C. (1994, August 19). Sex case against father dropped. *St. Petersburg Times,* pp. 1B, 6B.

40 Ibid.

41 Ibid.

42 De Vlaming, D. (1995). Interview by author.

43 Ibid.

44 Laign, J. (1991, September/October). Idol Gossip. *Changes: For and About Adult Children,* 4.

45 Bradshaw, J. (1995). *Family Secrets: What You Don't Know* Can *Hurt You.* New York: Bantam Books, 292.

46 Pittman, C. (1994, August 19). Sex case against father dropped. *St. Petersburg Times,* pp. 1B, 6B.

47 Bass, E., & Davis, L. (1988). *The Courage to Heal,* 88.

48 Ofshe, R. (1995, October). Interview by author.

49 "Recovered Memories": Recent Events and Review of Evidence—An Interview with Harrison G. Pope, Jr., M.D. (1994, July). *<Currents in Affective Illness>,* pp. 5-12.(From <Mental Health 1994> [SIRS Researcher CD-ROM Fall 1997, Art. No. 15]. Boca Raton, FL: SIRS, Inc. [Producer and Distributor].)

50 Neisser, U., & Harsch, N. (1992). Phantom flashbulbs: False Recollections of Hearing the News about the *Challenger.* In E. Winograd & U. Neisser (Eds.), *Affect and Accuracy in Recall: Studies of Flashbulb Memories.* New York: Cambridge University Press, 9-31.

51 Lawrence, V. (1993, June). Interview by author.

52 Bradshaw, J. (1995). *Family Secrets,* 287.

53 Ibid., 286.

54 Ibid., 289.

55 Ibid.

56 Gardner, R. (1992, November). Interview by author.

57 Ofshe, R. (1995, October). Interview by author.

58 Ibid.

59 Pope, H., & Hudson, J. (1995, January). Can memories of child sexual abuse be repressed? *Psychological Medicine, 25(1),* 121-126.

60 Ibid., 122.

61 Ibid.

62 Ibid., 123.

63 Ibid.

64 Ibid.

65 Ibid.

66 Ibid.

67 Ibid.

68 Ibid., 123-124.

69 Ibid., 124.

70 Ibid., 124-125.

71 Ibid., 124.

72 Ibid.

73 Ibid., 125.

74 Ibid., 125-126.

75 Legget, J. (1993, April 16-18). Lecture given at False Memory Syndrome Foundation National Conference: *Memory and Reality: Emerging Crisis,* Valley Forge, PA.

76 Ibid.

77 Ibid.

78 Ibid.

79 Ibid.

80 Ibid.
81 Ibid.
82 Ibid.
83 Ibid.
84 Ibid.
85 Brooks, G. (1993, March). Interview by author.
86 Leshner, J. (1993, June). Interview by author.
87 Ibid.
88 Hammond, D.C. (Ed.). (1990). *Handbook of Hypnotic Suggestions and Metaphors*. New York: W.W. Norton & Company, 347.
89 Ibid.
90 Childs, J. (1993, June). Interview by author.
91 Ibid.
92 Ibid.
93 Tom. (1993, June). Interview by author.
94 Ibid.
95 Ibid.
96 Ibid.
97 Ibid.
98 Ibid.
99 Ibid.
100 Ibid.
101 Ibid.
102 Ibid.
103 Ibid.
104 ASCA Co-Dependency Centers. (1992, August). [Advertisement]. *Changes: For People in Recovery 7(4)*.
105 Tom. (1993, June). Interview by author.
106 Roch v. Arkansas, No. 86-130, slip op. (June 22, 1987).
107 Tom. (1993, June). Interview by author.
108 Ibid.
109 Ibid.
110 Ibid.
111 Childs, J., & Cheryl. (1993, June). Interview by author.
112 Ibid.
113 Ibid.
114 Ibid.
115 Ibid.
116 Meacham, A. (1993, April). Presumed Guilty. 71-78.
117 Ibid.
118 Childs, J. (1993, June). Interview by author.
119 Tom. (1993, June). Interview by author.
120 Nathan, D., & Snedeker, M. (1995). *Satan's Silence: Ritual Abuse and the Making of a Modern American Witch Hunt*. New York: Basic Books, 107.
121 Perrin, R.D., & Parrott, L. (1993, June 21). Memories of Satanic Ritual Abuse: The truth behind the panic. *Christianity Today, 37(7)*, 21-23.
122 Ibid., 21.
123 Ibid.

124 Ibid.

125 Ibid.

126 Ibid.

127 Ibid.

128 Ibid., 21, 23.

129 Childs, J. (1993, June). Interview by author.

130 Schoener, G.R. (1992, February). Interview by author.

131 Ibid.

132 Boyd, H. (1992, April). Interview by author.

133 Haldane, E.S., & Ross, G.R.T. (Trans.). *The Philosophical Works of Descartes.* (Vol. 1). New York: Cambridge University Press, 6-7.

134 Ibid., 7.

135 Schoener, G.R. (1992, February). Interview by author.

136 Gleitman, H. (1993, April 18). *Reflections on Memory.* Presented at the False Memory Syndrome Foundation National Conference.

137 Ibid.

138 Kaminer, W. (1990, February 11). Chances Are You're Codependent Too. *New York Times Review of Books,* Section 7, p.1.

139 Ibid.

140 Ibid.

141 Ibid.

142 Ibid.

143 Ibid.

144 Wegscheider-Cruse, S. (1990, August 26-29). Speech given at The Second Annual National Conference on Co-dependency: *Discover the Miracles: Strategies for Healing in Recovery,* Scottsdale, AZ.

145 Mitchell, J. (1993, April). One on One with John Bradshaw. *Changes, The Magazine for Personal Growth,* 47.

146 Ibid.

147 Kaminer, W. (1992). *I'm Dysfunctional, You're Dysfunctional: The Recovery Movement and Other Self-Help Fashions.* Reading, MA: Addison-Wesley Publishing Company, Inc., 88.

148 Ibid., 97-98.

149 Ibid., 99.

150 Loftus, E. (1998, February 13). *New Ways to Create False Memories.* Presented at the symposium: *False Memory Creation,* sponsored by the Eleanor and Elliot Goldstein Foundation and Florida Atlantic University, Boca Raton, FL.

151 Ibid.

152 Ibid.

153 Ibid.

154 Ceci, S. (1998, February 13). *Is Truth in Jeopardy?* Presented at the symposium: *False Memory Creation,* sponsored by the Eleanor and Elliot Goldstein Foundation and Florida Atlantic University, Boca Raton, FL.

155 Schacter, D. (1998, February 13). *The Cognitive Neuroscience of Illusory Memories.* Presented at the symposium: *False Memory Creation,* sponsored by the Eleanor and Elliot Goldstein Foundation and Florida Atlantic University, Boca Raton, FL.

Chapter 9

1   Schaef, A.W. (1986). *Co-Dependence: Misunderstood, Mistreated.* San Francisco: Harper Collins Publishers, 3.
2   Ibid.
3   Ibid.
4   Hutchinson, J. (1992, August 9). Well-known psychotherapist settles malpractice suit for client intimacy. *Sunday Camera.*
5   Moody, V. (1995, November). Interview by author.
6   Ibid.
7   Moody v. Schaef, Fassel, and Wilson-Schaef Associates, No. 91CV610 (Boulder County, CO. 1991). [letter]. Denver, CO: Coffman & Company.
8   Moody, V. (1995, November). Interview by author.
9   Schaef, A.W. (1986). *Co-Dependence,* 5.
10 Schaef, A.W. (1989). *Escape From Intimacy: The Pseudo-Relationship Addictions —Untangling the 'Love' Addictions: Sex, Romance, Relationships.* San Francisco, Harper & Row, Publishers, 76-77.
11 Benetin, J. (1995, June). Interview by author.
12 Kaminer, W. (1992). *I'm Dysfunctional, You're Dysfunctional: The Recovery Movement and Other Self-Help Fashions.* Reading, MA: Addison-Wesley Publishing Company, Inc., 26.
13 Ibid., 13-14.
14 Tavris, C. (1992). *The Mismeasure of Woman.* New York: Simon & Schuster, 173.
15 Bradshaw, J. (1990). *Homecoming: Reclaiming and Championing Your Inner Child.* New York: Bantam Books, 20.
16 Ibid., 39.
17 Whitfield, C.L. (1990). *A Gift to Myself: A Personal Workbook and Guide to Healing My Child Within.* Deerfield Beach, FL: Health Communications, Inc., 1.
18 Levine, P. (1992, February). Interview by author.
19 Bradshaw, J. (1988). *Bradshaw On: Healing The Shame That Binds You.* Deerfield Beach, FL: Health Communications, Inc., 67.
20 Ibid., 95.
21 Ibid., 88.
22 Bradshaw, J. (1988). *Bradshaw On: Healing The Shame That Binds You,* 93.
23 Sheldrake, R. (1995). *The Presence of the Past: Morphic Resonance and the Habits of Nature.* Rochester, VT: Park Street Press.
24 Bradshaw, J. (1995). *Family Secrets: What You Don't Know Can Hurt You.* New York: Bantam Books, 79.
25 Yapko, M. (1992). Interview by author.
26 Ibid.
27 Yapko, M. (1995, October). Interview by author.
28 Ibid.
29 Ibid.
30 Ibid.
31 Ibid.

32 Jacobs, A. (1995, October). Interview by author.

33 Ibid.

34 Jaffé, A. (Ed.). (1979). *C.G. Jung: Word and Image*. Princeton, NJ: Princeton University Press, 228.

35 Fredrickson, R. (1992). *Repressed Memories: A Journey to Recovery from Sexual Abuse*. New York: Simon & Schuster, 113.

36 Bass, E., & Davis, L. (1988). *The Courage to Heal: A Guide for Women Survivors of Child Sexual Abuse*. New York: Harper & Row, Publishers, 14.

37 Fredrickson, R. (1992). *Repressed Memories*, 15.

38 Ibid., 78.

39 Ibid., 85.

40 Ibid., 14.

41 Ibid., 15.

42 Ibid., 164-165.

43 Ibid., 165.

44 Ibid.

45 Ibid., 164.

46 Bradshaw, J. (1995). *Family Secrets*, 294.

47 Fredrickson, R. (1992). *Repressed Memories*, 164.

48 Bradshaw, J. (1995). *Family Secrets*, xix.

49 Ibid., 80.

50 Repressed memory theory fails Kelly-Frye test in California. (1995, October). *FMS Foundation Newsletter, 4(9)*, 7.

51 Michigan Supreme Court limits the use of expert opinion testimony in child abuse cases (1995, October). *FMS Foundation Newsletter, 4(9)*, 9.

52 Ibid.

53 Gardner, R.A. (1993, Fall). Sexual Abuse Hysteria: Diagnosis, Pathogenesis, and Treatment.<*Academy Forum*>, pp. 2-5. (From<Corrections 1997>[SIRS Researcher CD-ROM Fall 1997, Art. No. 16]. Boca Raton, FL: SIRS, Inc. [Producer and Distributor].)

54 Loftus, E. (1998, February 13). *New Ways to Create False Memories*. Presented at the symposium: *False Memory Creation*, sponsored by the Eleanor and Elliot Goldstein Foundation and Florida Atlantic University, Boca Raton, FL.

55 Bradshaw, J. (1995). *Family Secrets*, 280.

56 Ibid.

57 Ibid., 86.

58 Ibid.

59 Ibid., 292.

60 Ibid.

61 Ibid., 294.

62 Ibid., 120-122.

63 Ibid.

64 Ibid., 85.

65 Ibid., 89.

66 Bradshaw, J. (1990). *Homecoming*, 209.

67 Bradshaw, J. (1995). *Family Secrets*, 95.

68 Whitfield, C.L. (1990). *A Gift to Myself*, 35.
69 Whitfield, C.L. (1994, January 15). *Statement of Safety* [Pamphlet]. False Memory Debate Conference, Seattle, WA.
70 Pendergrast, M. (1995). *Victims of Memory: Incest Accusations and Shattered Lives.* Hinesburg, VT: Upper Access, Inc., 494.
71 *FBI Study of Childhood Ritual Abuse.* (1996, November 19). [Online]. http://web.canlink.com/ocrt/ra_rep03.htm
72 Bradshaw, J. (1995). *Family Secrets,* 259.
73 Goldstein, E., & Farmer, K. (1993). *True Stories of False Memories.* Boca Raton, FL: SIRS, Inc., 68-69.
74 Gerry. (1993, June). Interview by author.
75 Ibid.
76 Personal Communication (1993, January).
77 Personal Communication.
78 Meacham, A. (1993, April). Presumed Guilty. *Changes: The Magazine for Personal Growth, 8(2),* 76.
79 Mitchell, J. (1993, April). One on One with John Bradshaw. *Changes: The Magazine for Personal Growth, 8(2),* 47-48.
80 Bradshaw, J. (1992). *Finishing Our Business with Mother.* [cassette recording, tape #4]. Houston, TX: Bradshaw Cassettes.
81 Ibid.
82 Halpern, D. (1992, December). Interview by author.
83 Ibid.
84 Bradshaw, J. (1988). *Healing The Shame That Binds You,* 82.
85 Jacobs, A. (1992). *Reparenting and Mind Control.* Unpublished manuscript, 7-8.
86 Meacham, A. (1989, September/October). Losing your Soul to a Cult. *Changes: For and About Adult Children (4)5,* p.72.
87 Ibid.
88 Jacobs, A. (1994, January). Theory as Ideology: Reparenting and Thought Reform. *Transactional Analysis Journal, 24(1),* 48.
89 Jacobs, A. (1992). *Reparenting and Mind Control,* 11.
90 Ibid., 11-12.
91 Jacobs, A. (1994, January). Theory as Ideology, 44.
92 Jacobs, A. (1992). *Reparenting and Mind Control,* 14.
93 Jacobs, A. (1994, January). Theory as Ideology, 50.
94 Court permanently enjoins Schiff rehabilitation project. (1971, September 2). *The Freelance Star,* p. 9.
95 Ibid.
96 People v Aaron Schiff, No. 15904 (Contra Costa County, CA, 1972) (Testimony of Carl Fjelle). [Transcript]. Charno, Willens, Jouras, and Willens, 89.
97 Ibid (Testimony of Jacqui Lee Schiff)., 160.
98 Ibid (Testimony of Sara Hartwell)., 226.
99 Ibid., 227.
100 Ibid., 210.
101 Ibid (Testimony of David Richman, M.D.)., 113.
102 Ibid (Testimony of Sara Hartwell)., 220.
103 Ibid., 221.

104 Ibid.
105 Ibid (Testimony of Carl Fjelle)., 89.
106 Ibid.
107 Ibid., 71.
108 Ibid., 72.
109 Ibid (Testimony of Aaron Schiff)., 46.
110 Ibid (Testimony of Carl Fjelle)., 73.
111 Ibid.
112 Ibid (Testimony of Aaron Schiff)., 49.
113 Ibid (Testimony of Carl Fjelle)., 83.
114 Ibid., 77.
115 Ibid (Testimony of Jacqui Schiff)., 167.
116 Ibid.
117 Ibid (Testimony of Carl Fjelle)., 79.
118 Ibid (Testimony of David Richman, M.D.)., 111.
119 Ibid (Testimony of Sara Hartwell)., 228.
120 Ibid.
121 Ibid.
122 Ibid (Testimony of Joan Wexler)., 8.
123 Ibid (Testimony of Carl Fjelle)., 87.
124 Ibid (Testimony of Joan Wexler)., 9.
125 Ibid (Testimony of Jim Freund)., 148.
126 Ibid (Testimony of Joan Wexler)., 10.
127 Ibid (Testimony of Sara Hartwell)., 219.
128 Ibid., 222.
129 Ibid (Testimony of David Richman, M.D.)., 112.
130 Wexler, J. (1992). Interview by author.
131 Ibid.
132 Ibid.
133 Jacobs, A. (1992). *Reparenting and Mind Control.*
134 Boyd, H. (1992, March) Interview by author.
135 Ibid.
136 Thattil, J. (1992, March). Interview by author.
137 Welsh, C. (1992). Interview by author.
138 Ibid.
139 Jones, R. (1991, August 15). The Strange 'Babies' of Small Heath. *The Birmingham Evening Mail,* p. 5.
140 How the Cathexis Therapy was Born. (1991, August 15). *The Birmingham Evening Mail.*
141 Pilkington, E. (1991, November 23-24). Mother and Child Reunion. *Weekend Guardian,* pp. 12-14.
142 Stein, M. (1991, November). Combatting Cathexis. *National Schizophrenic Fellowship,* Kingston Upon Thames, Surrey, England, *4,* 15.
143 Ibid.
144 Freeman, P. (1991, August 16). Clinic's Pledge on Childhood Therapy. *The Birmingham Evening Mail.*
145 Ibid.
146 Ibid.
147 Jones, R. (1991, August 15). The Strange 'Babies' of Small Heath, p.5.

148 Ibid., p.1.
149 Pilkington, E. (1991, November 23, 24). Mother and Child Reunion, p.13.
150 Ibid., p.12.
151 Ibid., p.14.
152 Robinson, J. (1992, January 11). *Evidence to the Registered Home Tribunal* (report).
153 Ibid (report item no.17).
154 Ibid (report item no. 21).
155 Jones, R. (1991, August 15). Break the Mind Cure. *The Birmingham Evening Mail.*
156 Smith, S. (1987). Regressive Work: Definition, Description, and Clinical Application. *Dissertation Abstracts International.* (University Microfilms No. LD01204).
157 Ibid.
158 Bradshaw, J. (1992). *Finishing Our Business with Mother.* [cassette recording, tape #5]. Houston, TX: Bradshaw Cassettes.
159 *Center for Creative Living (CCL) Ethical Policy.* St. Paul, MN: Center for Creative Living.
160 Joyce Sankey v Alfred Wiger and The Center for Creative Living, Inc. (Dakota County, MN. October 25, 1990). [complaint].
161 Carlson, E. (1995, September). Interview by author.
162 Bradshaw, J. (1988). *Bradshaw On: Healing The Shame That Binds You,* 105.
163 Ibid., 41.
164 Haldane, E.S., & Ross, G.R.T. (Trans.). *The Philosophical Works of Descartes.* (Vol. 1). New York: Cambridge University Press, 6-7.

Bibliography

Alcoholics Anonymous: The Story of How Many Thousands of Men and Women Have Recovered from Alcoholism. (3rd ed.). (1976). New York: Alcoholics Anonymous World Services, Inc.

American Psychiatric Association. (1987). *Diagnostic and statistical manual of mental disorders.* (3rd ed.). Washington, D.C.

Ansbacher, H., & Ansbacher, R. (Eds.). (1956). *The Individual Psychology of Alfred Adler: A Systematic Presentation in Selections from His Writings.* New York: Basic Books.

Bass, E., & Davis, L. (1988). *The Courage to Heal: A Guide for Women Survivors of Child Sexual Abuse.* New York: Harper & Row, Publishers.

Baum, L.F., & Hague, M. (1988). *The Wizard of Oz.* New York: Henry Holt and Company.

Beattie, M. (1992). *Codependent No More: How to Stop Controlling Others and Start Caring for Yourself.* (2nd ed.). Center City, MN: Hazelden Educational Materials.

Becker, R.A. (1989). *Addicted to Misery: The Other Side of Co-Dependency.* Deerfield Beach, FL: Health Communications, Inc.

Berger, P.L., & Luckmann, T. (1966). *The Social Reconstruction of Reality: A Treatise in the Sociology of Knowledge.* Garden City, NY: Doubleday & Company, Inc.

Bissell, L., & Royce, J.E. (1987). *Ethics for Addiction Professionals.* Center City, MN: Hazelden Foundation.

Bradshaw, J. (1988). *Bradshaw On: Healing The Shame That Binds You.* Deerfield Beach, FL: Health Communications, Inc.

Bradshaw, J. (1990). *Homecoming: Reclaiming and Championing Your Inner Child.* New York: Bantam Books.

Bradshaw, J. (1995). *Family Secrets: What You Don't Know Can Hurt You.* New York: Bantam Books.

Bradshaw, J. (1996). *Bradshaw On: The Family—A New Way of Creating Self-esteem.* (Rev. Ed.). Deerfield Beach, FL: Health Communications, Inc.

Bufe, C. (1991). *Alcoholics Anonymous: Cult or Cure?* San Francisco: See Sharp Press.

Canetti, E. (1962). *Crowds and Power.* New York: The Noonday Press.

Canfield, J. & Hansen, M.V. (1993). *Chicken Soup for the Soul.* Deerfield Beach, FL: Health Communications, Inc.

Carnes, P.J. (1991). *Don't Call It Love: Recovery from Sexual Addiction.* New York: Bantam Books.

Carnes, P.J. (1992). *Out of the Shadows: Understanding Sexual Addiction.* (2nd ed.). Minneapolis, MN: CompCare Publishers.

Castine, J. (1989). *Recovery from Rescuing.* Deerfield Beach, FL: Health Communications, Inc.

Cermak, T. (1988). *A Time to Heal: The Road to Recovery for Children of Alcoholics.* New York: Avon Books.

Cermak, T. (1989). *Diagnosing and Treating Co-Dependence.* Minneapolis, MN: Johnson Institute.

Co-Dependency. (1984). Deerfield Beach, FL: Health Communications, Inc.

Conroy, P. (1987). *Prince of Tides.* New York: Bantam Books.

Corsini, R.J. (Ed.) (1994). *Encyclopedia of Psychology.* New York: John Wiley & Sons.

Cosell, H. (1985). *I Never Played the Game.* New York: William Morrow and Company, Inc.

Deikman, A.J. (1990). *The Wrong Way Home: Uncovering the Patterns of Cult Behavior in American Society.* Boston: Beacon Press.

Dorland's Illustrated *Medical Dictionary*, (28th ed.). (1906). Philadelphia: W.B. Saunders Company.

Dr. Bob and the Good Old Timers: A biography with recollections of early A.A. in the Midwest. (1980). New York: Alcoholics Anonymous World Services, Inc.

Dyer, W.W. (1976). *Your Erroneous Zones.* New York: Funk & Wagnalls.

Eliot, T.S. (1955). *The Waste Land and Other Poems.* Orlando, FL: Harcourt Brace.

Ellis, A. (1963). *Reason and Emotion in Psychotherapy.* New York: Lyle Stuart.

Fick, P.M. (1995). *The Dysfunctional President: Inside the Mind of Bill Clinton.* Secaucus, NJ: Birch Lane Press.

Fingarette, H. (1988). *Heavy Drinking: The Myth of Alcoholism as a Disease.* Berkeley, CA: University of California Press.

Fredrickson, R. (1992). *Repressed Memories: A Journey to Recovery from Sexual Abuse.* New York: Simon and Schuster.

Gerstein, D.R., & Harwood, H.J. (Eds.). (1990). *Treating Drug Problems: A Study of the Evolution, Effectiveness and Financing of Public and Private Drug Treatment Systems.* Washington, D.C.: National Academy Press.

Ginzberg, L. (1909). *The Legends of the Jews* (Vol. 1). Philadelphia, PA: The Jewish Publication Society of America.

Goldstein, E., & Farmer, K. (1992). *Confabulations: Creating False Memories—Destroying Families.* Boca Raton, FL: SIRS, Inc.

Goldstein, E., & Farmer, K. (1993). *True Stories of False Memories.* Boca Raton, FL: SIRS, Inc.

Goodman, J.C., & Musgrave, G.L. (1992). *Patient Power: Solving America's Health Care Crisis.* Washington, D.C.: Cato Institute.

Grimm, The Brothers. (1992). *Little Red Riding Hood.* Kansas City, MO: Ariel Books.

Haldane, E.S., & Ross, G.R.T. (Trans.). *The Philosophical Works of Descartes.* (Vol. 1). New York: Cambridge University Press.

Hammond, D.C. (Ed.). (1990). *Handbook of Hypnotic Suggestions and Metaphors.* New York: W.W. Norton & Company.

Hassan, S. (1988). *Combatting Cult Mind Control.* Rochester, VT: Park Street Press.

Hatterer, L.J. (1984). *Encyclopedia of Psychology* (Vol. 1). (Raymond J. Corsini, Ed.). New York: Wiley.

Jaffe, A. (Ed.). (1979). *C.G. Jung: Word and Image.* Princeton, NJ: Princeton University Press.

James, W. (1902). *The Varieties of Religious Experience: A Study in Human Nature.* New York: The Modern Library.

Kaminer, W. (1992). *I'm Dysfunctional, You're Dysfunctional: The Recovery Movement and Other Self-Help Fashions.* Reading, MA: Addison-Wesley Publishing Company, Inc.

Kaufmann, W. (Ed.). (Trans.). (1956). *Existentialism from Dostoevsky to Sartre.* New York: The World Publishing Company.

Kelley Blue Book Used Car Guide; Consumer Edition, 1983-1997. (1997). New York: Kelley Blue Book.

Kellogg, T., & Harrison, M. (1991). *Finding Balance: 12 Priorities For Interdependence And Joyful Living.* Deerfield Beach, FL: Health Communications, Inc.

Kobler, J. (1973). *Ardent Spirits: The Rise and Fall of Prohibition.* New York: G.P. Putnam's Sons.

Kritsberg, W. (1985). *The Adult Children of Alcoholics Syndrome: From Discovery to Recovery.* Deerfield Beach, FL: Health Communications, Inc.

Kuhn, T.S. (1962). *The Structure of Scientific Revolutions.* Chicago: University of Chicago Press.

Larsen, E. (1983). [Audio cassette] *Basics of Co-dependence.* Brooklyn Park, MN: E. Larsen Enterprises.

Lee, J. (1987). *The Flying Boy: Healing the Wounded Man.* Deerfield Beach, FL: Health Communications, Inc.

Lerner, R. (1986). *Daily Affirmations: For Adult Children of Alcoholics.* Deerfield Beach, FL: Health Communications, Inc.

Lifton, R.J. (1986). *The Nazi Doctors: Medical Killing and the Psychology of Genocide.* New York: Basic Books.

Lifton, R.J. (1987). *The Future of Immortality and Other Essays for a Nuclear Age.* New York: Basic Books.

Loftus, E. (1991). *Witness for the Defense: The Accused, the Eyewitness, and the Expert Who Puts Memory on Trial.* New York: St. Martin's Press.

Middleton-Moz, J. & Dwinnel, L. (1986). *After the Tears.* Deerfield Beach, FL: Health Communications, Inc.

Miller, J.E. (1989). *Addictive Relationships: Reclaiming Your Boundaries.* Deerfield Beach, FL: Health Communications, Inc.

Miller, J.K. (1987). *Sin: Overcoming the Ultimate Deadly Addiction.* San Francisco: Harper & Row, Publishers.

Nathan, D., & Snedeker, M. (1995). *Satan's Silence: Ritual Abuse and the Making of a Modern American Witch Hunt.* New York: Basic Books.

Newman, J.H., Turner, F.M. (Ed.). (1996). *The Idea of a University.* London: Yale University Press.

O'Hanlon, W.H., & Weiner-Davis, M. (1989). *In Search of Solutions: A New Direction in Psychotherapy.* New York: W.W. Norton & Company.

Peck, M.S. (1978). *The Road Less Traveled.* New York: Simon & Schuster.

Peele, S. (1989). *Diseasing of America: Addiction Treatment Out of Control.* Boston: Houghton Mifflin Company.

Peele, S. & Brodsky, A. (1975). *Love and Addiction.* New York: Taplinger Publishing Co., Inc.

Pendergrast, M. (1995). *Victims of Memory: Incest Accusations and Shattered Lives.* Hinesburg, VT: Upper Access, Inc.

Perera, S.B. (1986). *The Scapegoat Complex: Toward a Mythology of Shadow and Guilt.* Toronto: Inner City Books.

Piper, W., Hauman, G., & Hauman, D. (1978). *The Little Engine that Could.* New York: Gross & Dunlap.

Russell, D.E.H. (1986). *The Secret Trauma: Incest in the Lives of Girls and Women.* New York: Basic Books, Inc.

Ryder, D., C.C.D.C., L.S.W. (1992). *Breaking the Circle of Satanic Ritual Abuse: Recognizing and Recovering from the Hidden Trauma.* Minneapolis, MN: CompCare Publications.

Schaef, A.W. (1986). *Co-Dependence: Misunderstood, Mistreated.* San Francisco: Harper Collins Publishers.

Schaef, A.W. (1987). *When Society Becomes an Addict.* New York: Harper & Row, Publishers.

Schaef, A.W. (1989). *Escape From Intimacy: The Pseudo-Relationship Addictions—Untangling the 'Love' Addictions: Sex, Romance, Relationships.* San Francisco: Harper & Row, Publishers.

Schaef, A.W. (1990). *Laugh! I Thought I'd Die (if I Didn't): Daily Meditations on Healing Through Humor.* New York: Ballantine Books.

Schaef, A.W. & Fassel, D. (1988). *The Addictive Organization.* San Francisco: Harper & Row, Publishers.

Schiff, J.L. (1970). *All My Children.*(1970). New York: M. Evans.

Sheldrake, R. (1995). *The Presence of the Past: Morphic Resonance and the Habits of Nature.* Rochester, VT: Park Street Press.

Stamas, D.T. (1981). *The Trap Man: How to Trap the Alcoholic.* Lombard, IL: Eureka Alcoholism Publishers.

Stark, R., & Bainbridge, W.S. (1985). *The Future of Religion: Secularization, Revival and Cult Formation.* Berkeley, CA: University of California Press.

Stratford (1991). *Satan's Underground.* Gretna, LA: Pelican Publishing Co.

Subby, R. (1987). *Lost in the Shuffle: The Co-dependent Reality.* Deerfield Beach, FL: Health Communications, Inc.

Szasz, T.S. (1970). *The Manufacture of Madness: A Comparative Study of the Inquisition and the Mental Health Movement.* New York: Dell Publishing Co., Inc.

Szasz, T.S. (1984). *The Myth of Mental Illness: Foundations of a Theory of Personal Conduct.* (Rev. ed.). New York: HarperCollins Publishers.

Tavris, C. (1992). *The Mismeasure of Woman.* New York: Simon & Schuster.

Thomas, T. (1990). *Surviving with Serenity: Daily Meditations for Incest Survivors.* Deerfield Beach, FL: Health Communications, Inc.

Thomsen, R. (1985). *Bill W.* New York: Harper & Row, Publishers.

Tillich, P. (1965). *Ultimate Concern.* New York: Harper & Row, Publishers.

Trimpey, J., & Ellis, A. (1996). *The Small Book*: *A Revolutionary Ap-*

proach to Overcoming Drug and Alcohol Dependence. New York: Dell Publishing.

Twelve Steps for Christians—From Addictive and Other Dysfunctional Families: Based on Biblical Teachings. (1988). (Friends in Recovery). San Diego, CA: Recovery Publications.

Wallace, J. (1989). *John Wallace: Writings.* Newport, RI: Edgehill Publications.

Wassil-Grimm, C. (1995). *Diagnosis for Disaster: The Devastating Truth About False Memory Syndrome and Its Impact on Accusers and Families.* Woodstock, NY: The Overlook Press.

Wegscheider-Cruse, S. (1981). *Another Chance: Hope and Health for the Alcoholic Family.* Palo Alto, CA: Science and Behavior Books.

Wegscheider-Cruse, S. (1985). *Choicemaking: For Spirituality Seekers, Co-dependents and Adult Children.* Deerfield Beach, FL: Health Communications, Inc.

Wegscheider-Cruse, S. (1989). *Another Chance: Hope and Health for the Alcoholic Family.)*(2nd ed.). Palo Alto, CA: Science and Behavior Books, Inc.

Wegcheider-Cruse, S., & Cruse, J. (1990). *Understanding Co-Dependency.* Deerfield Beach, FL: Health Communications, Inc.

Whitfield, C.L. (1989). *Healing the Child Within: Discovery and Recovery for Adult Children of Dysfunctional Families.* Deerfield Beach, FL: Health Communications, Inc.

Whitfield, C.L. (1990). *A Gift To Myself: A Personal Workbook and Guide to Healing My Child Within.* Deerfield Beach, FL: Health Communications, Inc.

Whitfield, C.L. (1991). *Co-Dependence: Healing the Human Condition—The New Paradigm for Helping Professionals and People in Recovery.* Deerfield Beach, FL: Health Communications, Inc.

Whitfield, C.L. (1995). *Memory and Abuse: Remembering and Healing the Effects of Trauma.* Deerfield Beach, FL: Health Communications, Inc.

Wholey, D. (1984). *The Courage to Change.* Boston: Houghton Mifflin Company.

Williams, M. (1958). *The Velveteen Rabbit.* New York: Doubleday.

Wilson, B. (1967). *As Bill Sees It: The A.A. Way of Life...Selected writings of A.A.'s co-founder.* New York: Alcoholics Anonymous World Ser vices, Inc., 199.

Wilson, Lois (1979). *Lois Remembers.* New York: Al-Anon Family Grou Headquarters, Inc.

Winograd, E., & Neisser, U. (Eds.). (1992). *Affect and Accuracy in Recall: Studies of Flashbulb Memories.* New York: Cambridge University Press.

Woititz, J. (1983). *Adult Children of Alcoholics.* Deerfield Beach, FL: Health Communications, Inc.

Woititz, J. (1986). *Struggle for Intimacy.* Deerfield Beach, FL: Health Communications, Inc.

Index